ENVIRONMENT AND THE POOR: DEVELOPMENT STRATEGIES FOR A COMMON AGENDA

H. Jeffrey Leonard and contributors:

Montague Yudelman
J. Dirck Stryker
John O. Browder
A. John De Boer
Tim Campbell
Alison Jolly

Series Editors:
Valeriana Kallab
Richard E. Feinberg

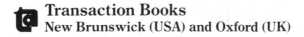
Transaction Books
New Brunswick (USA) and Oxford (UK)

Library of Congress Catalog Number 89-20202
ISBN: 0-88738-282-7 (cloth)
ISBN: 0-88738-786-1 (paper)
Printed in the United States of America

Library of Congress Cataloging-in-Publication Data

Environment and the poor: development strategies for a common agenda / H. Jeffrey Leonard and contributors, Montague Yudelman . . . [et al.].
    1. Environmental policy—Developing countries. 2. Economic development—Environmental aspects. I. Title. II. Series: U.S.-Third World policy perspectives: no. 11.
HC59.72E5L46   1989
338.9'009172'4—dc20

Photo Copyrights and Credits:

Sean Sprague/Panos Pictures, NEPAL (p. ii);
Mark Edwards/Still Pictures, ETHIOPIA (p. 2);
Inter-American Development Bank Photo, COLOMBIA (p. 48);
Inter-American Development Bank Photo, BRAZIL (p. 60);
Felix Ashinhurst/CARE Photo, MALI (p. 86);
Dennis Allen Glick/World Wildlife Fund, HONDURAS (p. 110);
E.G. Huffman/World Bank Photo, ECUADOR (p. 134);
Mark Edwards/Still Pictures, KOREA (p. 164);
Russell Mittermeier/World Wildlife Fund, MADAGASCAR (p. 188).

Map Credit and Copyright:

Map of Madagascar (p. 192), based on Eaux et Forets survey 1949–1958 after Humbert and Cours Darne 1965 and Tattersall 1988; revised, with permission, from Alison Jolly, *A World Like Our Own* (New Haven, Conn.: Yale University Press, 1980), p. xii. © Yale University Press.

Design Credit:
John Kaljee

Environment and the Poor

Acknowledgments

Guest Editor:
H. Jeffrey Leonard

Series Editors:
Valeriana Kallab
Richard E. Feinberg

The Overseas Development Council gratefully acknowledges a special grant from the Jessie Smith Noyes Foundation for the project leading to the publication of this volume; the support of The Pew Charitable Trusts for the ODC's U.S.-Third World Policy Perspectives series, of which this volume is part; and the support of The Ford Foundation, The Rockefeller Foundation, and The William and Flora Hewlett Foundation for the Council's overall research and outreach program.

The editors wish to express special thanks to John W. Sewell for his steadfast commitment to advancing the public policy debate on the interrelationship of the issues of poverty and environment and joint approaches to their solution. Special thanks for advice and critique at the planning and execution stages of the project and publication are also due to John P. Lewis, ODC Senior Advisor and Chairman of the ODC Program Advisory Committee and to members of that Committee; to Sheldon Annis, ODC Senior Associate; and to Patti Petesch, ODC Associate. On behalf of ODC and the contributing authors, the editors also extend special thanks to the World Wildlife Fund/The Conservation Foundation for co-sponsoring the series of discussion workshops at which drafts of the chapters were presented and debated by participating experts from both the environment and development communities.

The editors also wish to acknowledge and thank Melissa Vaughn, Patricia Masters, and Danielle M. Currier for editorial and production assistance; and Joycelyn V. Critchlow for processing the manuscript.

Contents

Foreword, by John W. Sewell ix

Overview:
Environment and the Poor: Development Strategies
for a Common Agenda
H. Jeffrey Leonard 3

    Introduction 3
    The Changing Nature of Poverty 9
    Where Poverty and Environment Collide 16
    A Common Agenda for Attacking Poverty and
        Environmental Destruction 29
    Conclusions 42

Summaries of Chapter Recommendations 49

1. Sustainable and Equitable Development
in Irrigated Environments
    Montague Yudelman 61

    The Scope of Irrigation 63
    The Performance of Irrigation Projects 65
    Environmental Costs Related to Irrigation 69
    Future Challenges 73
    Recommendations: Toward Efficient, Equitable, and
        Environmentally Sound Irrigation 74
    Conclusion 84

2. Technology, Human Pressure, and Ecology in the
Arid and Semi-Arid Tropics
    J. Dirck Stryker 87

    Poverty and Environment in Dry Areas 88
    Forces for Change 90
    Environmental Problems and their Causes 93
    Development Strategy in Dry Areas 99
    Recommendations 101

3. Development Alternatives for Tropical Rain Forests
    John O. Browder 111

    Rural Poverty and Tropical Deforestation 113
    Current Commercial Uses of Tropical Forests 114
    Development Alternatives for Tropical Forests 118
    Natural Forest Management 123
    Conclusions and Recommendations 128

4. **Sustainable Approaches to Hillside Agricultural Development**
A. John De Boer   135

The Himalayas: An Overview   138
Environmental Degradation in the Himalayas   138
Poverty and Environment in the Himalayas   141
The State of Hillside Agricultural Development   143
Public Policy and the Long-Term Future
   of Hill Agricultural   149

5. **Urban Development in the Third World: Environmental Dilemmas and the Urban Poor**
Tim Campbell   165

Issues and Trade-Offs   165
Urban Development and Poverty:
   The Magnitude of the Problem   167
The Environment of Human Shelter   170
Environmental Trade-Offs in the Cityscape   175
Dealing With Dilemmas: Social and Economic Dimensions
   in Strategies for Environment and Development   183

6. **The Madagascar Challenge: Human Needs and Fragile Ecosystems**
Alison Jolly   189

Madagascar: A Unique Ecosystem Under Siege   193
World Bank Policies for Development
   and Environment in Madagascar   201
Policies to Preserve Biodiversity with
   Sustainable Development   211

About the Overseas Development Council, the Editors,
   and the Authors   217
The ODC's U.S.-Third World Policy Perspectives Series   222

Foreword

An emerging "global agenda" of interrelated issues—growth, poverty, environment, and political pluralism—is becoming the central focus for development cooperation for the next two decades. Global poverty remains as serious as ever, despite marked progress over the last three decades in improving human well-being. Environmental stress at both the local and international levels threatens irreversible deterioration of the earth's fragile environment. Continued high levels of population and economic growth exacerbate both poverty and environmental degradation. And the increase in political openness throughout the world poses both dangers and opportunities.

There is now a growing awareness among policymakers that eliminating global poverty and sustaining the environment are inextricably interlinked. There is little agreement, however, on the necessary policy responses to such global-level environmental problems as the warming of the earth's atmosphere, or to such local-level problems as deforestation, soil erosion, and degradation, or the provision of urban water and sanitation.

This Policy Perspectives volume, *Environment and the Poor: Development Strategies for a Common Agenda,* is ODC's first attempt to sort out the complex interrelationships between several equally desirable policy goals: eliminating absolute poverty, slowing population growth, and safeguarding the environment. The central message of the study is important: Six out of every ten of the world's poorest people are being inexorably pushed by agricultural modernization and continuing high population growth rates into ecologically fragile environments—tropical forests, dryland and hilly areas, or the slums of the great urban areas. Unless development strategies support the capabilities of these people to ensure their own survival, the nearly 500 million poorest people in these fragile areas will be forced to meet their short-term needs to survive at the cost of long-term ecological sustainability and the well-being of future generations.

The contributors to this volume call for new policies and new forms of collaboration across a range of sectors and among participants at the local, national, and international levels. We hope that the many individuals who are part of the solutions to both poverty and environmental problems—population planners, water engineers, health professionals, trade negotiators, local activists, bankers, agroforesters, aid administrators, resource managers, economists, waste-disposal technicians, political leaders, and others—find the policy recommendations stimulating and practical.

Environment and the Poor: Development Strategies for a Common Agenda marks a new stage in the Overseas Development Council's long-standing concern with poverty-oriented development strategies. The study follows two earlier policy studies: *Development Strategies Reconsidered,* which examines the debate between inward- and outward-oriented development strategies; and *Strengthening the Poor: What Have We Learned?* which assesses the experiences of governments and aid agencies in implementing poverty-oriented development strategies over the last two decades. Both volumes were prepared under the direction of ODC's Senior Advisor, John P. Lewis. The interrelationships among policies to eliminate poverty, sustain the environment, restore necessary economic growth, and promote political pluralism will form a major part of the Council's work program over the next several years.

ODC was fortunate to involve H. Jeffrey Leonard as the director of the project that resulted in *Environment and the Poor.* Dr. Leonard, who is a Vice President of the World Wildlife Fund/The Conservation Foundation and director of its Fairfield Osborn Center for Economic Development, is the author of numerous books and studies; perhaps most important, he is one of the few who presently possess a clear and specific view of the close linkages between eliminating poverty and sustaining the environment.

This project was stimulated and made possible by a grant from the Jessie Smith Noyes Foundation. The Foundation's President, Stephen Viederman played a major role in catalyzing our thinking about the contents of this volume. In addition, support for this project came from the funds for work on poverty-oriented development strategies generously provided by Lutheran World Relief, the Christian Children's Fund, and The Hunger Project. The Policy Perspectives series of which this study is part enjoys generous support from The Pew Charitable Trusts and from core support for ODC's work from the Ford, Rockefeller, and Hewlett Foundations.

John W. Sewell, *President*
Overseas Development Council

August 1989

Overview

Environment and the Poor: Development Strategies for a Common Agenda

H. Jeffrey Leonard

Introduction

Two critical challenges have been thrust to the top of the development agenda for the 1990s: the reduction of poverty and the protection of the environment. First, debt-service obligations, declining terms of trade, high costs of capital, structural adjustment, and reduced development assistance have severely penalized the poorest developing countries. Concern about their plight has renewed international focus on poverty reduction as a priority for international development assistance.[1] Second, recent scientific evidence of global environmental threats—such as climate change due to increases in carbon dioxide in the earth's atmosphere—and growing recognition of the consequences of rampant natural resource destruction in tropical countries have for the first time placed protection of the environment in the mainstream of development policy objectives.[2] Indeed, the leaders of the world's seven leading industrial democracies, in what has been dubbed the first "Green Summit," agreed at their July 1989 meeting to redouble efforts to assist developing countries to preserve their resources and avoid deterioration of their ecological systems.

The problems of poverty and environmental degradation are both complicated and made vastly more urgent by the relentless increases in sheer numbers of people living in developing countries. Many developing countries experiencing rapid population growth find that per capita incomes are falling even in years of reasonable aggregate economic growth. In some high-population-growth countries, the capacity of the

3

land and its resources to provide poor people with food and life's basic needs is being exceeded in areas that once yielded ample sustenance.

Widespread poverty and environmental destruction threaten to block economic and social progress in many developing countries in the coming decades. Enduring poverty at the urban periphery and in the hinterlands of many middle-income countries, and pervasive poverty and hunger in the lowest income countries, severely constrain overall economic growth. The clearly visible scars associated with the destruction of forest, soil, and water resources throughout the developing world mark both the extreme waste of economic productivity already lost and the reduced productive potential of these resources for the future.

The depreciation of human capital by poverty and the depletion of capital stocks of natural resources assume even graver significance in light of the continuing scarcity of investment capital facing many developing countries. Net capital outflows to developed countries (as debt service, profit repatriation, and flight capital) have seriously constrained developing countries' economic expansion in the 1980s.[3] Improvements in human productivity and more efficient use of natural resources (including land) are two of the main avenues by which developing countries could generate internally some of the surplus capital necessary for growth in the absence of sufficient external investment capital.

The Clash of Poverty and Environment

Despite growing acceptance that alleviating poverty and protecting the environment are *both* critical to long-term economic growth, development economists often believe that the relationship between poverty and environment is akin to that between inflation and unemployment, as postulated by the Phillips curve. Many development economists argue that this relationship prevents developing countries from dealing with both problems simultaneously or through a single set of policy instruments, and that policies adopted to redress one problem will inevitably exacerbate the other. The point is often made, for example, that only after poor farmers increase their incomes can they turn their attention to reducing soil erosion and other long-term environmental problems.[4] Similar beliefs have often been expressed by developing-country leaders. Indira Gandhi, for example, held that extremely poor people and countries must make an explicit trade-off, accepting long-term environmental degradation to meet their immediate needs for food and shelter.

In short, the challenges of poverty reduction and environmental protection are often seen as antithetical—at least in the short-term horizon within which most poor people are forced to live. As with virtually anything that diverts even incremental energies or resources of subsistence-level people, a pause to protect or repair the environment can literally take food out of the mouths of hungry families.

Yet the real conflict is often less between what is good for the environment and what is good for the poor than between what is good for the poor of today and the poor of tomorrow. In many marginal, rural areas growing numbers of poor people inevitably have to degrade the environment a little more each day just to make ends meet. But in doing so, they take not only from nature's bounty but also from the well-being of future land-dependent generations. Consequently, even when the short-term trade-off between immediate hunger and environment is stark, the urgency is growing for developing-country governments and international donors to promote appropriate policy instruments to reduce the conflicts. As World Bank President Barber Conable has described the stakes: "The stubborn fact of the eighties is that growth has been inadequate, poverty is still on the rise, and the environment is poorly protected. Unchanged, these realities would deny our children a peaceful, decent, and livable world."[5]

The Ecological "Marginalization" of Poverty

More than anything else, three major demographic factors interact to place long-term environmental protection concerns in conflict with the short-term survival strategies of the poor:

- Rapid population growth,
- Land consolidation and agricultural modernization in fertile agricultural areas, and
- Prevailing inequalities in land tenure.

These factors have induced growing numbers of very poor people to migrate to new lands or to already burgeoning urban areas. In many rural areas characterized by traditional technology and few off-farm opportunities, growing populations continuously subdivide a resource whose potential to yield food, fodder, and fuel is relatively fixed.

A basic premise of this book is that, over time, this process causes environmental degradation and intractable poverty to become more and more closely intertwined in particular geographic areas with fragile environmental conditions. The world's poorest people are thus increasingly clustered in two types of areas: remote and ecologically fragile rural areas and the edge of growing urban areas.

Agricultural production, and therefore average income, has risen dramatically in many of the most fertile and easily reached regions of the developing world. But the stagnation of agricultural productivity in other areas and the push of landless people out of areas undergoing agricultural modernization have placed great pressures on poor people throughout the developing world to occupy and exploit more and more marginal lands. These include arid and semi-arid lands, hillsides, moist tropical forests, and other ecologically sensitive areas that were previously not exploited or were exploited less intensively.

Though not necessarily unfarmable, many of these lands are highly susceptible to ecological deterioration unless they receive investments of labor (or capital) to construct appropriate infrastructure and unless specially adapted agricultural technologies are introduced. Quite often, however, severe environmental degradation—manifested as soil erosion and loss of fertility, desertification, and deforestation—has accompanied the increasing pressures placed on such vulnerable lands. These environmental problems often undermine the livelihood of already impoverished, land-dependent people.

Environmental degradation and poverty clash in urban areas, too. Modern manufacturing industries, commercial centers, and service industries are concentrated at the core of many large cities in the developing world. Around them, large numbers of the poorest of the urban poor cluster in makeshift, ramshackle "shadow" cities at the urban periphery. As a result of absolute shortages of appropriate land or the high economic rents on "serviced" lands, these peripheral urban areas are often characterized by hazardous natural and man-made ecological conditions (some examples are flood plains, steep slopes, or vacant land adjacent to dangerous industries). The physically precarious conditions typical of urban squatter settlements in the developing world greatly magnify the vulnerability of the urban poor to a broad array of environmental sanitation problems (notably waterborne diseases), natural disasters (especially floods and mudslides), and man-made disasters (such as chemical plant explosions and urban fires).

In these geographical "poverty reservations," the need to reconcile anti-poverty and environmental improvement strategies is most urgent. The interaction of poverty and environmental destruction sets off a downward spiral of ecological deterioration that threatens the physical security, economic well-being, and health of many of the world's poorest people. Ironically, even as experts point out that the poorest people in developing countries have become "more bankable" by measure of their organization and human capacity, their lands are becoming "less bankable" by virtue of the pervasive deterioration of their productive capacity. This poverty and environment connection, depicted in Figure 1, also has significant implications for the "global" environmental concerns that have become widely publicized in the developed world during the 1980s: the prospects of global warming due to increased carbon and other "greenhouse" gases in the atmosphere and the destruction of a growing portion of the earth's biological diversity. While it is critical for the developed countries to enlist the developing countries in the "crusade" to save the world's environment, this will only be possible if developing countries perceive that poverty alleviation efforts are enhanced, not thwarted, by environmental protection plans.

Figure 1. The Poverty and Environment Connection

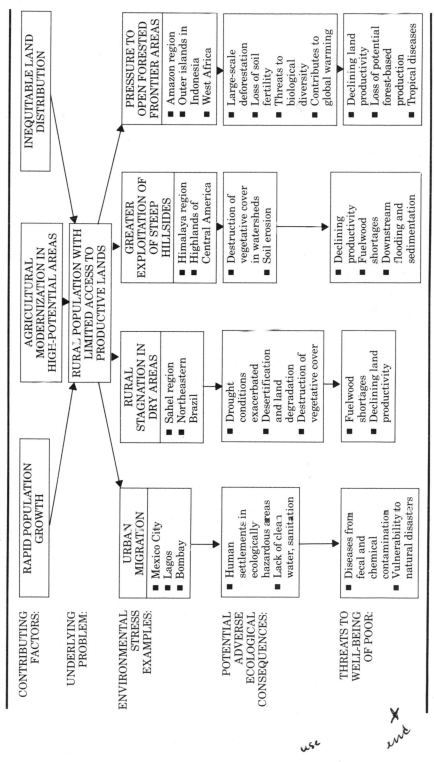

The Need for Joint Strategies

The international economic crisis of the 1980s has severely reduced the commitment by governments and international agencies to major anti-poverty initiatives in developing countries. The looming environmental crisis in the developing world is making it all the more difficult for poor people to eke out a subsistence living because the productivity of the natural resource systems on which they depend has been declining. The confluence of these two crises has set up one of the greatest challenges of development policy for coming decades. Few aspects of development are so complex as the need to reconcile anti-poverty and pro-environment goals. The policy linkages and choices to be made have not been sorted out. Neither international donors nor developing-country governments have been able to formulate a common policy agenda linking these two important concerns. Do both desired ends—poverty alleviation and environmental sustainability—come in the same package, or must painful choices be made between them?

One point is critical: Wherever the downward spiral described above already exists in particular geographic areas of the developing world, the primary target of development policies must be simultaneous alleviation of the constraints of poverty and environmental destruction. No long-term strategy of poverty alleviation can succeed in the face of environmental forces that promote persistent "erosion" of the physical resources upon which poor people depend. No environmental protection programs can make headway without removing the day-to-day pressures of poverty that leave people little choice but to discount the future so deeply that they fail to protect the resource base to ensure their own or their children's well-being.

The rest of this chapter examines the broad linkages between poverty and environmental destruction in developing countries. The changing nature of poverty, and of the poor themselves, is highlighted—with special attention to certain trends that heighten the urgency of *joint* poverty alleviation and environmental management strategies. An effort is made to identify the magnitude of the poverty problem in particularly vulnerable ecological areas of the developing countries and to demonstrate, in the aggregate, the range of the resulting severe environmental consequences. Finally, general policy guidelines and recommendations are developed for international development assistance agencies and national governments, which only recently have begun to grapple with the fact that poverty and environmental deterioration are inextricably linked.

Each of the following chapters explores the poverty-and-environment conundrum in a particular ecological area in greater detail. Montague Yudelman (Chapter 1) addresses the urgent need to increase the sustainability of agriculture in fertile, irrigated areas—both to protect the anti-poverty gains already made in these areas and to ease some of the poverty and environment pressures in more marginal ecological areas.

The especially difficult challenges of poverty alleviation in arid and semi-arid regions, where people depend completely upon a fragile land base, are explored by J. Dirck Stryker (Chapter 2). In regions such as the African Sahel or northeastern Brazil, the clash of environmental deterioration and poverty contributes most dramatically to human misery, starvation, and perhaps irreversible destruction of natural resources.

John O. Browder (Chapter 3) describes a variety of smallholder alternatives to deforestation that promise ecological and economic sustainability in tropical rain forest areas. Such alternatives—including modern adaptations of traditional forest management and agroforestry techniques—could help to reduce rampant deforestation in the Amazon region, the outer islands of Indonesia, West Central Africa, and other areas where large numbers of poor people have moved into tropical forests.

John De Boer (Chapter 4) outlines a strategy to assist and induce poor people in the densely populated hillside regions of the developing world (the greater Himalayas, Central America, and the Ethiopian highlands) to slow environmental problems—such as soil erosion due to tree-cover removal from steep slopes—that in the long term push local populations into deeper poverty.

Tim Campbell (Chapter 5) advances a series of low-cost and appropriate technology solutions to some of the environmental problems that threaten the health and economic well-being of poor people in urban areas.

Biologists have identified a small number of "hot spots" in tropical countries that harbor a large percentage of earth's total diversity of flora and fauna. Drawing on efforts under way in the island nation of Madagascar, Alison Jolly (Chapter 6) confronts the dilemma of whether the extremely poor residents' economic needs can be met without the loss of biologically unique species.

The Changing Nature of Poverty

A 1988 World Bank report estimated that more than 900 million people worldwide now live in a state of "absolute poverty." It defined this condition as characterized by "malnutrition, illiteracy, disease, short life expectancy and high rates of infant mortality."[6] Probably close to a billion more men, women, and children live along a subsistence margin that, while not life-threatening, precludes attainment of much beyond the minimal necessities.[7] Thus, the lives of nearly 2 billion of the world's 5 billion people still are controlled by the conditions of extreme poverty.

The vast majority—over 85 per cent—of the world's poorest people live in the developing countries of Africa, Asia, and Latin America. At least 80 per cent of those living below or near the level of absolute poverty in the developing world live in rural areas. These rural poor depend overwhelmingly on agricultural activities for their daily subsistence. However, urbanization is proceeding faster now than at any time in human history, and by early in the twenty-first century, most of the developing world's poor are likely to be living in urban areas. Regardless of their natural setting, the poor of Africa, Asia, and Latin America universally share the debilitating human environment of poverty: inadequate nutrition, poor shelter, lack of hygiene and health care, and a dearth of material assets or specialized skills.

Recent efforts to restore the issue of poverty alleviation to its position of the 1970s at the top of the development assistance agenda have called attention to the fact that the nature of poverty, and in many cases the needs of the poor as well, have since then changed in important ways. Except for small numbers of indigenous peoples in a few remote areas, most of even the poorest people have been exposed to some health care, technology, infrastructure, and communications that have improved their physical well-being and have limited the extent of starvation—at least on an emergency basis.

Perhaps more important than these improvements in social services and physical infrastructure, the human capacity of the poor has also improved in striking ways. Even in rural remote areas, the poor are "better educated, healthier, better organized, more experienced with institutional development—in a word, more 'investable.' "[8] Effectively, this means that the world has come closer to putting a floor under the poor. Hundreds of millions still suffer from absolute deprivation, but the relative success of poverty alleviation and food security programs in many developing countries has forestalled mass starvation, malnutrition, and extreme poverty on the scale that would have resulted from rapid population growth.[9]

Despite this progress, poverty in developing countries has become more entrenched and more structural in recent decades. More poor people are fed and live longer, and smaller percentages of poor people are absolutely poor in a life-threatening sense. The problem for the future is manifest. While the poorest of the poor—the poorest 20 per cent—may be reached by relief efforts, recent research has demonstrated clearly that they are generally beyond the reach of externally supported development projects or government-financed investment programs.[10] Thus, in many places where the worst symptoms of poverty—especially starvation—have been relieved, the poorest people still have not achieved any self-sustaining momentum toward prosperity through increased economic productivity. The lack of such momentum means that, despite progress in alleviating poverty, the poorest of the poor have been falling farther behind the rich—behind both rich countries and the rich people in their own countries.

As more poor nations progress toward relief of absolute hunger and construction of a social services safety net for many of those among the poor who live at the edge of starvation, closing the productivity gap that divides rich from poor will become the paramount challenge in coming decades. Closing that gap for those who remain in poverty while the world gallops ahead is, however, made more difficult because more and more of the poor live in households headed by women and because a growing number of the world's poorest lack access either to potentially productive land resources or to good employment opportunities. Indeed, three trends—the increasing numbers of women among the poorest of the poor, the growing problem of landlessness among the poor, and the massive need to create non-farm employment—are reshaping the nature of the challenge to alleviate poverty in developing countries. Each of these trends also has important consequences for the use or abuse of natural resources by poor people in their environments.

The "Feminization" of Poverty

One significant change in recent years—in reality and consciousness—is the increased recognition that poverty in developing countries has a gender bias, which requires different approaches to anti-poverty strategies. Recent studies, for example, have concluded that the numbers of poor households headed by women have expanded rapidly in rural Africa and in the urban slums of Latin America. These households were found, on average, to be poorer than other poor households.[11] For many reasons, poverty among women-headed households is usually deeper and more firmly entrenched than overall poverty. They generally have, for example, fewer working members, more dependents, less access to productive resources, more family and household-maintenance responsibilities concentrated on the head of household, and a high proportion of low-productivity employment.

In light of the high incidence of women-headed households among the world's poorest people—as well as the strategic importance of women's contributions to food production, household labor, and family income among all poor families—development assistance agencies and national governments have been pushed in recent years to focus anti-poverty strategies more explicitly on removing special burdens and constraints on women. Recent experience in attempting to design poverty alleviation programs to meet the needs of women shows that the most successful interventions have focused on raising the productivity of women themselves rather than on women as a part of households or families. The greatest successes appear to have been achieved in micro-enterprise and non-farm employment programs where women's entrepreneurial skills or wage earning capacity have been upgraded.[12]

Conversely, in rural agricultural areas, even where women's important roles as farmers and resource managers have been duly respected, increases in overall farm production or in physical employment opportunities for the landless have often had mixed welfare benefits for women in poor households and relatively less effect on women-headed households.[13] This is because incremental increases in external agricultural production or farm-related employment often result in greatly increased demand for women's unpaid labor or must come at the expense of critical household tasks—fuel gathering, foodcrop production, and food preparation.

In developing countries overall, women are thought to account for half the production of food. Women produce 75 per cent of Africa's food and devote probably more than 90 per cent of all time spent processing and preparing it. But women also are the primary collectors of essential resources—fuel and water—which poor people generally must provide for themselves in lieu of public services.

In this regard, women's multiple roles in poor households perpetually conflict with each other. For example, increased time spent on out-of-household chores or non-household employment can directly reduce the time women have for child-rearing and other household duties. Conversely, the time and energy devoted just to gathering fuel and water increasingly has been recognized as a major impediment to efforts to increase women's contributions to food production, household income, or family welfare.[14]

When confronted with environmental degradation that reduces the availability of fuelwood or water, or the productivity of the land which produces their food, poor women often have no other recourse but to work harder in an effort just to stay even. Thus, in many countries where deforestation has led to shortages of firewood, women have been forced to go farther afield and to expend much more time on collecting wood. Recent studies in Nepal have shown that, because of the roles played by women, serious adverse social and economic consequences such as peak-season shortages of labor, or declines in child nutrition, may be a direct result of deforestation.[15] This emphasizes the point that the links between environmental destruction and poverty, the concern of this volume, can be particularly pronounced for women-headed households, and that the burdens of "adjustment" or compensation for natural resource destruction may fall most heavily on women in many poor households.

A Rising Tide of Landlessness

The growing numbers of landless or near-landless agricultural workers and marginal farmers who do not have access to the productive resources necessary to provide for themselves and their families has become a major concern in development circles.[16] The degree to which landlessness or near-landlessness (access to plots of land too small to provide a minimal livelihood under existing land use patterns and technical capabilities) coincide with poverty is a source of debate among experts. Suffice to conclude, however, that most landless and near-landless in rural areas fall into several broad categories of generally poor people: agricultural laborers with little or no land of their own; small and marginal peasants who own or lease very small plots of land; people engaged in traditional rural artisan industries such as fishing and crafts; and shifting cultivators, nomads, and pastoralists.[17]

According to recent estimates, 13 per cent of all rural households in developing countries are landless, and almost 60 per cent have too little land to subsist (Table 1). On the basis of an average household size of 5.6 people, an estimated 935 million rural people live in households that have too little land to meet the minimum subsistence requirements for food and fuel. These data exclude China, which could add as many as 100–200 million more people to the category.[18]

The preponderance of landless and near-landless people live in Asia—most of them in Bangladesh, China (not included in Table 1), India, Indonesia, Pakistan, the Philippines, and Sri Lanka. In Asia, land scarcity and population pressure are the prime causes of landlessness. In Latin America, inequitable distribution patterns on arable lands are more of a problem. Although Africa generally has an abundance of land and less distorted patterns of land distribution, its emerging problem of landlessness is related to the combination of several factors. These include the technical, health, and financial obstacles to cultivation in humid tropical forests; the adverse effects of drought and desertification; and heavy population pressure in fertile river basins and rich rainfed soils.[19]

The Job Creation Challenge

With average rural household income lagging and falling in many countries and demographic trends pushing millions of increasingly landless entrants into the rural and urban labor force each year, poverty alleviation through employment generation is rising to the very top of most African, Asian, and Latin American countries' development priorities. During the 1990s, the developing nations must generate nearly 40 million new jobs every year just to absorb into the work force children already born.[20] India alone has to absorb almost 10 million new

Table 1. Landless and Near-Landless Households

Region	Total Households in Agriculture (millions)	Near-Landless millions	(% of total)	Landless (millions)	(% of total)
Total	232	136	59	31	13
Asia[a]	162	94	58	24	15
Africa	46	29	63	3	7
Latin America	24	13	54	4	17

[a] Not including China.
    Source: Adapted from Radha Sinha, *Landlessness: A Growing Problem* (Rome: Food and Agriculture Organization, 1984), Tables 1 and 2, p. 16.

entrants a year into its labor force in the coming decade. Indonesia needs 1.2 million new jobs a year, and Mexico more than a million. For comparison, in their peak growth year in the past 15 years, none of these countries generated even half as many jobs as they need to create each year in the 1990s.[21]

Thus while the preeminent objective of poverty alleviation efforts in the 1950s and 1960s was assuring that aggregate food production could keep abreast of exploding population, the central task for the 1990s and beyond will be to create enough jobs to employ billions of new workers throughout the developing world. Job creation on this scale— *and in the areas needing them*—poses an enormous challenge. Traditionally, industrial and service-sector jobs in urban agglomerations have been the magnets that have drawn poor migrants from the countryside. Urbanization will continue to grow faster than population in developing countries in coming decades, putting massive physical and environmental strains on cities and necessitating the creation of large numbers of industrial and service-sector jobs within urban economies. Yet, even if these urban areas grow as fast as expected, well-established demographic trends make virtually inevitable another quarter-century of rapid population growth in *rural as well as urban areas* in developing countries (Figure 2). Job creation efforts for new labor force entrants in many developing countries therefore must focus on both the urban and rural sectors.

To reduce the pace and costs of rapid urbanization, many developing countries and international donors in recent years have devoted greater attention to efforts to contain surplus populations in rural areas. At the same time, continuing agricultural modernization means

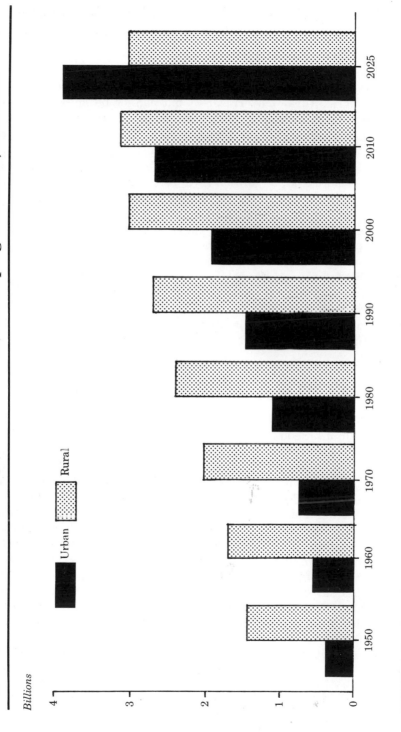

Figure 2. Rural and Urban Population Growth, Developing Countries, 1950-2025

Source: U.N. Centre for Human Settlements, Global Report on Human Settlements, 1986.

that agriculture itself offers less, not more, direct employment. This has brought even greater focus on the role of rural, *non-farm* employment—such as rural public works programs and agriculture-related industries.

Some countries, notably India and China, have experienced considerable success in creating rural non-farm employment to provide work for a greater portion of the poor people who have been turned off the land by agricultural modernization but cannot be accommodated in overcrowded urban areas. Even in these instances of successful rural job creation, only so many of the displaced rural labor force can be absorbed in meaningful non-farm work. For example, by giving highest political priority to a strategy of keeping people in the countryside, China boasts that it has more than 30 million rural people in non-farm jobs. Even so, this is only 10 per cent of the rural labor force.[22]

In short, optimism that rapid industrialization will absorb surplus rural populations is on the wane, the ability of the rural sector to sustain employment through non-farm employment is constrained, rapid population growth continues in both urban and rural areas, and more and more people are being pushed into landlessness or near-landlessness by agricultural modernization. As a result, it appears almost inevitable in coming decades that "the magnitude of rural as well as urban unemployment . . . is immense and will continue to grow unabated."[23]

Where Poverty and Environment Collide

The extreme difficulties that developing countries will have keeping up with the simultaneous need to create huge numbers of urban and rural jobs do not bode well for poverty alleviation or environmental protection efforts. Land is the provider of last resort in rural areas—and often even in peripheral urban areas. Lacking jobs to give them purchasing power, poor people seek land anywhere they can get it for subsistence food production and fuelwood. Often the lands where the itinerant poor end up are those that were previously only sparsely settled because of their remoteness, marginal nature, or ecological fragility. The point is that economic progress in the world at large, and successful economic development within middle-income developing countries, have resulted in the gradual emergence of de facto "poverty reservations" in geographical areas that have higher propensities than other areas to be the receptacles of the world's poorest people.

Poverty's Geographical Retreat

Table 2 shows where the poorest 20 per cent of the total population in the developing countries currently live. As can be seen, the majority of these 780 million "poorest of the poor" live in South Asia and Sub-Saharan Africa. Indeed, half of the developing world's poorest people live in South Asia, which includes the subcontinental countries of Bangladesh, Bhutan, India, Nepal, Pakistan, and Sri Lanka. This region also has the highest percentage of the developing world's total population (37 per cent) in the poorest-of-the-poor category. In Sub-Saharan Africa, with one-fifth of the developing world's poorest, more than a quarter of the population lives perpetually at the edge of starvation. If the Sahelian and northeast African countries were isolated in these figures, the percentage of population among the hungry poor would of course go up dramatically.

Thus the masses of the world's poorest people are more tightly clustered by regional location than they were several decades ago when poverty was pervasive throughout the developing countries.

Yet absolute poverty has also been on the retreat within the borders of most countries of the developing world. The combination of "green revolution" technologies, fertile alluvial soils, and adequate supplies of water has raised incomes substantially—if not always equitably—for the many poor people lucky enough to live in areas of high agricultural potential that have been reached by these inputs. The biggest disparities in the emerging economic development and well-being in rural areas of developing countries are not between rich and poor within those high-potential, already developed areas. Rather, the gap is widest between areas that—by dint of location, political influence, or high fertility—*have* benefited from agricultural modernization and infrastructural investment, and the areas that *have not* done so.[24]

Two types of rural areas in the developing world have not yet experienced the green revolution:

- Areas whose good agricultural potential has not been tapped because of a lack of investment capital, remote location, or a variety of social and economic circumstances (regional or tribal politics, cultural concerns);
- Areas whose limited agricultural potential (low soil fertility, terrain, lack of moisture, or other natural limitations) does not offer great promise for alleviating poverty under current agricultural technology.

For very poor people in underdeveloped areas with good natural potential for agriculture, the single best strategy for eliminating hunger and alleviating poverty must be a redoubling of efforts to provide the infrastructure, investment, agricultural research, and technological support necessary to adapt modern, high-yielding agricultural techniques to local conditions and circumstances. The ecological challenge in these areas must be to promote land and water management and

Table 2. The Poorest of the Poor[a], by Region (millions and percentages)

Region	Total Poorest of Poor in Region	As Percentage of:	
		Region's Population	Total Poorest of Poor in Developing Countries
South Asia	390	37	50
China	84	8	11
East Asia	33	7	4
Africa (Sub-Sahara)	156	30	20
Near East and North Africa	39	15	5
Latin America	78	17	10
Total	780	20	100

[a] The poorest of the poor are defined as the poorest 20 per cent among the total population of all developing countries.

Sources: Compiled and calculated from World Bank, *Social Indicators of Developments, 1988* (Baltimore, Md.: The Johns Hopkins University Press, 1988); and World Bank data.

environmental protection measures to ensure that increased agricultural development does not lead to long-term environmental degradation.

Figure 3 points to the good news on the global poverty front: nearly 280 million of the 780 million poorest people live in high-potential agricultural areas that can be "highly responsive to modern, production-increasing technology."[25] A reinvigoration of external capital flows and increasing support for specialized national agricultural research programs, if diligently pursued by international donors and national governments, could yield significant agricultural production increases in coming decades for poor people in "high potential" agricultural areas.

The flip side of this seemingly bright prognosis is that nearly two-thirds of the developing world's poorest people do not live in areas of high agricultural potential. The majority of these poor people are increasingly clustered in low-potential agricultural areas and squatter settlements on the periphery of large urban areas—the two types of areas that are becoming the major poverty reservoirs.

Approximately 370 million of the poorest live in rural areas judged by agricultural experts to have low agricultural potential—areas where limited soil fertility, adverse climatic conditions, or other natural factors inhibit success of modern agriculture. Here the challenges of poverty reduction are likely to be far more complex than in the high-potential areas. Moreover, as poverty reduction proceeds in the high-potential areas, the poorest of the rural poor are likely to be more and more confined to areas of low agricultural potential. High human fertility rates—together with the inflow of masses of poor people made landless by land consolidation and reduced demand for agricultural labor in high agricultural potential areas—will intensify human pressure in marginal areas.

Over 130 million of the developing world's poorest poor now live in urban areas. Demographers predict disproportionately faster developing-country population growth at the periphery of sprawling urban centers than in urban regions a whole. Overall population growth in the developing countries is about 2.1 per cent annually at present, but urban areas are growing by more than 3.5 per cent. Urban slums or squatter settlements that absorb the poorest of the new urban dwellers are growing at an estimated 7 per cent a year.[26]

Figure 3 underscores why the retreat of poverty into certain geographical areas increases strains on the natural environment. Poverty and environmental destruction are becoming inseparable twins less because the absolute numbers of people have grown than because the poorest people (who have the least access to investment capital and technology) occupy the lands that need the most infrastructure, management, and external inputs if their utilization is not to result in land degradation and environmental destruction.

A striking fact that has not been widely appreciated within the major international development assistance agencies is that approximately 470 million (or 60 per cent) of the developing world's poorest people live in highly vulnerable ecological areas. These include arid lands, limited fertility soils, steep slopes, and poorly serviced urban lands where too many land-dependent people or improper land utilization can cause environmental problems that further undermine their income and well-being of the people who live there.

Figure 3 shows the extent to which the poorest people in each of the major regions occupy ecologically vulnerable lands. Today, 63 million of Latin America's poorest people (80 per cent), 327 million of Asia's poor (60 per cent), and 80 million of Africa's poor (51 per cent) live in areas where they are highly susceptible to the consequences of soil erosion, soil infertility, floods, and other ecological disasters.

That coming decades are likely see the continuing "retreat" of poverty into the low-potential agricultural areas and the exploding peri-urban areas that are ecologically vulnerable is evidenced by the relegation of the poor in a number of middle-income countries of Latin

Figure 3. WHERE THE POOREST OF THE POOR LIVE

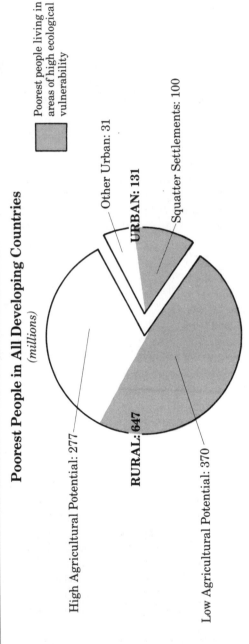

Poorest People in All Developing Countries
(*millions*)

Poorest people living in
areas of high ecological
vulnerability

Other Urban: 31

URBAN: 131

Squatter Settlements: 100

High Agricultural Potential: 277

RURAL: 647

Low Agricultural Potential: 370

A total of some 470 million people, or 60 per cent of the
developing world's 780 million *poorest* people, live in rural or
urban areas of high ecological vulnerability—areas where
ecological destruction or severe environmental hazards threaten
their well-being.

Note: Totals may not add up due to rounding.

ᵃThe "poorest of the poor" are defined as the poorest 20 per cent among the total population of all developing countries.
   Sources: Population and poverty figures compiled and updated from World Bank, *Social Indicators of Development, 1988* (Baltimore, Md.: Johns
Hopkins University Press, 1988), and from World Bank data files; estimates of the agricultural potential of rural lands occupied by the poorest
people are based upon preliminary figures compiled by the International Food Policy Research Institute (IFPRI); estimates of the numbers of the
poorest urban people living in squatter settlements are based on figures compiled from World Bank data files and the U.N. Centre for Human
Settlements.

Poorest People by Region
(millions)

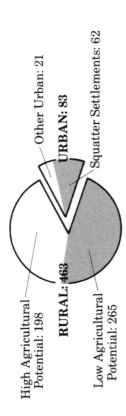

ASIA
(including China and the Near East)

In Asia, 327 million people, or 60 per cent of the region's *poorest* people, live in rural or urban areas of high ecological vulnerability—areas where ecological destruction or severe environmental hazards threaten their well-being.

Other Urban: 21

URBAN: 83

Squatter Settlements: 62

High Agricultural Potential: 198

RURAL: 463

Low Agricultural Potential: 265

SUB-SAHARAN AFRICA

In Sub-Saharan Africa, 80 million people, or 51 per cent of the region's *poorest* people, live in rural or urban areas of high ecological vulnerability—areas where ecological destruction or severe environmental hazards threaten their well-being.

Other Urban: 7

URBAN: 16

Squatter Settlements: 9

High Agricultural Potential: 69

RURAL: 140

Low Agricultural Potential: 71

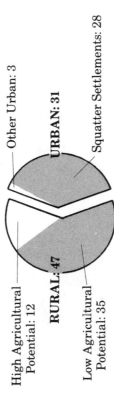

LATIN AMERICA

In Latin America, 63 million people, or 80 per cent of the region's *poorest* people, live in rural or urban areas of high ecological vulnerability—areas where ecological destruction or severe environmental hazards threaten their well-being.

Other Urban: 3

URBAN: 31

Squatter Settlements: 28

High Agricultural Potential: 12

RURAL: 47

Low Agricultural Potential: 35

America and Asia predominantly to these areas. Moreover, in middle-income countries, rising population stresses in low-potential and peri-urban areas cannot be divorced from the significant development that has taken place in areas with *high* agricultural potential. Inevitably, the modernization of agriculture in many prime agricultural areas has led to decreasing labor requirements in agricultural production. In southern Brazil or irrigated regions in Asia, millions of poor tenant farmers and landless laborers have been turned off the lands they used to help to till or harvest. This is virtually inevitable; although some initial steps in modernization (such as technology or infrastructure that permit double cropping) may *create* employment, a growing farm sector *sheds* labor.[27] Moreover, the productivity increases in many well endowed agricultural areas have indirectly added to economic difficulties for poor farmers in more marginal areas. Where commodity prices have fallen as a result of increased production in irrigated areas, for example, incomes have sometimes fallen for farmers outside those areas who have not boosted their production.[28]

Thus poverty alleviation in high-potential areas through agricultural modernization will always to some extent "succeed" at the expense of poor people in other areas. Simultaneous strategies therefore must be devised for low-potential agricultural areas and urban areas that absorb growing numbers of poor to accomplish two objectives: increasing human productivity through gainful employment, and relieving extreme environmental stress on their fragile resource bases.

To sum up, the combination of development achievements in many fertile areas and increasing population pressures in areas that were previously not heavily exploited has changed the nature of poverty in the developing world in recent decades. Instead of being ubiquitous across the landscape, poverty is in many developing countries more and more concentrated into definable geographical areas. In many of these areas, poor people occupy marginal or ecologically vulnerable lands that lack appropriate infrastructure and technology.

Ecosystems Under Stress

The growing concentration of poor people in precarious environments is a major cause of the severe environmental destruction that has been documented in developing countries by numerous recent studies. The strains of increasing exploitation by the poor correlate directly with severe environmental problems in many moist tropical forest, hillside, arid, and semi-arid areas. In urbanizing areas, environmental disasters have in the past decade underscored the degree to which poor people suffer when development proceeds without infrastructure and land preparation. Though not generally caused by poverty, the loss of agricultural productivity due to poor land and water management practices in many fertile agricultural areas threatens to reverse the gains of people who only recently pulled above the poverty level and to reduce the availability of cheap food for the urban poor.

This section draws on international data to provide a general picture of poverty-linked environmental destruction occurring in broad ecological zones found in the developing world and an estimate of the numbers of people whose livelihood and well-being may be thus jeopardized. Figure 4 shows the relative severity of problems associated with land degradation in different ecosystems in the developing world. The potential adverse consequences of such extensive environmental destruction on the prospects for future agricultural development can hardly be exaggerated.

Tropical Forests. Tropical deforestation has received a great deal of international publicity—in part because it is the environmental problem in developing countries that most directly affects the world at large—by threatening extinction of many valuable plants and animals and by contributing to the greenhouse effect. Humid tropical forests, including jungle, rain forest, cloud forest, swamps, and mangroves, cover 1.2 billion hectares, an area equivalent in size to almost two-thirds of the landmass of Latin America.[29]

It is estimated that at least 7.5 million hectares of this closed tropical forest is being cut down each year in developing countries. Up to two-thirds of tropical deforestation occurs for the purposes of increasing agricultural production, but because they are shallow and subject to hardening and to the leaching of nutrients, forest soils often lose their fertility after short periods of cultivation. Between a third and a half of the 5 million hectares of tropical forest cleared yearly for agriculture experience fertility declines of greater than 50 per cent within the first three years.[30]

Perhaps 80 per cent of this clearing is attributed to the slash-and-burn agriculture being practiced by poor settlers in these regions. Yet, as John O. Browder discusses (Chapter 3), not all poor people who live in tropical moist forest regions practice destructive forms of slash-and-burn agriculture. Many traditional users of the forest have developed methods of utilization that are ecologically stable under low population densities. Moreover, the attribution of the destruction to impoverished slash-and-burn agriculturalists in many tropical forest areas is misleading because it focuses only on the proximate causes. In many areas, especially the lowland forests of South and Central America, poor settlers may wield the machetes and torches that initially clear the forest, but the ultimate beneficiaries are the large landholders and companies that buy up small tracts of cleared or abandoned land and take advan-

Figure 4. Land Degradation in Developing Countries

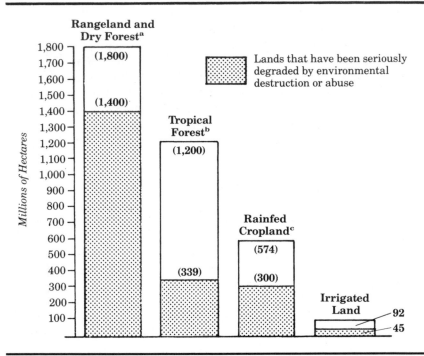

[a]Excludes deserts and cropland.
[b]Total tropical forest in developing countries; degraded portion indicates land that has been deforested since 1960.
[c]Rainfed cropland in current production.

Sources: United Nations Environment Programme (UNEP), *The State of the World Environment, 1987* (Nairobi: UNEP, 1987), pp. 23-32; World Food Council, "Sustainable Food Security": "Action for Environmental Management of Agriculture," Report presented at the 14th Ministerial Session of WFC, Nicosia, Cyprus, May 23-26, 1988, pp. 4-8; Food and Agriculture Organization, *Agriculture: Toward 2000* (Rome; FAO, July 1987), C 87/27, p. 255; United Nations Environment Programme, "The Disappearing Forests," *UNEP Environment Brief,* No. 3, 1988.

tage of subsidies to cattle ranching and other agricultural activities that would be unprofitable without government support.[31]

The absolute numbers of people who live in the world's tropical forest areas and depend on agriculture-related activities are still relatively low—probably about 200 million people.[32] Ominously, however, more and more of these people are very recent and poor immigrants from other areas. Governments in many countries with tropical forests—especially around the Amazon region, the Caribbean slope of Central America, the outer islands of Southeast Asia, and West and Central

Africa—have been purposely relocating people into these areas to relieve population pressures in other regions. Tropical forests have become the "safety" valves for countries facing a rising tide of landlessness because of overpopulation in good agricultural areas (Indonesia); limited urban absorption of persons displaced by agricultural modernization (Brazil); or grossly inequitable distribution of other arable lands (Central America). These poor settlers, often left abandoned by the false promises of government agricultural programs, pose far greater threats to tropical forests than do traditional forest dwellers.

Hillsides and Dry Lands. The clearest correlations between poverty and environmental destruction can be made in the mountainous and dry regions of developing countries. In these regions, growing population pressure has greatly increased the demand for food and fuelwood. Food production has moved onto areas traditionally used for seasonal grazing or onto steep upland slopes. The clearing of trees for agriculture and the increased demand for fuelwood have exacerbated environmental problems (such as soil erosion) that threaten food production and have forced people to spend far greater time gathering fuelwood.

Recent studies by several United Nations organizations have identified areas in the developing world where agricultural and wood production are insufficient to provide food and fuel to current populations because the carrying capacity of the land is being exceeded under existing agricultural technologies. In general, resultant food insecurity and fuelwood shortages tend to be most acute in dry and hilly areas of developing countries. For example, according to a recent World Food Council report, the regions where rural environmental deterioration and food production clash most sharply include: the Sahelian countries; the Horn of Africa and East Africa; much of Southeast Asia and Afghanistan; parts of South Asia, Java, and the Philippines; the Andes, Northeast Brazil, El Salvador, Guatemala, and Haiti.[33]

Another measure of the extent of the poverty and environment crisis in hillside and dry areas is provided by those areas experiencing acute shortages of fuelwood. The Food and Agriculture Organization's Forestry Department found that 69 of 95 developing countries studied faced fuelwood shortages. The researchers concluded that there is "a disturbing degree of correspondence between the areas at risk of desertification and deficient in fuelwood and those areas having inadequate land resources to feed their populations."[34] The principal technical advisor to the United Nations Development Programme remarked recently that "a map of absolute poverty in Africa . . . coincides with the areas that have been deforested."[35]

The FAO estimated in 1983 that, all told, nearly a quarter of a billion people (roughly 100 million in rural areas and 150 million in urban areas) suffered from acute shortages of fuelwood as a result of forest destruction. The most critical areas were the dry zones of the Sahelian countries, as well as much of East and South East Africa, the arid mountainous zones in the Himalayan and Andean countries, and the arid areas of the Pacific coast of Latin America. The study estimated that nearly 1.3 billion additional people (a billion in rural areas) lived where they could meet current demand for wood only by cutting trees faster than they were being regenerated. Over 700 million of these people lived in the countrysides and small towns of Asia, mainly in the great plains of the Indu and Ganges rivers and in Southeast Asia. This led FAO to conclude that, by the year 2000, as many as 3 billion poor people who depend upon firewood for their principal source of energy will face acute shortages.[36]

The environmental consequences of these trends are massive. In many arid and semi-arid areas, the pressures of wood gathering, inappropriate farming techniques, population growth, and overgrazing contribute to the spread of desert-like conditions that further decrease the productivity of marginal lands and make the rural poor even more susceptible to drought and other natural disasters. The productive potential of almost 900 million hectares of drylands in the developing countries (nearly 20 per cent of the total) already is severely degraded by desertification. At least 850 million people live in dry areas, where desertification is causing productivity to decline, and 230 million of these people are estimated to occupy desertified land.[37] In Sub-Saharan Africa alone, 65 million hectares of once productive grazing lands have been turned into unproductive deserts in the past half-century, affecting some 100 million people who currently live in these areas.[38]

Expanding cultivation out of the plains and valleys onto hillsides has caused serious erosion of an estimated 160 million hectares of upland watersheds in tropical developing countries in recent years. Some of the most devastated areas include the highlands of Ethiopia; the uplands of the Andean region; virtually the entire upper Himalayan watersheds; the central highlands of much of Central America; and Haiti, the Dominican Republic, and several other Caribbean nations. Thus some 500 million people are thought to occupy hillside areas at risk because of destruction of vegetative cover and soil erosion.[39]

Another reason for concern about environmental deterioration in the upland watersheds of the developing countries is that up to 40 per cent of all agricultural production in developing countries takes place in valley floors and deltas downstream, according to John De Boer (Chapter 4). It is estimated that the livelihood of 400 million farmers living in those downstream lowland areas in developing countries is threatened by soil erosion in upland watersheds.[40] Substantial investments in upstream land and water conservation may become critical less for the production they will yield in the upland watersheds than for the protection against excessive flooding and sedimentation they will give downstream producers.

Prime Agricultural Lands. Land degradation in fertile agricultural areas of developing countries threatens to reverse many gains from agricultural development. After a generation of large infrastructural projects to promote development of high-potential areas, development assistance agencies and governments are having increasing difficulty ensuring that these dams, irrigation systems, and other projects fulfill their productive potential annually and remain in good repair for their expected lifetimes. As a result, many developing countries cannot maintain the productivity gains from completed agricultural development projects. In India, Pakistan, Egypt, the Philippines, Sri Lanka, and other countries, waterlogging and soil salinization have removed nearly as much irrigated agricultural land from production as has been opened by new irrigation projects in recent years.[41]

FAO estimates that because of salinity or poor drainage, as much as 45 million hectares of irrigated land in developing countries requires reclamation—almost half of the 92 million hectares of irrigated land in the developing world.[42] According to Montague Yudelman (Chapter 1), at least a billion people in the developing countries have benefited from recent advances in irrigation; the threat of lost productivity due to land degradation is thus extremely serious. Millions of previously very poor families that have experienced less than one generation of increasing wealth due to rising agricultural productivity could see that trend reversed if environmental degradation is not checked.

Environmental deterioration is also serious in rainfed agricultural areas that could, with good land management practices, sustain long-term high-productivity agriculture. FAO estimates that without long-term conservation measures, 544 million hectares of rainfed cropland in the developing countries are threatened. Regionally, 10 per cent of South America's rainfed cropland, 30 per cent of Central America's, 17 per cent of Africa's, 20 per cent of Southwest Asia's, and 36 per cent of Southeast Asia's face soil erosion and soil fertility problems that could remove these lands from production by the year 2000.[43] These lands may encompass many of the 250 million poor people who still live in good agricultural lands—such as the black soils of India—that have not yet been served by modern agricultural technologies and infrastructure.

The Urban Periphery. Close to 100 million very poor people in the developing world live on the periphery of urban areas in settings where they may be threatened periodically by environmental disasters created or abetted by their own living conditions. The cumulative degree of environmental destruction that has occurred is difficult to assess and the total number of victimized people difficult to estimate. The anecdotal evidence, however, is that the numbers are substantial.[44] Numerous ecological disasters (floods, mudslides, industrial explosions) have occurred throughout the developing world in recent years, and their death tolls, economic costs, and ensuing health problems have been well publicized.

In Rio de Janeiro, for example, according to planning authority estimates, 3 million people (nearly two-thirds of all *favela* dwellers) live on the steep slopes surrounding the city. Mudslides, claiming hundreds of lives and leaving thousands homeless, have become commonplace during the annual rainy season—after squatter settlements strip away vegetation, destabilizing the hillside soils. A 1987 study concluded that the municipal government would have to spend nearly a billion dollars just to make basic infrastructural improvements to reduce the constant threat of floods and mudslides.[45]

During three months in 1984, three major industrial disasters in developing countries together claimed the lives of nearly 3,000 people— the leak of deadly gaseous chemicals in Bhopal, India; the explosion of a petroleum storage facility in Mexico City; and the incineration of a natural gas pipeline in Cubatão, Brazil. Despite their different causes, each of these disasters shared one common trait: Virtually all of the victims were extremely poor people who occupied previously vacant lands adjacent to major industrial facilities in heavily urbanized areas. In all three cases, had these squatter settlements not been so close to the industrial facilities, the death and injury toll from the disasters most probably would have been substantially lower.[46]

A Common Agenda for Attacking Poverty and Environmental Destruction

The changing physical circumstances of poverty in the developing world—who poor people are, where they live, and how much and what kind of land they have access to—require different responses from the international community than when poverty was pervasive throughout the developing countries and investment opportunities abounded in areas of high agricultural potential.

In many countries where the flat, fertile, irrigable lands have been developed, more marginal areas such as hilly, arid, and humid tropical areas are under increased population and development pressure. Such areas have become the repositories of some of the most enduring rural poverty in the developing world. Because these are often highly susceptible to ecological deterioration, their improved environmental management is becoming increasingly critical for development strategies.

Inevitably, international donors and developing-country governments need to make more concerted efforts, first, to formulate joint strategies to address the twin challenges of poverty and environment and, second, to differentiate the objectives of physical development strategies according to the productive capacity of the environment and the economic circumstances of the populace.

Fundamentally different approaches to development may be required to solve *both* the poverty and the environment problems that are rampant in many ecological areas where the world's poorest people are being remanded. At the same time, the success or failure of anti-poverty and environmental protection strategies in the well endowed agricultural areas, in marginal or fragile lands, and in urban squatter settlements is clearly interdependent.

Increasing Production in Well Endowed Areas

As a strategy for poverty alleviation, as well as for overall environmental protection, donors and national governments must redouble their efforts to raise overall agricultural output by investing in areas with the highest agricultural potential. A quarter of a billion of the world's poorest and hungriest people live in flat lowlands, alluvial valleys, and other areas with good agricultural potential. Under optimal conditions, these areas alone could produce enough food to meet regional demand of their growing populations. These lands represent unfinished business from the green revolution.

Very large increases in production can, and must, still be achieved in areas such as the central plains regions of India, the fertile plains and savannah belt of Africa, and the high savannah and Pacific lowland plains of the Central American and South American countries. These advances must underpin and be linked to efforts to reduce poverty and control environmental degradation in the areas where the other two-thirds of the poorest people live—the marginal rural areas and poorly developed urban settlements.

Environmentalists must recognize that these areas can only achieve their potential capacity through substantial investments in construction and land improvements, and that intensive development in good agricultural areas is perhaps the single biggest prerequisite for long-term conservation in other areas. It is also the only way to ensure abundant, affordable supplies of food for the growing masses of the urban poor.

Development assistance agencies must at the same time recognize that the next generation of physical development calls for more subtle responses than the past decades of helter-skelter large irrigation and agricultural development projects. Questions of long-term sustainability and smaller scale adaptation to local ecological conditions can no longer be ignored.

The keys to the promotion of joint poverty and environment strategies in high-potential agricultural areas are also the cornerstones to maximizing long-term agricultural output: intensification, innovation, construction and rehabilitation, and soil and water conservation.

Intensification. Agricultural production on the best farmlands of the developing world must be greatly intensified. This is especially true in Latin America, where land distribution and sociocultural factors often have resulted in less than maximal cropping patterns in fertile valleys and coastal plains. Across the developing world, notably in irrigated areas, gross inefficiencies still severely curtail production on land with high agricultural potential. Development assistance agencies need especially to confront the tremendous gap that exists between actual yields achieved in the fields and the yields made possible by modern science and technology. This will require far more focus on implementation and long-term maintenance in conjunction with agricultural development projects.

Technological Innovation. Continued technological innovation is needed to raise yields of major food crops to ensure food security for growing poor populations. Across Asia, in particular, the green revolution has run out of steam and must be broadened and deepened. Continued development of new high-yielding varieties of cereals (especially rice, which remains the staple food of hundreds of millions of the poor) is critical to feed growing rural and urban populations. Technological advances, which quadrupled wheat and rice yields in irrigated areas, need also to be duplicated for other food crops grown in rainfed agricultural areas. Given their great importance in the diets of poor people, especially in Africa, roots, tubers, and starchy bananas have received low-priority attention from the international agricultural research community. Breakthroughs in these and other regionally important food crops have proven far more complex and demand much more extensive adaptation to local circumstances and much greater attention to socioeconomic circumstances that inhibit production. In addition, an agricultural research agenda to meet the economic needs of poor people may not always be dictated by efforts to maximize crop yields. Quite often, poor people will benefit even more from technological breakthroughs that reduce such external threats to production as crop pests and disease (notably in Sub-Saharan Africa) or that lower demand for costly external inputs such as chemical fertilizers and pesticides.

Infrastructure. Infrastructure serving high-potential agricultural areas needs to be extended, improved, and rehabilitated. The availability and quality of infrastructure in the form of roads, canals, terraces, and electricity is probably the single most important determinant of the way people in developing countries use land. Research has demonstrated that farmers with access to good infrastructure use land more efficiently, adapt modern techniques and inputs more thoroughly, participate more in market economies (buying and selling), and employ more labor than do farmers with poor infrastructure.[47] In areas of good agricultural potential not yet served by infrastructure, construction of roads and other infrastructure would benefit millions of farmers who, for example, keep cattle in areas where crops could fetch a higher return because cattle, unlike produce, can walk to market. At the same time, as environmentalists have often argued, the construction of infrastructure often creates large adverse environmental impacts. Much greater environmental protection efforts must ensure that the ecological damage resulting from the next generation of infrastructure construction is radically reduced.

Land and Water Management. The failure to institutionalize long-term management of land and water resources as part of agricultural development programs in fertile agricultural areas is increasingly recognized as a major impediment to continuing increases in agricultural output. Indeed, the gains of even the many erstwhile poor people who have benefited from agricultural modernization in irrigated areas are threatened by salinization, alkalinization, and waterlogging—the ecological silent scourges—and by poorly maintained infrastructure. Montague Yudelman (Chapter 1) points out that marginal beneficiaries, not wealthier farmers, often suffer the most if these problems are ignored. Yudelman examines in more detail ways of maintaining and extending the agricultural progress of the past 30 years in irrigated agriculture so as to benefit the poor and protect the natural resource base.

The generation of on-farm and off-farm employment also needs much greater attention to absorb the growing numbers of landless poor in rich agricultural areas. These people will otherwise migrate to urban squatter settlements or to less well endowed and more ecologically fragile areas. When combined with food-for-work opportunities, conservation and rehabilitation projects that promote long-term soil and water conservation could employ many landless laborers.

Environmental Strategies for Poor People in Marginal Areas

Equipping people with basic life skills and facilitating outmigration to relieve pressures of excessive human exploitation may well be the best strategy for many marginal agricultural areas. Many development experts in fact point to the experiences with development in marginal regions, such as Appalachia in the United States or Wales in the United Kingdom, to argue that scarce development capital should not be wasted in developing areas that should, in the long run, be removed from agricultural production. However, the changing nature of poverty makes "benign neglect" an inadequate and unrealistic response to the environmental problems that are rampant in fragile, remote areas of the developing world. Few developing-country economies have realistic prospects in coming decades of creating enough urban and industrial jobs to pull the poorest people away from hillsides, arid lands, and tropical forests where they are currently destroying the environment and languishing in poverty in their efforts to survive.

The stark reality is that until well into the twenty-first century, the number of poor people with little technology or investment capital who need first and foremost to satisfy their basic food needs are likely to continue to increase in ecologically vulnerable agricultural lands. In the quest for subsistence, these poor people create environmental problems that further impoverish themselves and their land, that threaten downstream production in higher potential areas, and that contribute to global ecological problems such as species extinction and the greenhouse effect. These problems are becoming so acute that alternative development strategies must be found to address the human needs of the nearly 370 million of the world's poorest people who occupy such fragile ecological areas. Lacking alternative means of livelihood, these people will continue to overexploit the resources at hand, further enmiring themselves and their lands in poverty. Any development strategy to deal with this reality must focus simultaneously on raising the productivity of these people—either directly in agriculture or through other income-generating activities—*and* reducing the stress that poor marginal farmers place on fragile environments.

Thus the rationale for investing in agricultural and rural development outside the most fertile and densely populated areas is not that aggregate food needs cannot be met unless these lands are brought into production. If food production potential can be maximized in good agricultural areas, the world should be able to feed itself without the marginal production that can be eked out of fragile areas. The rationale is one of livelihood for the hundreds of millions of people who will remain in these areas and environmental protection for the resources that will continue to be heavily exploited as a result.

Marginal and ecologically sensitive areas need different approaches to poverty alleviation, food production, agricultural development, and employment generation. Instead of focusing on one goal—increasing food production, for example—a variety of strategies must be devised to disrupt the vicious cycles of poverty and environmental degradation. In some areas, this may be possible by investing in infrastructure and technology to increase the productivity and sustainability of agriculture, though not necessarily food production. In others, the focus will need to be on income generation through on-farm wage employment, or through non-farm rural employment in enterprises or public works programs. In the final analysis, some regions may make scant progress in breaking the connection between poverty and environment until the inevitable is facilitated—migration from marginal areas to more fertile areas (where possible) or to urban areas (where necessary).

From Subsistence to Sustainable Agriculture. The socioeconomic and demographic forces here described and the increasing determination of governments to promote national territorial development have swept multilateral development banks and bilateral assistance agencies into a tide of large projects intended to open up virgin and sometimes marginal lands for agriculture and livestock in recent decades. Often, these ambitious efforts to exploit previously undeveloped lands have not been premised on the introduction of new techniques for increasing or sustaining production. Such attempts—as in projects for resettlement in the tropical forests of the Amazon or Indonesia, or for range management in Botswana and the Sahel—have often resulted in spectacular and widely publicized ecological disasters.[48]

The underlying cause of failure is that poor farmers have not been provided with sustainable alternatives to subsistence agriculture or their pastoral lifestyles. The problem is multifaceted. First, many poor farmers who have moved into frontier areas simply do not receive the economic and physical infrastructure necessary to move beyond subsistence agriculture. For example, the million poor migrants who moved into Rondonia, Brazil, in the early 1980s deforested an area larger than the state of West Virginia. Enticed there by the offer of free land and government support under the Polonoroeste Project, they continue to practice destructive subsistence agriculture that soon depletes soil fertility, leaving them again poor and on the move. For example, according to recent reports, almost half of the settlers who came to outlying areas of the project in 1985 had by 1988 abandoned their lands. Although many of these settlers have moved to urban areas, many others have joined other newcomers in extending slash-and-burn agriculture deeper into the forest frontiers in Acre and Amazonas.

Many Brazilian agricultural development experts now realize that the type of farming likely to be economically and ecologically sustainable in the cleared areas of Rondonia does not revolve solely around subsistence crops and must include intensive cultivation of perennial bush and tree crops (such as coffee, nuts, cocoa, and rubber). This type of agriculture requires more capital inputs and better transportation for marketing but is more likely to protect soil fertility and produce a surplus for small farmers in the long term. Over time, this more intensive pattern will concentrate agriculture in the most fertile areas, decrease the unit costs of public services, stimulate a more active rural trading system, encourage closer economic ties between rural areas and rapidly expanding urban areas, and reduce the strain on the remaining forested areas.[49] Unless and until these settlers receive the support and investment necessary to make this transition, they will continue to practice ecologically destructive and economically unsustainable forms of agriculture.

Second, too little effort has been made to test and introduce agricultural techniques that are adapted especially to overcome the specific ecological constraints of many fragile localities where the poor have settled. Recently, field projects at the International Institute of Tropical Agriculture (IITA) in Ibadan, Nigeria, have demonstrated that the combination of rows of leguminous trees alternated with rows of annual crops can provide organic nutrients and other benefits that can prolong the productivity of acid, infertile soils found in much of the humid tropics.[50] Much progress has been reported by ecologists and small private voluntary organizations in the introduction of sustainable agroecological systems in developing countries.[51] However, many of these efforts remain relatively small-scale and limited in replicability by dependence upon externally provided expertise; the challenge is to move from the demostration project and model village phase to widespread introduction of these techniques. Development assistance agencies need to put greater resources into advancing such agroecological techniques and to adapting them to meet the needs of poor farmers who cultivate marginal soils and do not have access to chemical inputs.

Third, too little attention has gone into developing long-term plans for promoting a transition from slash and burn to sustainable land use and land management techniques in areas where conventional continuous cultivation is not appropriate, especially for poor people who cannot afford the infrastructure and fertilizers that would be necessary to correct for nature's deficiencies. Although the overall sustainability of agriculture is a primary long-term objective, agricultural development efforts in some areas of limited fertility or ecological fragility may require a succession of unsustainable steps. This is the case, for example, in some tropical soils where long-term nutrient limitations and soil qualities appear to necessitate higher inputs (such as fertilizers) or lower levels of exploitation (perennial or tree crops) if agriculture is to be sustained. Experiments at Yurimaguas in the Peruvian Amazon have demonstrated a succession of input-lowering techniques that can give poor farmers a critical "bridging" period. Although unsustainable in the long run, such techniques can prolong soil fertility declines for as long as five to seven years, while farmers make the transition to other long-term strategies of exploitation, such as perennial cropping or silviculture.[52]

All of these examples suggest that efforts to propagate subsistence food production in marginal areas may be far less successful than sequential cropping patterns that promote a long-term transition from traditional low-productivity, soil-degrading techniques, to more intensive, higher-production agriculture. To the extent that marginal areas remain in agricultural production, poor farmers may have to switch to perennials and other non-food crops that can better adapt to the ecological constraints than can rice, beans, squash, maize, various tubers, and other traditional food crops.

Environmentalists and advocates of "self-reliant" development strategies often criticize programs that promote market-oriented agriculture for poor farmers rather than concentrate on local food production. In reality, economic success for small farmers lies in a diversified strategy to ensure food security through a combination of food production and market orientation. Particularly in fragile environments, agricultural development efforts to meet poor farmers' needs should be concentrated on maximizing the sustainability of farming as a livelihood rather than narrowly focused on promoting individual household food self-sufficiency.

Multiplying Small Successes. International donors are under enormous pressure to tackle rural environmental problems that are directly linked to poverty at the project level. Indeed, they spent hundreds of millions of dollars in the 1970s and 1980s to support forest management, watershed protection, village woodlots, shelterbelts, and other forms of large environmental improvement projects. Yet these projects still have an extraordinarily high record of failure in most of Africa and in dry and hillside areas in Asia and Latin America.

One problem consistently cited in development literature is that the scale on which donors are used to dealing with large infrastructural projects is far too massive to promote the kinds of microbehavioral changes in on-farm management that are needed for long-term success of agroforestry, fuelwood and fodder production, or integrated pest management projects. Clearly donors must find better ways of supporting multitudes of small projects and working through nongovernmental organizations in order to duplicate small successes.

Yet simply helping governments and private voluntary organizations to dot the globe with small, decentralized projects is not likely to have enough impact to pull the poorest countries and people from the poverty and environment trap. A rush into small-scale, decentralized and nongovernmental approaches to poverty might leave untended the

questions of system-wide barriers.[53] A multitude of village-level reforestation projects does not add up to a strategy for solving a fuelwood
shortage on its current magnitude in much of Africa. Thus, a World
Bank forester observed, "The challenge remains how to multiply what
are in many cases relatively small-scale initiatives . . . into larger-scale
rural forestry programs that will penetrate throughout the rural areas
as quickly as possible. The current [1984] rate of tree planting in many
Bank countries is less than one-fifth . . . the rate needed to assure a reasonable supply of fuelwood, fodder and poles by the year 2000."[54]

An Agenda for International Agricultural Research. It was the
"Malthusian nightmare" of population outstripping food production
capability in the developing world more than anything else that stimulated the creation of the international network of agricultural research
centers in the 1960s and 1970s. The nightmare has not materialized,
and hunger is no longer regarded as a failure of food production or agricultural technology.[55]

This evolution, together with the environmental threats to agricultural production in many ecological areas in the developing world, has
enormous implications for donors, who contribute nearly $500 million
annually to support agricultural research in developing countries. As
CGIAR Chairman and World Bank Vice President W. David Hopper
recently noted to members of the Consultative Group on International
Agricultural Research (CGIAR): "Food abundance has been the overarching goal of the CGIAR since its inception. . . . Now a changing environmental context poses a new challenge . . . the sustainability of food
production in various environments."[56]

To meet these new challenges, the international community needs
to make a much more concerted effort to apply modern science and technology. Agricultural research must be targeted on the special needs of
such areas, and it must be appropriately adapted to specific social and
cultural settings, so as to increase agricultural productivity while
reducing environmental destruction in land fertility. Through the
CGIAR, international donors helped to revolutionize agriculture in the
irrigated areas of Asia and the Americas in the past two decades. Now
they should take the lead in promoting scientific research that increases
productive potential in the ecological areas where green revolution technologies have not been appropriate—arid and semi-arid zones, hillside
and tropical forest areas—and where some of the greatest poverty and
environmental destruction persists.

Traditionally, the international agricultural research centers have
concentrated on increasing single-crop yield potential through the
development of germplasm and appropriate management practices. In

the future, more research needs to be focused on increasing the long-term yield potential for more specialized agricultural production systems. This will require special attention to: the cumulative effects over time of cropping patterns and input use on land productivity; to the development of farming techniques for on-farm erosion control, soil conservation, and moisture retention (via vegetative measures and the introduction of tree crops); and to inexpensive, safe means of pest control in practically every agricultural setting.

Resource-poor farmers—who can least afford the inputs that help raise and sustain agricultural productivity—often congregate on resource-poor lands where fertility is most difficult to sustain without external inputs and productive infrastructure. Cropping patterns, biological techniques for nutrient fixing and pest control, and other agricultural innovations that lower the requirements for external inputs may be as important for many poor farmers as those that raise yields under conditions that can only be achieved with high inputs of fertilizers, pesticides, and other measures that may correct soil constraints artificially. Donors concerned with poverty and environment need to push the agricultural research community to devote much greater attention and resources toward input-lowering technologies that permit the sustainable exploitation of marginal soils in areas of increasing population pressure.

In addition, despite the special focus of the international research community on the collection and preservation of germplasm, remarkably little scientific attention has been devoted to the potential for similar tree-crop research. There is widespread consensus among agricultural experts that any "sustainable" effort to introduce or stabilize productive agricultural systems in fragile areas depends heavily upon widening the use of agroforestry techniques, growing trees alongside pastures and crops. Much greater international research should be focused in the coming decade on intensive efforts to improve collection, screening, selection, and production of fast-growing woody shrubs and trees for use by resource-poor farmers in marginal areas. The goal should be to promote the introduction of varieties (1) that not only tolerate low-fertility soils, but also contribute to soil improvement through nutrient fixing and soil stabilization, and (2) that provide additional farm produce such as nuts, fruit, fuelwood, or browse for livestock.

Another key area for emphasis in forestry research is the enhanced use of secondary forest species in the rehabilitation, stabilization, and (where possible) recovery of soil fertility in the millions of hectares of abandoned, degraded lands in the developing world. In degraded lands such as steep watersheds, humid tropical regions, and dry zones—wherever external pressures are removed before extreme degradation sets in—researchers have observed striking regenerative progress in the natural establishment of trees and grasses. Far more systematic assessment and screening for desirable characteristics such as fast growth and moisture retention will be valuable in years to come as more and more countries follow India's example in setting up special programs and agencies to rehabilitate degraded lands.

Under the International Center for Research in Agroforestry (ICRAF) and many other regional institutions, a variety of long-term research efforts are under way. This is one area of agricultural research where priority attention from international donors and virtually all of the international agricultural research centers could yield very substantial progress in the coming decade.

Appropriate Conservation Technologies for the Poor. Many donors and recipient governments have promoted large, engineering-based solutions to environmental problems and paid far less attention to local, on-farm, labor-intensive solutions. Even in labor-constrained circumstances, mechanized, labor-saving conservation techniques are not always appropriate in areas susceptible to natural resource degradation.

The economic and ecological obstacles to traditional, capital-intensive approaches are pronounced in on-farm soil conservation techniques and land-clearing for agriculture in forested areas.[57] Recent studies indicate that large cost savings and high rates of return could be realized in many countries by replacing conventional methods of constructing large earthworks with on-farm vegetative systems for soil erosion control and moisture retention.

The Indian government, with large external support from multilateral agencies, has responded to its massive soil erosion problem by spending more than $100 million to construct on-farm earthworks to reduce soil erosion. By 1987, diversion banks and waterways protected about 2 million hectares. However, some estimates indicate that up to 90 per cent of India's arable land (nearly 300 million hectares) eventually may need to be protected by such soil erosion control measures. India would have to spend an estimated $14 billion to extend the current strategy broadly enough to protect the agricultural land base from reduced productivity.[58]

A recent study by World Bank consultants proposed that, instead of the earthworks strategy of soil conservation, India should promote the use of a coarse perennial grass (Vetiver or khus grass) as the backbone of a soil conservation program based upon vegetative hedges and contour planting. The proposed techniques have been used for more than 30 years with striking success in several regions of India, as well as on Fiji and the steep-sloped areas of several Caribbean islands. The cost per hectare would range from one-hundredth to one-tenth of the cost of earthworks. Moreover, since the farmers could do the planting themselves and the grass could be cultivated in on-farm or local nurseries, poor farmers could internalize many of the costs instead of borrowing or reducing current consumption to initiate these soil conservation measures on their own farms.[59]

A strategy of introducing vegetative conservation measures to help stave off India's soil erosion problems could provide benefits not only to small landholders who cannot afford mechanized soil conservation means, but also to India's growing landless population. Local non-farm employment—in the form of hired labor and small enterprises for nursery production of plant material—would increase in areas beset by the worst land degradation and poverty.

New Approaches to Developing Fragile Areas. The international donor community needs to acknowledge that maximizing agricultural production is not necessarily always the primary development objective in every ecological zone. This may be especially true in areas with essential upstream watershed protection functions and in critical habitats for unique flora and fauna.

Investment in the conservation of heavily exploited watersheds is increasingly seen by international donors as a critical complement to downstream efforts to raise agricultural production in fertile valley and lowland areas. Yet few attempts have been made to link upstream protection with downstream production at the project finance level. Instead, donors have launched major agricultural development projects without adequately assessing related actions such as reforestation, terracing, or soil conservation programs that upland watersheds may need. As a result, watershed protection projects most often respond to emerging crises and are financed by bilateral donors as concessionary loans or with outright grants-in-aid. Much greater attention needs to be devoted to internalizing the costs of upstream investments into the project financing for downstream agricultural development.

Donors often ignore the potential for promoting "low-level" utilization strategies in fragile and remote areas—especially those where indigenous peoples maintain distinct sociocultural systems in relative harmony with their natural surroundings. For example, individuals and communities in many remote tropical forest areas are tapping the resources of the forest—growing or maintaining natural forest species for fuel, fiber, fodder, medicines, and timber. Yet these activities can rarely be "scaled up," in size or intensity, without threatening to undermine other important objectives: the lifestyles and cultures of native populations, the protection of biological diversity, and the maintenance of watershed absorptive capacity through maximum tree cover. A challenge to donors is to find ways to balance the goals of increasing the productivity of low-level users of remote forests (rubber tappers, rattan collectors, fruit and nut collectors) without disrupting their socioeconomic systems and without threatening the integrity of the forest. John Browder (Chapter 3) examines some alternatives in tropical forest areas.

The international conservation community must also continue to see the protection of flora and fauna in developing countries as a battle that must be fought *outside* as well as inside the parks and protected areas of poor countries. A program cosponsored by the U.S. Agency for International Development and the World Wildlife Fund, for example, seeks to improve the quality of life of rural people through field projects that integrate the management of natural resources in "buffer zones" around protected areas with small-scale community development efforts. This Wildlands and Human Needs Program includes more than 20 projects in Africa, Asia, and Latin America.[60] Drawing on the experiences of World Wildlife Fund and other conservation organizations, Alison Jolly (Chapter 6) develops recommendations for reconciling economic development with the need to protect extremely fragile and unique natural resources based upon her experiences in Madagascar.

Promoting Resource-Efficient Urban Development

The ultimate solution to many serious environmental problems linked to severe poverty in rural areas of developing countries may depend as much on the rate of urbanization, and indirectly on the rate of industrial and service-sector expansion, as on location-specific investments to promote "sustainability." Simply put, both poverty and environmental destruction in marginal areas of the developing world are signs of the pervasive lack of non-farm, income-generating opportunities within many countries' economies. If industrial and rural non-farm employment were growing at faster rates, fewer people would stay on their marginal lands, desperately attempting to extract a subsistence living.

But the inevitable increases in industrialization and urbanization that will be necessary to reduce both rural poverty and natural resource destruction bring their own enormous poverty and environmental challenges. Ironically, while continued urbanization is both inevitable and necessary, cities create environmental distortions far beyond their borders. Their demand for food, water, energy, and waste disposal taxes natural resources in surrounding rural areas in many ways.

Tim Campbell argues (Chapter 5) that the answer is not to try to reverse the urbanization process that fuels such rapid and choking growth in developing countries. Urbanization, even growth of megacities, is part of the solution to both poverty and environmental degradation, even if it poses additional perils as well. If megacities and secondary cities throughout the developing world are to absorb the inevitable expansion of poor populations without further declines in sanitary conditions and increases in environmental hazards, developing countries will have to find ways to provide more cost-effective infrastructural services and to deliver and maintain these services with greater efficiency.

Low-Cost Environmental Technologies. Donors need to promote urban development planning processes that emphasize the introduction of low-cost, decentralized technologies to reduce ecological dangers to the urban poor. A recent U.S. Agency for International Development (USAID) report concluded: "In any city where there are problems of lagging employment and enterprise creation, inadequate municipal service provision, insufficient cost recovery by utilities, pollution, low productivity, or high welfare costs, major improvements are likely to be possible through greater resource efficiency."[61] On the basis of a series of demonstration projects in several cities around the world during the 1980s, USAID found that one of the key responses to the challenges of rapid urbanization and population growth, high energy costs, and increasing pressures on scarce resources must be for "growing cities with most of their growth and expansion yet to come [to] develop into the future using much more resource-conserving and economical approaches than had been practiced by the world's cities heretofore. Virtually all of the technologies needed to deliver more services for less, and thus [to] alleviate many of the most menacing environmental threats to poor people in urban areas, already exist in developing countries."[62] Donors need to undertake major rethinking of what urban development means, especially in poor areas. Tim Campbell makes some recommendations for accomplishing this, such as greater attention to decentralized waste treatment and more efficient cookstoves.

Packaging Public Services. The packaging and "clustering" of infrastructural services as a means of serving more people at lower unit costs needs to be more diligently pursued. Even the poorest urban people can usually construct basic shelters. The location of a dwelling and the services available are often more important to their quality of life than the physical structure of their homes. This is why many experts on urban poverty urge public authorities to concentrate on improving the supply of public services in urban areas rather than on improving the quality of housing as such.[63]

Donors widely acknowledge, too, that installing public services as a package, instead of delivering separate infrastructure for water, sewerage, electricity, and transportation would increase efficiency and decrease unit costs. The realities of land tenure in many low-income settlements, and public-sector agency bureaucratic rivalries and uncoordinated planning processes, mean that public services are usually not delivered as a package to poor people. Instead, such services are usually provided incrementally and in response to a major crisis or political confrontation.

Conclusions

The growing numbers of poor people living in more geographically focused poverty zones in the developing countries are not simply standing still, waiting to be touched by the magic hand of development. They are literally "losing ground" as their lands suffer more and more from the strains of too many people, inappropriate technology, or lack or "protective" infrastructural investment. Environmental destruction has become synonymous with poverty wherever poor people cluster together.

Environmental degradation—soil erosion, desertification, declining soil fertility, salinization, flooding, mudslides, fuelwood shortages, unhealthy water supplies—is now one of the most formidable constraints on productivity for rural and urban poor in developing countries. These problems sap the productive potential of the marginal and meager land resources available to poor people; they heap additional labor requirements on poor people (especially women) who already work very long hours just to meet basic subsistence needs; they threaten the physical security of people and their possessions; and they increase opportunistic diseases that debilitate adults and kill infants.

These environmental problems have dramatic implications for government finance in an era when investment capital is scarce. Larger doses of investment capital and remedial labor will be necessary to rehabilitate, maintain, or increase agricultural production on these lands than would otherwise be necessary. The World Bank noted this phenomenon: "The agricultural base has deteriorated in many parts of the world, and, if unchecked, the deterioration will increase the cost of agricultural production in these areas. Deforestation and soil erosion are already catastrophic in many regions."[64]

The longer these circumstances persist, the higher will be the remedial costs and the external social and economic costs for nations that can ill afford to foot the bill. The incalculable human suffering associated with this process and the destruction of invaluable wildlife and natural resources in the interim can never be recouped.

Notes

[1] See John Lewis and contributors, *Strengthening the Poor: What Have We Learned?* (New Brunswick, N.J.: Transaction Books in cooperation with the Overseas Development Council, 1988).

[2] World Commission on Environment and Development, *Our Common Future* (London: Oxford University Press, 1987); H. Jeffrey Leonard, ed., *Divesting Nature's Capital: The Political Economy of Environmental Abuse in Developing Countries* (New York: Holmes and Meier, 1985).

[3] The World Bank, *World Development Report 1988* (Washington, D.C., 1988) p. 27.

[4] See for example, L. D. Swindale, "The Impact of Agricultural Development on the Environment: An IARC Point of View," speech given to the Consultative Group on International Agricultural Research Mid-Term Meeting, West Berlin, 15–19 May 1988.

[5] Barber Conable, "Address to the Board of Governors" (Washington, D.C.: The World Bank, September 1980).

[6] The World Bank, *The World Bank's Support for the Alleviation of Poverty* (Washington, D.C., 1988), p. 1. An earlier report had designated at least 730 million "hungry poor"—those whose daily caloric intake was so low as to threaten starvation or chronic malnutrition. See The World Bank, *Poverty and Hunger: Issues and Options for Food Security in Developing Countries* (Washington, D.C., 1986), p. 16.

[7] The World Bank estimates that in the late 1980s about half of the world's population (more than 2.5 billion people) was living on $1 or less per day. Although a standard "global" poverty line based upon GNP per capita or other economic indicators would be virtually meaningless, most poverty-oriented international development assistance programs focus on reaching broader groups than merely the "hungry" poor or those living in "absolute poverty." UNICEF's 1989 report, *The State of the World's Children*, for example, argues that anti-poverty programs must ensure "that essential needs are reliably met not just for the one billion or more who are the absolute poor of the world in the 1980s and 1990s, but for the 1.5 to 2 billion people who will constitute the poorest third of the developing world's population." (Oxford, England: Oxford University Press for the United Nations Children's Fund, 1989), p. 65.

[8] Sheldon Annis, "The Shifting Grounds of Poverty Lending at the World Bank," in Richard E. Feinberg and contributors, *Between Two Worlds: The World Bank's Next Decade* (New Brunswick, N.J.: Transaction Books in cooperation with the Overseas Development Council, 1986), p. 37.

[9] For example, writing of the situation in India, where nearly a hundred million people live in absolute poverty today, Uma Lele points out that agricultural modernization and other interventions to promote economic development have succeeded in holding poverty "well below the levels that population growth otherwise would have caused." Uma Lele, "Empowering Africa's Rural Poor: Problems and Prospects in Agricultural Development," in Lewis and contributors, *Strengthening the Poor*, op. cit., p. 77.

[10] See Michael Lipton, "The Poor and the Poorest: Some Interim Findings," *World Bank Discussion Paper 25* (Washington, D.C., 1988).

[11] Mayra Buvinić and Margaret A. Lycette, "Women, Poverty and Development in the Third World," in Lewis and contributors, *Strengthening the Poor*, op. cit., pp. 150–51.

[12] Buvinić and Lycette, "Women, Poverty and Development in the Third World," ibid., pp. 156–57.

[13] See United Nations Development Fund for Women (UNIFEM), *Development Cooperation with Women: The Experience and Future Directions of the Fund* (New York: United Nations, Department of International Economic and Social Affairs, 1985); and Alice Stewart Carloni, "Lessons Learned from 1972–1985: The Importance of Gender for AID Projects," Draft paper prepared for the U.S. Agency for International Development (Washington, D.C., 1985).

[14] See Nafis Sadik, "Women As Resource Managers," in *State of the World Population 1985* (New York: United Nations Population Fund, 1988), p. 3.

[15] Shubh K. Khumar and David Hotchkiss, "Consequences of Deforestation for Women's Time Allocation, Agricultural Production, and Nutrition in Hill Areas of Nepal," *IFPRI Research Report 69* (Washington, D.C.: International Food Policy Research Institute, October 1988).

[16] See M. J. Esman, *Landlessness and Near Landlessness in Developing Countries* (Ithaca, N.Y.: Cornell Rural Development Committee, 1982); and Radha Sinha, *Landlessness: A Growing Problem* (Rome: Food and Agriculture Organization, 1984).

[17] The categories are roughly those adapted by the Cornell Rural Development Committee as outlined in Esman, *Landlessness and Near Landlessness in Developing Countries*, op. cit., p. 2.

[18] Food and Agriculture Organization, *Agriculture: Toward 2000* (Rome, 1987).

[19] See Sinha, *Landlessness: A Growing Problem,* op. cit., pp. 18-23.

[20] See U.S. Agency for International Development, *Development and the National Interest: U.S. Economic Assistance into the 21st Century* (Washington, D.C., 1989) p. 90.

[21] Werner Fornos, *Gaining People, Losing Ground: A Blueprint for Stabilizing World Population* (Washington, D.C.: The Population Institute, 1987), p. 11.

[22] International Fund for Agricultural Development, *Annual Report 1986* (Rome, 1986), p. 29.

[23] Sinha, *Landlessness: A Growing Problem,* op. cit., p. 8.

[24] See Consultative Group on International Agricultural Research (CGIAR), "Sustainable Agricultural Production: Implications for International Agricultural Research," (Rome: FAO, Technical Advisory Committee Secretariat, March 1988) pp. 41–42. Also, see John Mellor, "The Intertwining of Environmental Problems and Poverty," *Environment,* Vol. 3, No. 9 (November 1988).

[25] John Mellor, "Agricultural Development Opportunities for the 1990s—The Role of Research," address presented at the International Centers Week of the Consultative Group on International Agricultural Research, Washington, D.C., 4 November 1988.

[26] Peter M. Kimm, "The Challenge of Urbanization in the 1990s," paper presented at the 1989 International Development Conference, Washington, D.C., 20–22 February 1989. Also, Janice Perlman, "Global Urbanization: Challenges and Opportunities," paper presented at the International Workshop on Improving Urban Management, Honolulu, Hawaii, 9–13 January 1989.

[27] Helen Hughes, "Agricultural Development, Growth and Equity: 40 Years of Experience," Sir John Crawford Memorial Lecture, delivered at the World Bank, Washington, D.C., 4 November 1988, p. 26.

[28] Consultative Group on International Agricultural Research, (CGIAR), "Sustainable Agricultural Production," op. cit., pp. 56–57.

[29] United Nations Environment Programme, "The Disappearing Forests," *UNEP Environment Brief No. 3* (Nairobi, Kenya, n.d.).

[30] Ibid.

[31] In addition to Browder's chapter in this volume, see also Dennis J. Mahar, *Government Policies and Deforestation in Brazil's Amazon Region* (Washington, D.C.: World Wildlife Fund and The Conservation Foundation, 1989) pp. 7–9, and H. Jeffrey Leonard, *Natural Resources and Economic Development in Central America* (New Brunswick, N.J.: Transaction Books, 1987) pp. 123–25.

[32] International Task Force on Forestry Research, "A Global Strategy for Tropical Forestry," report sponsored by the Rockefeller Foundation, the United Nations Development Programme, the World Bank, and the United Nations Food and Agriculture Organization, (September 1988), p. 29.

[33] World Food Council, "Sustainable Food Security: Action for Environmental Management of Agriculture," report prepared by the United Nations Environment Programme in consultation with the World Food Council, 8 April 1988 (Rome: Food and Agriculture Organization, 1988/5/Add.1).

[34] Food and Agriculture Organization, *Land, Food and People* (Rome, 1984), p. 50.

[35] Chuck Lankester, as quoted in Kristen Helmore, "UN Tries to Slow Deforestation by Boosting African Timber Industry," *Christian Science Monitor,* 4 October 1988, p. 11.

[36] Food and Agriculture Organization, "Fuelwood Supplies in the Developing Countries," *FAO Forestry Paper 42* (Rome, 1983).

[37] United Nations Environment Programme, "General Assessment of the Progress in the Implementation of the Plan of Action to Combat Desertification: 1978–1984" (Nairobi, Kenya, 1984).

[38] Food and Agriculture Organization, *African Agriculture: The Next 25 Years, Annex II, The Land Resource Base* (Rome, 1986), pp. 4–5. Some estimates of the amount of dry land affected by desertification in all of Africa are as high as 742 million hectares, or one-quarter of the continent. See Rattan Lal, "Soil Degradation and the Future of Agriculture in Sub-Saharan Africa," *Journal of Soil and Water Conservation,* (November–December 1988), p. 445.

[39] World Food Council, "Sustainable Food Security," op. cit., p.5.

[40] International Task Force on Forestry Research, *A Global Strategy for Tropical Forestry,* op. cit., p. 7.

[41] United Nations Environment Programme, "Environmental Perspective to the Year 2000 and Beyond," Document produced as annex to United Nations General Assembly resolution 42/186 of December 1987, UNEP/GC.14/26 (Annex II), (Nairobi, Kenya, 1987) p. 102.

[42] Food and Agriculture Organization, *Agriculture: Toward 2000,* op. cit., p. 257.

[43] Food and Agriculture Organization, *Land, Food and People,* op. cit., pp. xi, 9.

[44] See, for example, Maria Elena Hurtado, "The Grim Hazards of Poverty," *South,* January 1989, p. 41

[45] Cited in United Nations Fund for Population, *The State of the World Population 1988* (New York, 1988), p. 7.

[46] See H. Jeffrey Leonard, *Pollution and the Struggle for the World Product* (New York: Cambridge University Press, 1988), pp. 119–20, 165–66, 194.

[47] John Mellor, "Agricultural Development Opportunities for the 1990s," op. cit.; for elaboration, see International Food Policy Research Institute, "Infrastructure and Agricultural Development," *IFPRI Policy Briefs 3* (Washington, D.C., September 1988).

[48] See especially, *Friends of the Earth, Financing Ecological Destruction: The World Bank and the International Monetary Fund* (London: Friends of the Earth, 1986, 1987, 1988); "The World Bank: Global Financing of Impoverishment and Famine," *The Ecologist* (Special Issue, 1985); Steve Schwartzman, "Bankrolling Disasters" (Washington, D.C.: Sierra Club, 1986); Bruce Rich, "The Multilateral Development Banks, Environmental Policy and the United States," *Environmental Law Quarterly,* Vol. 12, No. 4 (1985).

[49] See H. Jeffrey Leonard, "Environmental Hysteria May Hasten Amazon's Destruction," *Wall Street Journal* 16 October 1987, p. 29; and Ellen B. Geld, "Will Farming Destroy Brazil's Amazon Basin," *Wall Street Journal,* 13 January 1989, p. 27.

[50] "Alley Cropping: Six Years of Experiments and Farmer Use of the System," in International Institute for Tropical Agriculture, *Farming Systems Program* (Ibadan, Nigeria: IITA, 1985).

[51A] See Miguel A. Altieri, *Agroecology: The Scientific Basis of Alternative Agriculture* (Berkeley: University of California, Division of Biological Control, 1983); T.C. Edens, et al., eds., *Sustainable Agriculture and Integrated Farming Systems* (East Lansing: Michigan State University Press, 1985); Office of Technology Assessment, *Enhancing Agriculture in Africa* (Washington, D.C., U.S. Government Printing Office, 1988); and Roland Bunch, *Two Ears of Corn: A Guide to People-Centered Agricultural Improvement* (Oklahoma City: World Neighbors, 1982).

[52] Pedro A. Sanchez and Jose R. Benites, "Low Input Cropping for Acid Soils of the Humid Tropics," *Science,* Vol. 238 (11 December 1987), pp. 1521–27.

[53] The questions regarding the appropriate roles of decentralized "village-center" approaches in poverty alleviation, as well as the role of nongovernment organizations, are addressed by several chapters in Lewis and contributors, *Strengthening the Poor,* op. cit. See, especially, Lewis, "Overview," pp. 13, 21; Norman Uphoff, "Assisted Self-Reliance: Working With, Rather than for, the Poor," pp. 47–59; Samuel Paul, "Governments and Grassroots Organizations: From Co-Existence to Coalition," pp. 61–72, and Thomas W. Dichter, "The Changing World of Northern NGOs: Problems, Paradoxes, and Possibilities," pp. 177–88.

[54] John Spears, "Review of World Bank Financed Forestry Activity, FY 1984," (Washington, D.C.: The World Bank, 1984).

[55] See The World Bank, *Poverty and Hunger,* op. cit., p. 54.

[56] Consultative Group on International Agricultural Research, *1987–88 Annual Report,* (Washington, D.C.: The World Bank, 1988), p. ii.

[57] Michael K. Wade, et al., "Overcoming Soil Fertility Constraints in a Transmigration Area of Indonesia," *Trop Soils Bulletin* Number 88-01, December 1988.

[58] The World Bank, *Vetiver Grass: A Method of Soil and Moisture Conservation,* 2nd ed. (New Delhi, 1988) pp. 2–3.

[59] Ibid., pp. 4, 15–17

[60] See Dennis McCaffrey and Helena Landazuri, "Evaluation of the Wildlands and Human Needs Program," (Washington, D.C.: U.S. Agency for International Development, 1987).

[61] Avron Benavid Val, *More With Less: Managing Energy and Resource Efficient Cities* (Washington, D.C.: U.S. Agency for International Development, 1987), p. 91.

[62] Ibid., p. vii.

[63] Paul Streeten, et al., *First Things First: Meeting Basic Human Needs in Developing Countries* (New York: Oxford University Press, 1981), p. 145.

[64] The World Bank, *Poverty and Hunger,* op. cit., p. 16.

Summaries of Chapter Recommendations

Summaries of Chapter Recommendations

1. Sustainable and Equitable Development in Irrigated Environments (Montague Yudelman)

Irrigation has been and will continue to be a major factor in agricultural development and food production for the foreseeable future. The availability of irrigation has benefited hundreds of millions of poor people in recent decades by raising agricultural incomes within irrigated areas and by helping to make more abundant supplies of affordable food available to urban areas. Nevertheless, it is clear that water resources will have to be managed much more efficiently in the future than in the past as capital becomes scarcer and costs of irrigation are rising. Just as important, much more attention will have to be given to minimizing environmental damage than has been prevalent in earlier irrigation programs. To this end, it is recommended that:

- Project planners should give due attention to the rehabilitation of existing projects, many of which are operating well below their potential. The returns on investments with large sunken costs are usually higher than on new investments. At the same time, much more time and effort should be devoted to ensuring that existing and new projects are well operated and maintained. This will call for a change in the nature of investments in irrigation.
- Planners should be explicit in considering the size of a project when there are options between large-scale and smaller-scale investments. The advantages of smaller-scale investments are being stressed by economists and environmentalists; however, there are circumstances where there are no substitutes for large-scale irrigation efforts.

49

- Planners should have time enough to ensure that projects are adequately prepared before funds are committed for a project. In addition, the planning process should incorporate methodologies that take account of environmental consequences of investments in irrigation.

- All planning for irrigation projects should include due regard for requirements to limit waterlogging and salinization as well as health concerns and, where appropriate, involuntary resettlement. In addition, other upstream and downstream environmental issues should be identified by close cooperation among persons from different disciplines. These issues include the importance of watershed management as well as limiting harmful environmental consequences that follow from intensification of agriculture in irrigated areas.

- There should be greater international cooperation in overall planning for improving transnational water use. The World Bank and the regional multilateral development banks should take active steps to promote such coordination.

- There is a need for a much-enlarged research effort in improving water management. Donors should increase their contributions for water research under the auspices of the Consultative Group on International Agricultural Research (CGIAR). The International Irrigation Management Institute should be enlarged and admitted to the CGIAR system.

- International donors and governments should insist on heightened efforts to collect "water charges" to improve water use, to increase revenues, and to promote equity. At the same time, there should be renewed efforts to promote greater participation by water users in the management and maintenance of irrigation systems.

- In looking ahead, planners should begin to think about the issues raised by growing population pressures on existing, densely populated irrigated areas. New problems will soon arise from the merging of rural and peri-urban interests, which will require new approaches to irrigation development.

- Planners should also keep abreast of the information and research on climatic change as they consider alternatives among options for long-term, large-scale investment in irrigation.

2. The Arid and Semi-Arid Tropics: Technology, Human Pressure, and Ecology (Dirck Stryker)

Growing population pressure, increased economic activity, and improved technology have severely complicated the maintenance, enforcement, and adjudication of land-use rights in the dry regions of the world. At the same time, the undermining of local authority by colonial regions and national governments, and the tendency within these governments toward centralized authority, has weakened traditional systems for managing the use of natural resources. These trends have led to range degradation, depletion of soils and woodlands, erosion by wind and water, and in some instances desertification. Despite these problems, economic development of arid and semi-arid regions has helped to reduce poverty and to protect the poor by diversifying sources of income, spreading risks associated with subsistence food production, and increasing mobility for pastoralists in time of adversity.

The major poverty and environment dilemma in dry areas, therefore, is whether the advantages of development and reduced poverty have been outweighed by the losses associated with their adverse impact on the natural resource base and what can be done to minimize these losses. While the problems associated with environment and poverty in the arid and semi-arid tropics cannot be fully overcome without a much better understanding of their causes, there are a number of specific actions that can be taken immediately.

- National governments should turn control of scarce ground and surface water over to local political authorities or, failing this, should institute water charges or other controls on the use of water and rangeland resources.

- Governments should assess taxes on the transportation of fuelwood into urban areas, since it is often the high demand for cheap fuelwood in cities that leads to excess tree cutting in dry regions.

- Governments should retain or institute modest fertilizer subsidies in countries where the problem of soil depletion has been identified and where the budget and foreign exchange earnings are adequate to satisfy demand for fertilizer at the subsidized prices. Studies should be undertaken to determine optimal subsidy rates on different kinds of fertilizer suited to local soil conditions.

- National governments and donors should design and implement a series of pilot projects in arid and semi-arid regions that will produce highly valued manufactured products for export to exterior markets. The policy environment for these projects should be modified so as to avoid bias against exports and efficient investment.

- National governments and donors should support projects to improve animal health in arid and semi-arid regions. At the same time, the impact of livestock projects on the rangeland should be more closely monitored.
- National governments and donors should continue to invest in transportation and other infrastructure in arid and semi-arid areas.
- Land legistlation should be reviewed, simplified, and brought into conformity with local custom, with particular attention paid to women's rights. Unambiguous procedures for expropriation and compensation should be defined. Other laws and regulations should be examined to identify any barriers to the establishment of local organizations for natural resource management. These organizations should have the power to make rules, apply sanctions, raise revenue, and regulate the use of natural resources in other ways.
- National governments and donors should promote close links between family planning and programs to improve maternal and child nutrition in arid and semi-arid regions. Women should be actively involved in all areas of planning and implementation.
- Donors should undertake a series of field studies in arid and semi-arid areas to assess the impact of commercialization and to assist in the design of effective interventions to preserve the environment and to alleviate poverty.

3. Development Alternatives for Tropical Rain Forests
(John O. Browder)

The destruction of tropical forests is among the most controversial environmental issues of our time. The underlying causes of tropical deforestation are many and complex. In many cases current uses of tropical forest lands for livestock production, agricultural settlement, and commercial timber extraction have not proven to be financially viable or ecologically sustainable. Development alternatives for tropical rain forests have focused on three broad types of activities: plantation forestry to meet growing industrial fuelwood needs; stabilizing conventional small-scale farming through agroforestry; and natural forest management for secondary forest products as well as commercial timber. Each of these alternatives provides different social and financial benefits, but their widespread adoption is constrained by various obstacles.

The nature of plantation forestry (high establishment costs, relatively long production cycles, low labor requirements) makes this the least attractive alternative from the perspective of poverty alleviation. Moreover, the replacement of biologically heterogeneous natural forests with relatively homogeneous plantation forests is assailable on environmental grounds. Nevertheless, on a small-scale, plantation forests may provide economic benefits for poor people—with minimal (or at least acceptable) environmental trade-offs—by supplying essential energy sources for small urban communities and industries and creating off-farm employment.

Agricultural development and environmental conservation converge on three general objectives: improving productivity through intensification (higher yields or increasing frequency of cropping); diversifying production to enable year-round activity and income; and incorporating productive tree or forest components into farming. Much can be learned from indigenous traditions of agroforestry but, regrettably, few research funds have been devoted to exploring the range and operational aspects of traditional farming systems.

Natural forest management, which includes a wide variety of extractive activities, potentially offers some of the highest financial returns from tropical forest land use. Again, what little is known of traditional and indigenous systems of natural forest management is instructive. Generally, these management systems require low inputs of labor and capital, utilize diverse forest resources, preserve forest structure and ecological functions, and are extremely productive per unit of area and labor. The widespread adoption of traditional natural forest removal is constrained by market factors, diverse cultural contexts, inadequate knowledge of operational aspects, and policies that provide incentives for natural forest removal.

Donor organizations and governments are encouraged to focus their resources on three areas: the application of traditional natural forest management practices to non-traditional populations; the economic and biological recovery of secondary (disturbed) forest areas; and the biological diversification of production to fully exploit the biodiversity of tropical forests, which is their comparative advantage.

4. Sustainable Approaches to Hillside Agricultural Development (A. John De Boer)

Development strategies for the world's poor hill areas need to address the interrelated traits that are currently increasing poverty and environmental degradation in these regions. These traits include: widespread poverty; a poor resource base; low agricultural productivity; land tenure patterns in hill areas themselves; concentrated land ownership and the pursuit of mechanized export-oriented agriculture in the adjacent, better endowed and situated lowlands (which limit labor absorption from the hills); a lack of alternative local sources of income in the hills; male outmigration to distant off-farm employment to contribute to family subsistence through remittances; dense populations with a high proportion of women, the very old, and the very young; rapid rates of population growth (reinforced by short-term needs for more on-farm household labor to eke out a subsistence from a declining resource base); highly variable rainfall and soil types; a fragile balance of essential biological interrelationships between agricultural production, livestock production, and forests; poor transportation, marketing, communications, and basic services infrastructures; and isolation from national political processes.

A further challenge to policy is that it must deal with vast numbers of small-scale, natural-resource-using activities that, taken together, have a massive environment impact.

Five major policy thrusts recommended to improve the *long-term* future of hill populations and the natural resource base of hill areas are: (1) community-based forestry programs, (2) better land use planning and management, (3) active promotion of outmigration from the hills through a reallocation of public expenditures, (4) reform of institutional structures and policies to meet poor people's needs in the hills, and (5) widespread promotion of new and adapted labor-saving technologies, particularly targeted to reach the large numbers of women performing agricultural production and fuelwood collection and other support activities to meet household subsistence needs.

The focal point of effective poverty- and environment-minded policies must be increasing the low productivity—and income—of hill communities while simultaneously reducing labor requirements for the broad range of support activities that help maintain households. Specific recommendations toward this goal include:

- Promotion of continued outmigration to areas where labor productivity is greater;
- Allocation of capital away from subsidies and toward productive investments with strong employment-creating effects;
- Careful balancing of job-creation costs in hill areas and in more favored areas;
- Increased efforts to promote higher-value agricultural products along with better marketing infrastructure;
- More and better research focusing on the constraints and opportunities at the village and household levels;
- Greater emphasis on forestry to increase overall household productivity and reduce environmental stress;

- More work on alternative institutional structures and management practices to promote village-based forestry and agro-forestry to bring about a drastic reduction in overgrazing;
- Development of new sources of energy for remote areas; and
- Appropriate public policies that provide secure land tenure, promote long-term investments in trees, conservation structures, and improved livestock.

5. Environmental Dilemmas and the Urban Poor (Tim Campbell)

The powerful forces of urbanization will continue over the next several generations, concentrating nearly half the Third World's population in cities by the year 2010. Before then, the rapid pace of urbanization will result in nearly as many of the Third World's poor living in cities as in rural areas.

Serious urban environmental problems in developing countries—indoor air pollution, the lack of environmental sanitation, present ways of waste recycling, and urban resource mismanagement—put millions of poor families at risk of disease and increased mortality.

This chapter argues that, just as small changes in the macroeconomic context have had important, adverse environmental effects on the poor, narrowly conceived environmental policy can have adverse effects on their economic circumstances. The chapter does not attempt to catalog all of the dilemmas for policymakers regarding the poor and their environment; it focuses on a set of issues critical to the health and the survival of millions of the urban poor. Some of these critical issues present themselves at the small-scale household level; others, at the vast scale of the urban and regional environments:

- *Cooking and Fuel Substitution.* Indoor air pollution caused by incomplete combustion of biomass cooking fuels poses serious health threats to millions of the poor—particularly women and children. Better stoves and fuels could greatly increase heat energy and reduce contamination.

- *Environmental Sanitation.* Contamination of the household environment by human wastes affects millions of households even though, as an environmental issue, household sanitation is often ignored. Conventional water and sewerage is too expensive for most of the Third World's poor. Low-cost technologies are "on the shelf," but more needs to be done by assistance agencies and environmental groups to increase participation by the poor in the improvement of household sanitation and to expand investment in low-cost sanitation in cities.

- *Land Capability.* Most cities in developing countries are unable to prevent inappropriate uses of land such as settlement in swamps, on hillsides, in floodplains and on food-producing land. This causes long-run harm and often leads to loss of life and property in flooding, landslides, or industrial accidents. Donors need to strengthen local governmental capacity for land control and taxation. Nongovernmental groups can help by improving and simplifying techniques such as land capability and environmental impact analyses.

- *Food, Water, and Energy.* Few urban policies and development assistance strategies take into account the mutual interdependencies of major resource flows, such as energy-intensive support to food and water supply systems. More rational use of these resources would make urban systems more sustainable, but would also hurt the interests of the poor in the short run. Donors and environmental groups have to give greater weight to these macro-urban resource flows, to develop techniques of urban food production, and to improve the resource efficiency of water and energy use.

- *Materials Recycling.* Solid waste disposal and recovery have been neglected, and solid waste is almost certainly a serious source of contamination of groundwater supplies for many Third World cities. In addition, increasing numbers of the urban poor make a living by scavenging and recycling materials, exposing themselves and their children to dangerous conditions and toxic substances. Development assistance institutions should work on modifying standard management practices to incorporate the safe labor conditions and positive economic potential of materials recycling.

6. The Madagascar Challenge: Human Needs and Fragile Ecosystems (Alison Jolly)

Both policymakers and conservationists recognize the interdependence of human welfare and the immediate human environment. Wilderness areas and wild species also contribute to human welfare—in their roles as watersheds, climate regulators, gene pools, and as sources of natural products. In addition, people of many nations increasingly acknowledge the scientific and cultural value of biodiversity in terms of human wonder, enjoyment, and understanding. The world's richest and rarest wild species are found in major concentrations of biological diversity in the tropics. Many of these areas face mounting threats due to encroachment by impoverished people and the forces of modern economic development. In such areas, the value of wild species, as well as the need for economic development that provides sustainable benefits for human beings, may necessitate development policy priorities that differ from those of orthodox economic prescriptions.

The government of the Democratic Republic of Madagascar and a consortium of donor agencies are now accepting the challenge to preserve a rich national heritage in a poor country. The problems they face illustrate one case of the need to link a much improved quality of life with sustainable use of the human environment and with the benefits of preserving biodiversity.

Some policy recommendations for governments and foreign donors to aid developing countries to promote alternative forms of development in areas that are the repositories of valuable and unique flora and fauna include the following:

- Support and protect nature reserves.
- Support efforts, such as those by the World Wildlife Fund, to preserve buffer zones and marginal areas, encouraging an environmentally benign existence for people living on semi-wild land.
- Encourage wildlife tourism, planned extraction, and other sustainable uses of the wild, with revenue channeled to people living on semi-wild land.
- Greatly increase professional training and public education in conservation.
- Invest in productive activitites that emphasize local markets and support subsistence farmers through, for instance, improved land tenure, credit, fertilizers, and agricultural extension attuned to small-scale producers, including women.
- Support initiatives for reducing foreign debt and debt service. Paraphrasing Luis da Silva of Brazil, if rain forests are the lungs of the world, Third World debt is the world's pneumonia.
- Greatly improve and expand health measures, including better access to medicines, child nutrition, and access to and emphasis on family planning.

For their part, species-rich, financially poor developing countries should insist that donors:

- Promote an International Fund for Biodiversity. If poor nations set aside their land and use their scarce personnel to preserve a global heritage, they should expect commensurate contributions from the rich—perhaps through a United Nations-based Biodiversity Fund.
- Provide far greater resources to help them protect the earth's biodiversity. The debate is now polarizing negatively, with environ-

mental concerns becoming another conditionality that slows or stops aid. Species-rich countries could, instead, use their biodiversity as a lever to increase aid.

- Address public opinion in the rich countries directly, through scientists and journalists. Again, the debate is polarizing, with rich and poor blaming each other for environmental losses. A constituency of conservationists and the media across national lines can influence all governments to accept long-term environmental responsibility.

Environment and
the Poor

Chapter 1

Sustainable and Equitable Development in Irrigated Environments

Montague Yudelman

The years after World War II, especially the 1960s and 1970s, were years of explosive growth in the amount of land served by irrigation; over three decades, irrigated acreage almost tripled. Most of this expansion was in the developing countries and was part of a massive effort, strongly supported by international donors, to increase agricultural output. The increase was to come from providing millions of farmers with adequate and controlled supplies of moisture, improved seeds, and agrochemical inputs. The subsequent expansion of irrigation and the widespread diffusion of high-yielding varieties of rice and wheat seed, along with fertilizers, was one of the most successful efforts to transfer technology for increasing agricultural output in modern times. It also represented one of the largest ecological and sociological changes recently induced by mankind. The spread of the new irrigation-based technology has influenced the ecology of approximately 200 million acres and the lives at least 1 billion rural people, mostly in Asia.

The rapid expansion and improvement in irrigation increased food production and thus helped enhance food security for the population at large. This will probably continue to be the primary justification for expanding irrigation in the future, when absolute increases in population may well be more than 1 billion people every ten years (representing a 20 per cent increase of the 1988 population per decade). Most of the population increase will occur in the developing countries, and much of it will be urban, depending on marketed food rather than subsistence farming.

Given the seemingly limited prospects for substantial increases in production from dry-land agriculture, a good part of future growth in food supplies is expected to come from an expanded irrigation sector. The U.N. Food and Agriculture Organization (FAO) estimates that irrigation will have to increase by 40 per cent over the next twenty years— with current average yields rising by 60 per cent to meet projected demand.[1] On a national basis, the largest planned increase of irrigation is in India, where the Seventh Plan calls for an increase of 20 million hectares by the year 2000. Governments of such countries as Pakistan and China in Asia and Mexico and Brazil in Latin America, and a number of governments in the arid and semi-arid areas of North Africa and Western Asia, are also relying on extending the acreage under irrigation to help meet domestic demand for foodstuffs.

Although the costs of irrigation are rising, many governments are nonetheless planning to invest large amounts in irrigation infrastructure. In recent years, however, the expansion of irrigation has been seen to bring mixed blessings. Questions are being raised about the economic benefits, sustainability, and ecological side effects of irrigation. Critics have charged that scarce capital has been wasted by emphasizing investments in irrigation infrastructure that have given low returns. They argue that benefits often have been skewed toward wealthy farmers, and that predicted yields have not been attained due to poor land and water management practices. They point out that many thousands of poor people have been resettled to accommodate dams and reservoirs needed for irrigation schemes. They also contend that public health has been seriously threatened by the spread of waterborne or water-related diseases and parasites. Critics of irrigation further suggest that other environmental side effects have undermined the well-being of people and led to the abuse of natural resources outside the irrigated areas.

This chapter looks at some of these charges and considers how to reconcile the need to continue expanding irrigated production in the developing world with some of the environmental and human problems that have been associated with irrigation. It discusses the diversity and spread of irrigation and examines the record of economic performance of some irrigation projects supported in recent decades by the multilateral agencies (especially the World Bank), outlines some of the environmental issues associated with them, and looks at the question of which economic groups have tended to benefit the most from irrigation projects. Some of the long-term environmental costs and challenges are examined, including the adequacy of future supplies of water. The chapter concludes by offering a series of recommendations to help international donors and developing-country governments (a) meet the needs for increased output from irrigated areas in an era when capital and water may be more scarce than at present, and (b) reduce environmental damage and increase the benefits accruing to poor farmers in the irrigated areas.

The Scope of Irrigation

Diversity and Technology of Irrigation

Irrigation, defined as "the use of an artificial means to influence the supply of moisture to increase crop production," is practiced in many parts of the globe, in a wide range of climates, and with varying degrees of sophistication. Technically, irrigation helps to raise and stabilize crop yields per hectare by reducing plant stress during periods of water shortage. Irrigation is helpful in the humid tropics, where, by supplying needed moisture when it is not readily available because of unimodal patterns of rainfall, it enables double- or triple-cropping with high annual yields per hectare. At the other end of the climatic spectrum, irrigation is important for crop production in large parts of the semi-arid and arid tropics that otherwise would be too dry to sustain agriculture. By providing regular and timely supplies of water, irrigation reduces the risk of crop loss while encouraging farmers to invest in land improvements and to use purchased inputs. In many parts of the tropics, the spread of irrigation has gone hand in hand with the spread of technologies that rely on improved seed, fertilizers, and pesticides, as well as on regular supplies of water. The use of these technologies has increased average yields in irrigated areas even further.

Irrigation schemes are quite diverse, and they vary enormously in cost, size, and scope. The artificial means for controlling water range from sophisticated, capital-intensive systems to efforts of very modest proportions. The anatomy of a sophisticated irrigation scheme may well consist of gigantic dams to impound and store water, large pumping plants, extensive canals and pipe systems to distribute water to farmers' fields, and elaborate mechanical systems to apply water to the land. Such systems can cost hundreds of millions of dollars, involve thousands of users, and irrigate large acreages (hopefully at low cost per acre irrigated). On the other hand, a scheme may consist of something as simple as providing supplemental moisture for a few small plots of land—by using a series of shallow ponds to store rainfall and earthen jars to carry it to farms around the periphery of the ponds. Irrigation schemes can also vary depending on the source of water being distributed; they can store water and then distribute it by gravity flow; or they can depend on pumping underground water (water in aquifers below the earth's surface), which normally is continuously replenished by nature.

Arguably the most important change in irrigation technology in developing countries in recent years has been the very substantial expansion of the use of compact diesel or electric engines to extend the use of "low-lift" irrigation from watercourses, wells, and tube wells. This expansion has been most pronounced in Asia—especially with the proliferation of privately owned wells in South Asia and wells owned by individual communes in northern China. It is estimated that there are now more than 5 million small-capacity tube wells in these regions, representing an investment of more than $1 billion. This spread of power-driven pumps has made food production in Asia much more sensitive to the supply and costs of energy. It has also permitted much more flexibility and individual initiative in irrigation than was possible in state-controlled surface projects. More recently, there is increasing interest in schemes involving the conjunctive use of surface water and groundwater to promote greater efficiency in resource use. Such an approach, however, requires a higher degree of coordination in the planning and programming of water use than has been attained in most parts of the world.

Successful irrigation, whether on a large or a small scale, depends on an appropriate mix of agroclimatic, agronomic, engineering, and socioeconomic conditions. These conditions are present in many parts of Asia and the Middle East—regions with long irrigation traditions—and to a lesser extent in parts of Latin America. The necessary mix of conditions is strikingly limited to only a few areas of Sub-Saharan Africa. In this vast region, large-scale dams are needed to regulate the seasonal flows of most rivers. In addition, large entities of irrigable land are few, and there is little tradition of irrigated agriculture. Consequently, irrigation in Sub-Saharan Africa, unlike that in Asia, tends to be very costly and to give low returns.

The Expansion of Irrigation

Between 1950 and the mid-1980s, acreage under irrigation grew from around 90 million hectares to around 250 million.[2] Irrigated acreage increased by about 6 million hectares per year in the 1960s, by about 5 million hectares a year in the 1970s, and has continued to grow in the 1980s, though at a slower rate. The area under irrigation almost tripled between 1950 and 1970, with a faster rate of growth than that of population, especially in the most populous regions of the world. Currently some 160 million hectares of land, or two-thirds of all land irrigated, is in the developing countries. About 100 million hectares of this total is in Asia—mostly in China, India, and Pakistan. Relatively smaller acreages are under irrigation in Latin America (30 million hectares) and Africa (10 million hectares). Sub-Saharan Africa is the region with the smallest acreage under irrigation (somewhat less than 5 million hectares)—a fact not unrelated to the region's difficulties in the agricultural sector.

The very rapid expansion of land under irrigation has made irrigated acreage an increasingly important source of agricultural production. In Asia, the 45 per cent of the total area under cultivation that is irrigated provides nearly 60 per cent of the region's food production. Nearly 80 per cent of Pakistan's food, 70 per cent of China's, and more than 50 per cent of India's and Indonesia's food is produced on irrigated land. Even in regions where acreage under irrigation is not so extensive, for example in South America, the irrigated areas still produce a high proportion of agricultural output—more than 50 per cent in the case of Chile and Peru. The same applies to a number of countries in North Africa and the Middle East.

The Performance of Irrigation Projects

Economic Efficiency

The increases in total agricultural output that have accompanied the spread of irrigation are indisputable. However, by themselves these figures indicate very little about the economic performance of the irrigated subsector and the efficiency of resource use. In the context of resource-use efficiency, irrigation can be viewed as an investment—and can be subject to the usual tests, such as the economic rate of return, for appraising and evaluating costs and benefits from any output-generating investment. The largest single investor in irrigation in recent years, the World Bank, takes the economic rate of return seriously and seldom approves an irrigation project with an expected rate of return of less than 10 per cent—on the grounds that this would indicate too low a return to the economy from the use of scarce resources. The World Bank also uses the rate of return as an important criterion in ex post evaluation of its projects to determine whether they have met expectations. A series of these evaluations conducted by the World Bank gives a mixed picture of the efficiency of resource use in irrigation projects undertaken in the 1960s and 1970s; they show that investments in irrigation have been relatively successful, but less so than they might have been. Around three-quarters of the projects had rates of return of more than 10 per cent.[3]

A "second look" evaluation of some of the projects well after their completion, though, highlights the problem of sustainability once Bank financing ends. Over time, poor operation and maintenance had reduced the efficiency of a number of projects. For example, some reservoirs were silting up sooner than anticipated; equipment and canals had fallen into disrepair; waterlogging and salinization were spreading;

and, in some instances, water supplies had become irregular and uncertain, leading to a reduction in the area irrigated and in yields. At the same time, the evaluations indicated that many *governments* had made very little provision for rehabilitation and for providing resources—including recurrent expenditures—for maintenance. Cooperation between administrations and water users to maintain systems had not been promoted, and the users themselves were contributing very little to the costs of the system's upkeep. These evaluations made it clear that there was far more to efficient irrigation than having a well-designed system, and that both improved system management and the involvement of water users were important for the sustained success of these projects.

The World Bank evaluations also showed in many instances that higher-than-expected costs per hectare irrigated were offset by higher-than-expected prices for output; while costs in a number of projects exceeded expectations by more than 40 per cent, so did output prices. This was most fortunate, but gives pause for reflection about future investments. The real costs of new irrigation are rising, but the prices of most staples have not risen in recent years, nor are they expected to increase very dramatically. Discussions with Bank staff indicate that average costs per additional hectare irrigated by some new projects have increased from less than $1,000 to over $5,000, and in a few cases have even reached $10,000. Since commodity prices have not risen substantially, it will be increasingly difficult to justify new investment on economic grounds unless much more attention is paid to improving the cost-effectiveness of systems, facilitating the achievement of greater productivity at the farm level (or unless commodity prices rise above former levels).

Poverty Alleviation and Equity

One of the stated objectives of increased investment (by donors) and expansion of irrigation is to contribute to the alleviation of poverty and to promote greater equity in rural areas. Obviously the reduction—or worsening—of poverty and the distribution of gains from investments in irrigation will vary from place to place, as they depend on a host of differing circumstances. These range from levels of taxes and subsidies to rights to land and water. It is nevertheless possible to draw some broad conclusions about the impact of irrigation on the distribution of benefits and on poverty alleviation. These conclusions tend to parallel the much-researched findings on the economic impact of the spread of irrigation and of biological and agrochemical technology.

First, consumers have gained from the expansion of irrigation and the accompanying yield-increasing technology. Furthermore, it is arguable that *poor* consumers have gained more, proportionately, than richer consumers. Irrigation-based technology has raised on-farm productivity and lowered the costs of production of widely consumed staple commodities such as rice. Lowered production costs and expanded capacity have led to a sustained increase in the supply of rice and to a secular decline in its price. Poor people, especially the urban poor, typically spend a higher proportion of their low income on basic foods, such as rice, than do the rich. Consequently, a fall in the price of a commodity like rice is proportionately more significant to the poor consumer than to the rich.

The distribution of gains from irrigation can also be looked at in a spatial or geographic context. Most farming areas with widespread irrigation are more prosperous than adjacent or comparable areas that depend on rainfed or dry-land agriculture. Irrigation has provided the leading edge for agricultural and economic growth and increases in employment and incomes in areas as diverse as the Punjab in India, Sonora in Mexico, and the irrigated areas of Morocco. In most instances, though, fiscal policies do *not* exist for redistributing incomes between regions; more generally, water users in public sector projects in the richer areas contribute little to the direct costs of providing or maintaining these systems, which are subsidized by taxpayers at large.[4]

Gains also differ *among* water users in the areas that benefit from investments in irrigation, in both the private and the public sector. In some countries, for example Sudan and Pakistan, the larger, more prosperous farmers have the means to acquire tube wells and have enough land—usually ten to fifteen hectares—to gain from economies of scale. Smaller, poorer producers have neither the credit rating nor the land holdings to enable them to acquire pumps and use them productively, even though the pumps are often subsidized. Consequently, they have to buy water from larger farmers, often at monopoly prices. Personal observations in India and elsewhere make it obvious that not all water users in public-sector surface projects have equal access to water. The poorest producers, usually the furthest from the main outlets, seldom have the same access to regular and timely supplies of water as the larger, politically powerful producers who have close alliances with the managers of large systems.

A recent study of Bangladesh illustrates the complexity of determining whether poverty has been alleviated and equity improved within the irrigated sector. According to the study, access to irrigation has been the key to technological change. The study shows that:

> Small farmers and tenants [in the irrigated areas] adopted the new technology as readily as did medium and large ones [and] the yield per acre was higher on smaller farms. But profits and family incomes were lower on smaller farms, because they paid 25 per cent higher water charges and about 10 per cent higher wage rates than the large farms. The profits were substantially less on rented land,

since the tenant has to pay 50 per cent of the gross produce as rent
. . . but the profits per acre on tenant farms were higher for the
modern varieties. . . . Diffusion of the new technology thus
increases income for all groups of farmers but also increases the
inequality in the distribution of agricultural income among farm
households.[5]

The study also concludes that employment and wages increased in the
irrigated areas.

In summary, then, the gains from investments in irrigation seem to
have gone to consumers, to the inhabitants of irrigated areas, and to
those farmers with access to water. Generally, water users have been
subsidized by the taxpayers at large. Within irrigated areas, the larger
producers have gained more than the smaller producers, poverty has
probably diminished, but income inequality has probably worsened.
Within this context, moreover, some disadvantaged groups will have
suffered more than others—for example, female household heads who
have no legal rights to water, small farmers who pay discriminately
high prices for water, and those who are exploited by tenurial arrangements.

Maintaining Gains

A number of signs point to the need to pay increasing attention to maintaining those gains which have accrued from past investments. One
such sign is the need for premature rehabilitation of many surface
schemes. Studies in India, for instance, show that seepage from unlined
canals is increasing, so that about 45 per cent of the water is lost before
reaching farmers' fields; in Pakistan, somewhere between 20 and 70 per
cent of the water is lost. Elsewhere, for example in Indonesia, crumbling
irrigation structures and the near collapse of secondary and tertiary
canals have led to serious inefficiencies in the use of water.[6]

Considerable capital is required for the rehabilitation of existing
projects—especially for the modernization of systems developed many
years ago to provide security against famine rather than to increase
marketed output. Funding is less readily forthcoming for such purposes,
however, than for new projects, which usually have the support of many
vested interests—politicians, government officials, farmers, contractors, and, very often, aid-giving agencies. Similarly, as has been pointed
out, timely and adequate maintenance of irrigation infrastructure is
essential to the efficient operation of the system. But even though all
parties agree on this, actual practice has differed from stated views.
One reason has been the higher status and support given to the infrastructure builders—usually central governments—compared with the
infrastructure maintainers and operators, who are decentralized. Fur-

thermore, maintenance often involves the provision of recurrent expenditures and the organization of groups of water users to take care of decentralized facilities. These are hardly popular issues among donors—or among the engineers and bureaucrats who manage many public irrigation systems.

Environmental Costs Related to Irrigation

The rapid expansion of irrigation has had many direct and indirect effects on the environment and on the quality of life of millions of human beings. For present purposes, the emphasis will be on three environmental impacts that are *directly* attributable to the spread of irrigation: (1) the increase in salinization, (2) the spread of disease, and (3) the involuntary resettlement of those whose land is inundated. Other indirect environmental impacts will be briefly discussed.

Salinization and Waterlogging

The most obvious direct environmental cost to society from the manner in which irrigation has been extended has been the debilitation of natural resources due to salinization and waterlogging. These problems are most prevalent in the arid and semi-arid regions. For instance, one study indicates that around 75 per cent of the irrigated land in Pakistan suffers to varying degrees from salinity, waterlogging, or both—with a pronounced reduction in the yield of most crops.[7] It is estimated that productivity in India has been reduced on 20 million hectares of land irrigated by canals because of salts, and that a further 7 million hectares of land now lie unused because of the accumulation of excess salts. The affected area represents 5 per cent of the country's most productive terrain. In Egypt, a land-scarce economy, almost half of the cultivated area—mainly in the western part of the Nile Delta— is saline and salt-affected at levels sufficient to affect crop production, reduce yields, and lead to the temporary or permanent abandonment of irrigated areas. Other semi-arid countries with irrigated lands that have always had a degree of salinization in their irrigated areas—for example, Turkey and Iraq—now suffer from extensive salinization.

The phenomenon of salinization is also present in South America. In Peru, 30 per cent of the best land in the irrigated coastal area is affected by salinity, and existing data indicates that salinization has increased in the past fifteen years. In Mexico, about 10 per cent of the smaller irrigated acreages suffer from varying degrees of salinity; about 55,000 hectares have been abandoned because of soil salinity. One estimate is that the annual loss of output in Mexico due to salinization is equal to 1 million tons of food grains, or enough to provide basic rations for 5 million people.

Although waterlogging and salinization arise from complex causes, many of which are largely the result of human intervention, there has long been an understanding of what is required to prevent or correct the rise in the water table and subsequent soil degradation and to reclaim salted areas. Waterlogging and salinity can be prevented or reduced by two basic techniques—employed individually or together. The first is reducing the application of water in excess of crop needs and reducing seepage from canals. The second is supplementing the natural drainage capacity by constructing tube wells or subsurface drains. Once waterlogging has taken place, lost production capacity can be regained by enhancing drainage using vertical and horizontal methods.

Since the 1950s there has been growing recognition of the importance of lining canals to prevent seepage and incorporating drainage into some large-scale irrigation projects to facilitate runoff of surplus moisture, thus preventing the water table from rising and salinization from taking place. Despite this understanding, there has been and continues to be widespread neglect of canal improvements and the provision of drainage in the development and utilization of water for raising and sustaining agricultural productivity. The reasons for this are complex. One plausible explanation, based on personal observation, is that engineers and designers of projects are overly optimistic in their initial appraisals. Many argue that it could take as long as twenty to thirty years before new irrigation promotes waterlogging, and there is no need to install drains before they are necessary. Drainage may not even be required, they reason, and the deleterious effects of a lack of drainage and maintenance only appear in the years after a project is completed. Consequently, planners tend to postpone provisions for drainage and maintenance, with potentially damaging results. Similarly, few direct pressures—such as charging producers for the use of water—discourage over-irrigating and waterlogging the soil.

Health Effects

Other costs to society, such as the impact of irrigation projects on health, generally receive less attention than warranted. Where it has coincided with the provision of safe drinking water, irrigation has had some important positive effects on health, but there can be little doubt that the watercourses and drains of some canals have become health hazards. Sicknesses associated with the spread of irrigation include endemic chronic diseases such as malaria, onchocerciasis, schistosomiasis (or bilharzia), and tilariasis; and endemic diseases such as cholera and diarrhea. No one knows the direct and indirect costs of these diseases, but they are grim burdens to over 100 million people, and they weigh heavily on many aspects of daily human existence.

Attempts, albeit limited, have been made to include health components in the design and operation of irrigation programs. These components have included large-scale efforts to eliminate or control the carriers of disease, such as schistosomiasis-bearing snails and malaria-carrying mosquitoes. The results of these efforts have been mixed: Despite short-term gains, control often has broken down because of high costs and lack of sustained effort due partly to the shortage of funds to finance needed services.

It is now widely accepted that public health measures and health education programs—especially for rural women, who come into contact with water more than men in the course of household management—can reduce the prevalence of diseases such as schistosomiasis. The necessary measures include the provision of potable water systems, as well as sanitary toilet and sewage disposal systems. Also needed are rural health centers and the expertise to deal with both the disease and the education of the populace about the importance of abandoning traditional ways of disposing of human wastes. It is clear that reducing the prevalence of schistosomiasis and other waterborne afflictions will be very difficult unless there is a commitment by public health authorities to mount a major attack on such diseases.

The World Health Organization (WHO) has made considerable efforts to encourage those concerned with the development of irrigation to incorporate disease-preventing measures in their projects. Despite these attempts, however, health concerns are not sufficiently integrated into the planning, operation, and maintenance of irrigation schemes. One reason for this is that the traditional managers of these projects— usually engineers, agronomists, and economists—have yet to accept that health is indeed a matter of serious concern. Health issues clearly need to be given greater weight in thinking about future irrigation projects, and this will require much greater collaboration between different interest groups than has occurred in the past.

Involuntary Resettlement

The voluntary resettlement or relocation of displaced people has been a major consequence of dam construction, especially in the case of large-scale projects. The building of the Aswan Dam, for example, involved the relocation of 100,000 or more people.[8] More recently, between 1979 and 1985, the World Bank approved the financing of forty projects for agricultural and hydropower development that will cause the relocation of at least 600,000 people in twenty-seven different countries.[9] According to the Bank's chief sociologist, compulsory resettlement has had devastating consequences for the health and well-being of the displaced persons—as well as fostering environmental degradation, especially of forest lands used for resettlement.[10] The pitfalls of managing resettlement include: chronic underestimation of the number of people involved (partly due to obsolete data and partly due to a wish to minimize the importance of the problem); the prevalence of an engineering-agricultural production bias that ignores the social dimensions of planning; underestimation of financial costs; failure to take into account the wishes of the host population receiving the settlers; and excessive pressure on the environment.

Fortunately the question of forced resettlement is now receiving increased attention from donors and host governments. Efforts are being made to see relocation as part of a *development process* rather than as a relief operation. To this end, it is expected that in future the means will be made available as part of an investment program to relocate agriculturists to become productive farmers, and that care will be exercised to minimize damage to the environment. However, as with other attempts to improve the content of projects, these efforts will add to project costs as well as require skills that are not usually associated with the development of irrigation systems.

Other Environmental Concerns

A number of more general environmental costs result from the development of irrigation. Some of these costs, such as, the degradation of irreplaceable natural habitats, can arise from careless construction. They can occur upstream—for example, from the consequences of man-made lakes to impound water—leading to the destruction of riverine life that cannot adapt to lake conditions. Downstream effects include the alteration in the flow of rivers, which leads to riverbank erosion and changes in land use from the shifts in the timing and volume of silt deposits. Irrigation projects can also influence the quality of the water, thus affecting both fisheries and downstream urban consumers.

Numerous environmental problems also follow the intensification of agricultural production resulting from the spread of irrigation. One serious concern is that the diffusion of modern, genetically uniform varieties to increase yields, for instance, has decreased the genetic diversity of a vast acreage of cereals and increased the vulnerability of large areas to pests and disease. Many proposed solutions involve a trade-off between higher yields and greater security—for example, the use of multiline strains of cereals that will reduce risk but lower output. Other environmental concerns include the consequences of increased resort to agrochemical fertilizers to raise yields and pesticides to cope with the proliferation of pests that usually accompanies denser stands of plants. The increased use of fertilizers, especially soluble nitrates, sometimes has resulted in the contamination of drinking water drawn from aquifers; and the increased—and often excessive—use of pesticides has polluted the atmosphere in some areas and has harmed workers as well as consumers, especially where poisonous residues have accumulated on plants.

Policies to reduce salinization, reduce health hazards, and promote voluntary resettlement are all part of dealing with the expansion of irrigation. The policies adopted to check any environmental excesses following from intensification of production—such as removal of subsidies on purchased inputs, banning the use of harmful pesticides, and promotion of integrated pest management—are usually distinct from policies concerning irrigation itself. Nonetheless, they are an important part of any overall approach for reducing the environmental damage arising from the spread of irrigation.

Future Challenges

The Supply of Water

Will there be enough fresh water in the future to meet the needs of a vastly increased world population? In the 1960s, some feared that there would be a global water crisis, with demand exceeding available supply. These projections now appear overly pessimistic. Revised unpublished estimates made by consultants to the World Bank in the 1970s and 1980s indicate that the world as a whole has more than enough fresh water to meet its agricultural, municipal, and industrial needs well into the next century. There is no global shortage per se, but as is apparent, there are areas of scarcity and those of plenty. What is of growing concern is that the natural balance is being disturbed in some drier areas because of competition for limited water supplies. Underground water resources are being depleted more rapidly than they are replenished. This is true in areas where there has been a surge in the use of pumps and unregulated pumping of groundwater—often the same areas where there have been rapid increases in agricultural output. The projected increases in demand for water for irrigation will add to the pressure to deplete resources even further. Costs will rise as the water table falls, and in due course economically usable supplies may well be exhausted. This outcome can only be avoided if policies are adopted that treat water as a *renewable* resource—a relatively scarce commodity that should be husbanded. The introduction of regulations limiting the pumping and spacing of wells and the imposition and collection of water charges in surface schemes will make it clear that water is not a free good and will help conserve supplies. The importance of the rational use of water will grow over time—as will the need to value water accordingly.

Climatic change is another factor that may well influence future supplies of water and policies on irrigation, and it raises many issues that need further study. For instance, a gradual warming of the climate could increase drought and water shortages in many parts of the world, including most areas that are already classified as semi-arid. The potential hazards of climatic change give added impetus for reviewing non-fossil energy options such as nuclear, solar, and hydroelectric power—since the use of fossil fuels contributes to the depletion of the atmosphere. The ecological advantages of using hydroelectric power may lead to a more favorable disposition toward multipurpose projects that include hydropower, provided they are relatively cost-effective. Prudence dictates that decisionmakers be alert to these broader concerns when they consider the longer-term effects of large-scale investments in irrigation.

The Supply of Capital

The need for sustained increases in food production will require a very substantial investment in irrigation—some $100–150 billion—over the next twenty years. It is likely that there will be greater rather than fewer constraints (internal and external) on the ready availability of funds for development purposes, including funds for irrigation. At the same time, as has been pointed out, the costs of extending irrigation are rising. In addition, taking account of environmental concerns such as health, resettlement, and salinization will add even more to the cost of projects. Thus development strategies will have to give increasing weight to raising revenues, reducing subsidies, ensuring cost-effectiveness, and promoting selectivity in investment so that the available limited resources can be used to best advantage.

Recommendations: Toward Efficient, Equitable, and Environmentally Sound Irrigation

Project Planning

Circumstances vary greatly in the irrigated areas of the world, but within broad constraints policymakers have a number of options that can meet environmental, production, and equity concerns.

Maintenance and Rehabilitation. Most policymakers tend to favor investments in new projects. This is usually much more politically attractive than improving old projects and is strongly supported by both national government departments and outside donors—as well as by contractors, who have a vested interest in setting up new works rather than the less glamorous business of rehabilitating and maintaining older projects. This often leads to the distortion of priorities, misallocation of resources, and continued inefficiency.

This is not a moot issue; new projects are frequently initiated even though many existing projects are performing poorly and could be improved with modest increases in investments in rehabilitation and maintenance. A number of examples in Asia (as in Pakistan and Sri Lanka) and elsewhere (as in Mexico) illustrate that modest incremental expenditures can give high returns by building on the substantial sunken costs in poorly performing irrigation works and related infrastructures.

Experience does, however, present an important caveat in considering the desirability of investing in rehabilitation. A project may give a low return because agricultural policies inhibit production. For example, prices may be too low to provide water users with incentives to increase output (as has been the case in recent years in the irrigated areas of Sudan). Or it may be that agricultural services—for example, those providing inputs or credit—are inadequate (as has been the case in parts of Bangladesh in recent years). In such cases, the power to correct deficiencies lies outside of the irrigation subsector—in large part on actions by bodies such as agricultural departments.

It is also necessary to distinguish between a deteriorating physical capacity due to depreciation of capital and poor performance due to inadequate maintenance. Reservoirs, canals, weirs, pumps, and the like depreciate over time and must be replaced or rehabilitated. Replacements of this kind will become increasingly significant in the years ahead. However, if a system's poor performance is traced to poor management and inadequate maintenance, then investment in replacement and physical rehabilitation may be bypassing the main obstacles to improved efficiency. In this event, the remedy may well lie in improving the existing system through a better "social design" of projects. This might involve upgrading the bureaucracy concerned with managing systems, training and funding an expanded maintenance staff, and organizing the participation of local water users—women as well as men—in maintenance activities.

Balancing Large and Small Projects. If policymakers are expanding irrigation, then they should weigh the advantages of smaller projects over large, capital-intensive ones. Most environmental activists have a bias against large projects, as do many economists. There are some good reasons for this. Many large projects have been far more costly than anticipated and have disturbed the ecology with harmful side effects. Also, large projects incorporate an element of inflexibility; the economic environment can change (the costs of energy might rise or fall), but large multipurpose projects involving heavy fixed costs cannot be modified. Scarce capital can be tied up without the massive project producing energy because of a gross miscalculation of demand. Moreover, large projects often involve the displacement and resettlement of many poor farmers because of the need to inundate storage areas.

In contrast, small projects are favored because they involve limited investments and offer more flexibility. They can be "written off" without too much loss if they are poorly designed; and, it is claimed, they can be developed without displacing people or damaging the environment. Small projects also engender a much larger element of local involvement.

It is also easier to organize smaller numbers of water users than larger numbers. For example, cooperative efforts through farmers' groups and water users' groups have been more effective in small-scale indigenous schemes in Indonesia and elsewhere than in larger projects.[11] Also in Indonesia, the author's observations confirm that cooperative action by water users has been successful in groundwater schemes that serve less than 150 farmers, while schemes that serve up to 250 farmers per tube well have performed less than satisfactorily. An important reason for this appears to be that increasing numbers lead to increasing managerial and organizational problems.

Finally, small projects are often preferred because the level of managerial and technical skill required for their operation and maintenance is smaller than for large projects—an important consideration in some developing countries and regions, especially in Africa. However, it must be borne in mind that small projects often are not adequate substitutes for large projects; hydrologic and storage requirements to trap runoff may call for large-scale investments to capture economies of scale. Consequently, while many considerations point toward upgrading existing projects and investing in small-scale endeavors, this should not preclude investment in large-scale projects. The essential requirements in all cases are realistic, cost-effective preparation and implementation based on sound data—fully taking into account environmental and ecological conditions.

The Pace of Investment. Where policymakers do exercise the option of expanding irrigation, the pace or rate of investment becomes an issue of some concern. The very rapid expansion of irrigation has represented a major commitment to increase agricultural output but, as has been stressed above, many investments have not performed as well as expected, and some have represented a gross misallocation of resources. Cost overruns and delays from a variety of causes—including poor project design—have led to fewer hectares being irrigated than should have been the case and higher costs per hectare, with unnecessarily low returns. The cumulative costs to society from the underutilization of capital—especially borrowed capital—have been substantial.

The pressure to move ahead and make new investments has often resulted in poor project design. This pressure has come from external donors anxious to commit funds to meet the demands of their constituencies, and from developing-country governments eager to expand the capacity to irrigate even if it does not represent the most effective use of capital.

Because of this pressure, investments have been made on the basis of very limited and often inadequate information about physical, social, and economic conditions in the area concerned. Gathering baseline information on soils, rainfall, and other agroclimatic conditions is tedious; time is needed to determine optimum crop mixes in irrigated areas; gathering information on socioeconomic conditions, taking account of issues such as health and the prevention of deforestation, and enlisting the cooperation of water users in projects also requires time.

A conflict exists between the desire to increase investment in agriculture, especially in irrigation, to meet perceived needs on the one hand, and the effective use of that investment on the other. In general, it would seem that a strategy of "making haste slowly" is both appropriate and prudent. Resources will be used to greater advantage where there is adequate preparation and careful project design.

Improved Cost-Benefit Methodology. Large-scale investments in irrigation have to involve regional planning to take account of the role of watersheds and other areawide linkages. Within this context, though, one of the continuing concerns is the need to improve the means available for assessing the environmental impact of investments in irrigation.[12] Currently most investments in irrigation are appraised and evaluated on the basis of cost-benefit analysis or its derivatives, such as analysis of the economic rate of return to the economy from an investment.

The inclusion of environmental concerns as part of such a methodology raises a number of practical and conceptual issues. The first of these is the problem of identification of the environmental impact of an investment in irrigation. The more evident environmental effects from irrigation, such as the spread of salinization and waterborne diseases and forced resettlement from inundated land, as well as the often less apparent upstream and downstream effects already have been mentioned. Clearly the identification of the diverse forms of environmental impact always will be problematic; equally clearly, though, the traditional analysts of irrigation projects will have to rely on the cooperation and experience of environmental specialists to help in this effort.

The second problem is the valuation of indirect benefits and costs. Project analyses focusing on production usually have concentrated on the more easily measured direct costs and benefits from projects. These have been valued on the basis of market costs and in terms of an economic rate of return. The incorporation of environmental concerns brings a number of *indirect* benefits and costs into the picture—and many of these do not have a market price. For example, there is no market price for estimating the costs of erosion, or changes in the quality of water. Yet a number of techniques have been developed that can measure and attach a value to many of these indirect effects. Despite the ingenuity of the analysts, though, there are a number of values that defy quantification. These include the value of a human life (or the benefit of saving a life) and the value of saving an irreplaceable asset such as a rain forest or an endangered species. These values can only be assessed in qualitative terms.

In addition, the economic rate of return deals with one project that, alone, may have only a marginal impact on the environment, while a number of similar projects together may have a disproportionately large impact. Nonetheless, even when data are incomplete and there are conceptual problems, the analysis is important because it assists decision-makers by informing them of all the costs and benefits involved in investing in an irrigation project and the gains or losses from including or excluding different components, including environmental elements, in the project.

Efficient Water Management

Water Charges. Water charges, or a fee on the volume of water used, are based on the principle that water is a relatively scarce resource and should be priced accordingly. The broader arguments in favor of having farmers pay for the water provided by public systems are compelling. They include:

(1) Waste reduction: One of the greatest problems in irrigated agriculture is over-irrigation, which reduces productivity and contributes to waterlogging and salinization. If farmers have to pay for water, they will reduce use and hence wastage. Also, if water is priced adequately, it will be used to grow higher-value crops rather than lower-cost products.

(2) Revenue contribution: Poor maintenance—often due to a perennial shortage of funds—is commonplace. Revenue from water users can be "earmarked" for maintenance, thus improving the efficiency of the system.

(3) Equity promotion: Water users who gain access to a valuable resource raise their incomes (or the value of their assets). They should contribute more toward the cost of providing the water than those who do not have access. Similarly, users of large volumes of

water—presumably large landowners—should pay more than small landowners.

(4) Cost recovery: The beneficiaries of a project should contribute toward its costs over the project's economic life. This follows standard economic practice based on reasonable depreciation schedules.

In general, market-oriented economists consider adequate water charges to be one of the most important, policy instruments (if not *the* most important one) for correcting the shortcomings of many public sector irrigation systems. Appropriate pricing would lead to better resource allocation and would reduce pressure to invest in unproductive irrigation systems. Appropriate pricing policies would also lead to more efficient water use at the farm level, greater equity, and better system maintenance.

However, the author's experience at the Bank has been that the application and collection of water charges has not been very successful.[13] One reason for low cost recovery is that there are strong political pressures against increasing the price of water. Large numbers of individuals have a vested interest in maintaining negligible rates. These include agricultural producers—large and small—as well as officials who have a stake in promoting the expansion of irrigation works. There are also technical arguments against charging fees based solely on the volume of water used. One of the most frequently advanced is the difficulty of measuring water used by volume; very few irrigation systems outside of the United States, Australia, Europe, and parts of North Africa have water meters and, in many instances, the costs of installing and policing meters are relatively high. Other technical issues involve the problems of measurement of water use, especially in flood irrigation systems and in areas of fragmented holdings.

The greatest obstacle to introducing and expanding water charges, however, is the lack of political will; given the pressing and overgrowing need to raise revenues and improve the efficiency of resource use, this will have to change. Suitable proxies will have to be found for metering as a means of measuring the volume of water used, for example, charging for water linked to turns in rotations and having bulk sales of water to users' associations.

Indeed, it may well become important that donors make the application of water charges and the collection of these charges a condition of structural adjustment or sectoral agricultural loans in the future. A minimum requirement might well be the collection of revenue sufficient to cover recurrent expenditures in public sector projects.

International Cooperation. International cooperation can serve the cause of efficient management of water resources through, for example, promotion of a more rational use of water carried by major rivers flowing through more than one country. International efforts have been made in the past, notably by the Mekong River Commission, which coordinated various governments' attempts to develop and use the water of the Mekong effectively. Currently there is some flickering interest in a more rational use of water in the Indian subcontinent, including transnational approaches to the India–Nepal and India–Bangladesh river systems. According to the former Minister of Agriculture in India, "existing arrangements are not merely suboptimal in terms of flood control, power generation and irrigation but positively harmful to the long-term ecological balance. Yet the barriers to cooperative action have so far proved formidable."[14] These formidable barriers have included national concerns about sovereignty over riparian rights and doubt about the economic advantages and disadvantages of transnational approaches. Given the fact that the Indian subcontinent will probably soon surpass China as the most populous region in the world, it would seem prudent to pay greater attention to using the relatively scarce waters of the region as effectively as possible. This is an area where, as has been suggested, the governments concerned could work with the United Nations and a regional institution such as the Asian Development Bank to examine possible avenues of cooperation for more effective use of the waters of the region.

The somewhat limited potential for low-cost irrigation in Africa will have to be exploited, but the issue is complicated by the international nature of many African rivers. More than fifty-seven major rivers or lake basins are shared by two or more countries: five are shared by six or more; the Nile, by nine; and the Niger, by ten. Most donors and governments in Africa have yet to formulate policies for cooperation and coordination in the development of international rivers. As in the Asian context, there would seem to be a case for a regionwide approach to using these resources to raise agricultural output. Such an approach might well be initiated by the region's major development institution, the African Development Bank. The process of analysis and negotiation would undoubtedly be long and complicated, but it could result in substantial dividends.

Water Management Research. In recent years, interest has increased in the role of research in promoting agricultural development. The flow of resources into agricultural research in the developing countries has greatly increased, especially for crop production. Much less research has been done on irrigation per se, and little research has been conducted on traditional irrigation which is still dominant in the developing world.

Many facets of irrigation in poorer countries could benefit from further research. Generally, the greatest shortcoming in improving irrigation in developing countries has been irrigation management. Irrigation management, as a discipline, might be said to embrace making a system work more effectively through its adaptation and innovations to local needs, rather than by adhering to rigid rules and procedures. Members of the international donor community recently established the International Institute for Managing Irrigation (IIMI) specifically to undertake research on irrigation management in developing countries. In contrast to the scale of the problem, the Institute is a very modest effort with an annual budget of $3–5 million a year. It would seem to warrant greater support from the international community as well as membership in the Consultative Group for International Agricultural Research (CGIAR).

The research agenda should also encompass many other issues that will be increasingly important in the future: how to promote multidisciplinary approaches to the development, implementation, and management of irrigation projects; what means of levying fair charges for water users are the most appropriate and effective; and what kinds of socioeconomic organization in densely populated irrigated areas can promote and safeguard the incomes of men and women who, increasingly, will be part-time farmers on fragmented, small-scale irrigated holdings.

Watershed Protection. Historically, many early gravity systems of irrigation were destroyed by the erosion and sedimentation of reservoirs and channels. These problems have become increasingly important in affecting water storage and distribution systems and have severely damaged many water storage reservoirs. Guaranteeing the permanence of some irrigation projects will require greatly reduced erosion in watershed areas. For example, it has been estimated that the life of the reservoir in the Rio Honda watershed in Ecuador can be doubled if erosion in the watershed can be controlled.[15] Many watersheds, however, are in areas far removed from the dams. Changes in land use in the tributary areas of the Nile in Ethiopia, for instance, have an effect on the volume of silt deposited in the Aswan Dam in Egypt. (There is as yet no careful study about how such changes might indeed alter the sedimentation rate.) Improvement in this context would probably depend on international agreements.

Policymakers concerned with irrigation are seldom involved in upstream watershed management. Usually the watersheds are in hilly areas that are used for natural or planted forests and for raising livestock. The ecology of these areas becomes disturbed when there is accelerated deforestation and overgrazing. Very often these activities are spurred by the poverty and lack of alternative opportunities that confront the forest dwellers and tenders of livestock. Usually, too, the only way of limiting the destruction of the natural resource base and subsequent erosion is through strict control over the exploitation of these regions' resources. This sets up a conflict between users of the watershed basin and the downstream beneficiaries of the irrigation system. One partial solution that has been tried under World Bank auspices in the Magdalena Valley of Colombia is for water users to pay a fee that goes to help provide alternative opportunities for the poor in watershed areas.[16]

The main lesson learned from the siltation and sedimentation of reservoirs, however, is that a regional approach must be employed in planning large-scale projects. Such an approach would have to extend beyond the narrow focus of control of the available supply of water to ensure that there will be limits on the sedimentation of the system. This in turn would involve active programs to control the actions of foresters and animal grazers—a far cry from the usual province of irrigation engineers.

Interdisciplinary Focus. One of the major requirements for a more comprehensive approach to irrigation such as that suggested in this chapter is that there be an interdisciplinary focus in dealing with irrigation. This applies to both planning and execution. Irrigation is increasingly recognized to be more than a means to increase production. It is also seen to have strong impact on equity and the environment. As yet, however, most donors and governments have not widened the focus beyond that of the engineer, agronomist, and economist (and in some cases, there is still little communication between engineers and agronomists). However, as has been pointed out, the medical profession, sociologists, political scientists, and ecologists play important roles along with members of the more traditional disciplines associated with irrigation projects.

The lack of interaction among these disciplines is serious. The damage done by lack of appreciation of the importance of watershed management has been considerable, and the costs of ignoring medical needs have been high. Perhaps the greatest need is for interaction among the designers of projects and those who are concerned with the contributions and rights of the users of water—both women and men. In the final analysis, as has been stressed, the human dimension is an important one, but it is often the one that is most neglected.

Meeting Equity Concerns and Anti-Poverty Objectives in Irrigated Areas

Much of the discussion about promoting greater equity in agriculture has revolved around redistributing assets, especially ownership and control of land. The most important factor that governs income distribution within irrigated areas is the pattern of ownership of land with access to water and the tenurial rights in the irrigated areas. All other things being equal, a more even pattern of ownership will lead to a more even distribution of income; similarly, if absentee ownership were abolished and tenants given a greater share of the output they produced, income distribution would be less skewed. Changing overall rights to land, however, usually involves a shift that is considered too radical by those within the power structures of many governments. Most governments with large irrigated acreages (outside of China) have eschewed such radical reform and have favored more modest efforts to discourage a worsening of income distribution—for example, setting upper limits on the size of family holdings and regulating tenancy arrangements.

A number of alternative steps can be taken to promote greater equity within existing systems. The first is to ensure that all producers in a system—usually a public sector surface irrigation system—have access to water and receive their prescribed allotments. Often this requires that users agree among themselves about the distribution of water and then band together to exercise their rights. In some instances this will involve a partnership between users and managers of the system, or the empowerment of users to run the system. For the most part, equitable access depends on the political power exercised by the users.

Fiscal policies can improve equity in irrigation areas. The removal of subsidies on equipment that is employed primarily by larger farmers—such as pumps and tractors—along with the reduction in subsidies for credit can contribute to greater equity. Similarly, the imposition and collection of water charges or some form of user levy based on the amount of water used could also make the system fairer and even out the net income earned.

Finally, investment policies could be oriented to promote greater equity. Irrigation projects can be designed and financed with this in mind. The layout of a project could be arranged so that a given volume of water is shared by more rather than fewer producers (who would still have enough to produce a surplus for the market). Other infrastructure, such as roads, can be located to ensure that low-income producers have access to markets; alternatively, there must be adequate storage facilities for poorer producers. In addition, investments in services such as research and extension can be designed to assist "resource-poor" producers.

Population Pressure

The increasing pressure of population on limited irrigated areas of land is adding new dimensions to the future role of irrigation. The most evident instance of this is the island of Java, which could well be the forerunner of similar situations elsewhere.

Currently, population density is around 710 people per square kilometer—or twice that of the Netherlands. The rapid growth of urban agglomerates has made a substantial part of the irrigated area peri-urban rather than rural. Very little land is unused, and the irrigation system provides water for agricultural and domestic uses. In addition, the majority of rice producers, male and female, are now part-time farmers, with most relying on other employment or activities to generate a large part of their income.

The situation in Java points to a future where there will be an islandwide population density equivalent to a low-density city-state. This raises questions about what kind of farming organization makes sense where irrigation will be partly a semi-urban phenomenon carried out by part-time workers. Thus far this issue has received little emphasis; it will become increasingly important as populations grow and attention has to be focused both on increasing the production *and* employment creation in situations where there are serious constraints on the supply of land.

Conclusion

Irrigation has been at the leading edge of the remarkable increases in food production in the tropics in the postwar years. It will continue to be important in coming years, as populations increase very substantially and as demand for staple foods rises. However, the costs of irrigation are rising, and resources are not as readily available as they once were. It behooves donors and others to ensure that these resources are used as effectively as possible to promote equitable, environmentally sound development. In their attempts to do so, donors may benefit from many lessons that emerge from the rapid development of irrigation in recent decades—including the importance of good project preparation and the need for maintenance, as well as the need to take into account concerns such as salinization of soils, health issues, and resettlement. Analytical techniques must be improved to incorporate environmental costs and benefits, and there needs to be much closer cooperation among traditional analysts and environmentalists. Water users must be more involved in planning to ensure sustainability, and attention has to be paid to watershed management. In addition, international initiatives on water sharing and research might be considered as the world moves into the twenty-first century. One of the overriding concerns for the future is that water be seen as a relatively scarce but renewable resource—and valued accordingly.

Looking ahead, it appears that the growing population pressure in some irrigated areas will make it necessary that irrigation be seen as a semi-urban phenomenon—a substantial challenge. This raises a number of new concerns about the organization of irrigated agriculture as a part-time activity where employment creation is a major preoccupation.

Notes

[1] Food and Agriculture Organization (FAO), *Agriculture Towards 2000* (Rome, 1985).

[2] Based on data in W. Robert Rangely, "Irrigation and Drainage in the World," in *Water and Water Policy in World Food Supplies,* Conference Proceedings, 26–30 May 1985, Texas A&M University, College Station, pp. 30–35.

[3] Montague Yudelman, "The World Bank and Irrigation," in *Water and Water Policy in World Food Supplies,* op. cit., pp. 419, 423.

[4] See Robert Repetto, "Skimming the Water," Research Report 4 (Washington, D.C.: World Resources Institute, 1986).

[5] Mahabab Hossain, "Nature and Impact of the Green Revolution in Bangladesh," Research Report 67, International Food Policy Research Institute (IFPRI) in collaboration with Bangladesh Institute of Development Studies, (Washington, D.C.: IFPRI, July 1988), p. 6.

[6] See W. R. Gasser, "Survey of Irrigation in Eight Asian Nations" (Washington, D C.: U.S. Department of Agriculture, 1981).

[7] The examples cited in this and the following paragraphs are drawn from papers presented at the Conference on Water and Water Policy in World Food Supplies, op. cit.

[8] Gilbert White, "The Environmental Effect of the High Dam at Aswan," *Environment,* Vol. 30, No. 7 (September 1988), pp. 5–28.

[9] Michael Cernea, "Involuntary Resettlement and Development," in *Finance & Development* (Washington, D.C.: The World Bank, September 1980), pp. 44–46.

[10] Michael Cernea, "Involuntary Resettlement in Development Projects—Policy Guidelines in World Bank-Financed Projects" Technical Paper 80 (Washington, D.C.: The World Bank, April 1986).

[11] However, there are illustrations of successful group participation in large projects; see Honorio B. Bautisto, "Experience with Organizing Irrigators' Associations: A Case Study from the Magat River Irrigation Project in the Philippines" (Sri Lanka: International Irrigation Management Institute, 1987).

[12] See John A. Dixon, "Economic Analysis of the Environmental Impacts of Development Projects" (Manila, Philippines: The Asian Development Bank, 1986).

[13] See Repetto, "Skimming the Water," op. cit., pp. 4, 5.

[14] C. Subramanoniam, "Making Institutions Work—Development Program," in *Water and Water Policy in World Food Supplies,* op. cit., p. 376.

[15] This estimate is given in an unpublished paper by Alfredo Sfeir-Younis (The World Bank, Washington, D.C., 1987).

[16] This condition was attached to a loan made to Colombia by the World Bank in 1978.

Chapter 2

Technology, Human Pressure, and Ecology in the Arid and Semi-Arid Tropics

J. Dirck Stryker

The tropical arid areas of the world average 100–400 millimeters of rainfall a year, with the 400-millimeter level roughly corresponding to the low end of the rainfall range necessary for cultivation without irrigation.[1] Arid regions are therefore basically pastoral in their orientation. In the semi-arid tropics, on the other hand, much of the land is cultivated, though both the quantity of rainfall (400–800 millimeters) and its duration (three to four months) severely limit the range of crops that may be grown and the yields produced. Strictly speaking, neither arid nor semi-arid regions include deserts, which typically receive less than 100 millimeters of rain a year. Yet many "deserts" are in fact arid or semi-arid lands that have been degraded by human activity. The result has been a loss of valuable natural resources and impoverishment of the inhabitants.

Major issues associated with environmental degradation and poverty in these drier areas of poor nations are the subject of this chapter. Although the scope is global, the analysis draws extensively on the author's experience in the Sahelian zone of West Africa. A broad description is first provided of the arid and semi-arid tropics, their ecologies, and the ways in which people have traditionally adapted to these environments. A discussion of the major forces of change that currently characterize these regions—population growth, increased demand for marketed products, the introduction of new technologies, and the displacement of local political authorities—then leads to an examination of the environmental problems that have resulted from these changes. An assessment is also provided of actual and potential strategies of natural resource management that have been or might be used to overcome these problems. A final section presents a series of policy recommendations.

A key assumption underlying the recommendations is that the primary goal is to reduce poverty in these regions—not to preserve the environment for its own sake or for its benefits to the rest of the world by maintaining biological diversity, avoiding climatic changes, or other reasons. These other objectives are laudable, but they are treated elsewhere. The focus here is on alleviating poverty and on the role of sound natural resource management in that process.

Poverty and Environment in Dry Areas

The Ecology of the Arid and Semi-Arid Tropics

The tropical arid and semi-arid regions are located principally in Africa north and south of the Sahara, Southern Africa, the Near and Middle East, central Asia, northeastern Brazil, and central Australia. In the arid areas, rainfall is generally inadequate and too variable—spatially, seasonally, and from year to year—for farming without irrigation. In semi-arid regions, somewhat more abundant and less variable rainfall makes cultivation possible, but the risks of crop failure are just as great as in arid areas because crops need moisture over the entire length of the growing season.

Within these zones, extensive areas are covered by exposed hard clay and lateritic soils of low fertility. Cultivation is therefore usually concentrated in depressions and other areas where deeper soils have been deposited through water and wind erosion. In the absence of degradation, natural vegetation generally includes a diffuse ground cover of such perennial species as trees, shrubs, and grasses. This protects the soil from wind erosion and compaction. Once degradation occurs, the soil loses water reserves, and these plants die.[2]

Major environmental difficulties often arise when dry-land farming encroaches onto arid lands, typically during a succession of good years with above-average rainfall. The fields are stripped of their indigenous perennials when the soil is cultivated, and natural ground cover is replaced with annual crops, such as millet, which fail if rainfall is less than average or badly timed. Cultivation is then abandoned, but the damage to the land has already been done.

Where rainfall is inadequate, irrigation may be used to replace or supplement it. The systems used range from large projects involving dams and extensive canal networks to small, hand-irrigated gardens. If irrigation is not carefully managed, however, it can lead to long-term environmental problems. For example, salinization and waterlogging of irrigated soils have led to the sterilization of huge areas in North Africa, the Near and Middle East, India, and elsewhere. (These problems are treated in Chapter 1.)

Excessive exploitation of scarce trees and shrubs for fuel, construction, and animal forage also seriously endangers arid and semi-arid lands by decreasing the vegetation that helps to hold the soil in place and to recycle nutrients in the ground. Soil fertility and humus content decline and the structure of the soil breaks down, leading to further erosion from wind and rain.

Traditional Economic Activity

In the most recent comprehensive study of the population of various ecological zones, it was estimated that, in 1975, the arid and semi-arid tropics were populated, respectively, by 132 million and 314 million people.[3] Worldwide population densities averaged 0.2 persons per hectare in arid areas and 0.7 persons per hectare in semi-arid zones, although there were large differences among the major regions of the world. For example, population densities in arid and semi-arid areas, respectively, averaged 1.0 and 1.9 persons per hectare in Southeast Asia, but only 0.08 and 0.22 persons per hectare in Africa.

Most people in these dry areas are very poor. Although there are no worldwide data on per capita income by ecological zone, the figures for countries with a large proportion of their land lying within these zones suggest how poor they are. Each of the Sahelian countries of West Africa, for example, has an annual per capita gross domestic product of less than $500—compared to the average of $600 for all developing countries.[4]

The major traditional economic activity in the arid tropics is nomadic or semi-nomadic pastoralism, which is highly adapted to the ecological conditions that characterize this zone. Spatial and temporal variations in rainfall are accommodated by animal movements. The most important of these is *transhumance,* the seasonal movement that occurs during the rainy season to fresh pasture in otherwise dry areas. This is followed by retreat to dry-season grazing near permanent water sources. Depending on the amount and distribution of rainfall from year to year, the pattern may be altered.

Animal movements are supplemented by species diversity to protect herders against the whims of nature. For example, cattle and sheep derive most of their nutritional intake from grasses, while camels and goats depend more on browse from trees and shrubs. Each food source is affected differently by the amount and distribution of rain.

Animal husbandry is also very important in semi-arid areas as a supplement to cultivation. Rainfed crops include millet, sorghum, groundnuts, and legumes. Yields are low and critically dependent on the quantity and timing of rain. Ownership of livestock allows farmers to diversify against the risk of drought and to maintain capital in the form of animals as a hedge against bad times. Animals are used in some areas for hauling and tilling, but livestock and cultivation generally are not well intergrated in a mixed farming system.

The Role of Women

The role of women is vitally important in arid and semi-arid regions beset by hardship and periodic famine. Survival often depends on the allocation of food within the household, and women make these decisions. Women who have outside sources of income are likely to allocate food purchased with this income according to need, giving priority to young children and pregnant or lactating mothers. To the extent that women gain greater opportunities to earn income by selling animals, making jewelry, and pursuing other economic activities, family nutrition is likely to be improved. This has important implications for government interventions designed to increase these opportunities.

The outmigration of men, seasonal or otherwise, also has important consequences for women, who must then take on additional agricultural tasks. Whether outmigration results in an improved standard of living for the family depends in part on the money sent home and the savings that are generated for investment in farming and other economic activities. In the meantime, it is women who must hold the family together.

Women are also the chief gatherers of household fuelwood. Tree planting and other conservation measures must therefore clearly involve them. Furthermore, policies under consideration—for example, a tax on the transport of firewood—need to be scrutinized for their specific impact on women.

Forces for Change

The major forces for change in arid and semi-arid regions are population growth, increased demand for marketed products, the introduction of new technologies, and the displacement of local political authorities by national governments. Each of these factors has important implications for the linkages between the environment and economic activity.

Population Growth

Population growth in arid regions is commonly believed to result in overgrazing and the destruction of shrubs and trees. The fragility of the environment and the weakness of the underlying resource base also imply a very limited capacity to absorb increased numbers of people— even from nomadic and semi-nomadic societies, whose reproduction rates are lower than those of farmers.[5] A recent World Bank study suggests that current levels of rural population in the arid zone of West Africa, for example, are already at or beyond the region's sustainable limit.[6]

To assess the environmental impact of population growth in this area, it is necessary to understand the ways in which population pressure is relieved.[7] Outmigration, temporary or permanent, is one important source of relief. Another is economic diversification, including commerce and handicrafts, which bring in cash income for purchases of cereals and other imports from outside the pastoral zone. Such income is critical to herders during periods of drought. Indeed, losses suffered during prolonged drought make it impossible for many herders to become reestablished afterward, forcing them out of the zone.

Pressure on arid lands is affected by population growth not only within this region but also in adjacent semi-arid areas, often more densely populated than either arid or more humid regions.[8] Semi-arid areas tend to be more populated for several reasons:

- Rates of population growth are generally higher among farmers than among herders, with higher fertility rates and lower mortality rates.

- More sparsely populated sub-humid and humid areas harbor animal and human diseases such as river blindness, which inhibits immigration.

- Powerful political entities in the semi-arid areas of West Africa and India have facilitated the maintenance of higher population densities through military protection of the people and control of the use of land.[9]

Population growth in the more densely populated semi-arid tropics has often pushed cultivation into drier arid regions, creating some of the environmental problems noted earlier. Population pressure has also increased the demand for scarce fuelwood, leading to increased soil degradation and desertification. These pressures have exacerbated conflicts beween farmers and herders, especially where permanent cultivation has been introduced in areas previously used by herders for seasonal migration. Finally, population growth in semi-arid areas has created pressures for the intensification of cultivation through a reduction in fallow periods and other traditional soil-conservation practices.

Demand for Marketed Animal and Cash Crop Products

With urbanization and income growth, the demand for animal products from arid and semi-arid regions has increased, causing prices—especially cattle and sheep prices—to rise. The result has been a shift away from subsistence herding to the raising of animals for sale. Farmers and herders have in this way earned income to purchase cereals and other foods.

One important consequence of this trend has been to increase the human carrying capacity of the land in some arid and semi-arid regions. Herders can survive with fewer animals, for example, by selling them in exchange for other foods instead of living solely off the milk and the meat. The expanding market has also shifted incentives in favor of raising cattle and sheep and away from the better adapted camels and goats, which are less susceptible to drought. The greater drought vulnerability of cattle and sheep tends to be offset, however, by their higher value in the marketplace.

The expansion of commercial activity and the monetization of the pastoral economy have altered patterns of ownership and created opportunities for saving and investment in ways that influence natural resource management. Animals are increasingly owned by farmers, traders, civil servants, and other non-herders. At the same time, capital accumulated by herders is being invested outside the livestock sector, allowing for greater diversification and lowering their risk—though at the same time reducing their stake in preserving the rangeland.

Similarly, cash-crop farming has opened opportunities for increased specialization in agriculture. In West Africa, for example, farmers who used to grow millet and sorghum for their own consumption began during the colonial period to shift some of their land and labor toward producing groundnuts for cash, while consuming imported foods, including rice. Although this trend was later reversed because of a decline in world groundnut prices, it nonetheless initiated an expansion of commercial activity, a reduction in food-crop production, and increased dependence on purchased food.

Introduction of New Technology

All arid and semi-arid regions have witnessed the widespread introduction of new technology over the past few decades. One of the most important innovations in Africa has been the development of an effective vaccine against rinderpest, which periodically used to devastate cattle herds. This has both raised herder productivity (by drastically reducing mortality from the disease) and increased pressure on grazing resources. Thus the reduction of rinderpest has heightened the need for appropriate land management in previously infested areas.

Other interventions, such as efforts to develop water resources and to improve herd management and breeding, have been less successful. For example, government-drilled and -owned wells and boreholes have made water freely available to all users, but animals have concentrated around these water points, especially during the dry season, and have destroyed the vegetation within a radius of several miles. Government ranches have been less successful in herd management and breeding than traditional herders, and they have taken over large tracts of valuable land that herders could use more productively.

In semi-arid areas, the major emphasis has been on improvements in cropping techniques. These efforts have suffered from the lack of an economically viable technical package. Some progress has been made in developing high-yielding sorghum varieties in India, but transplanting these to West Africa has proved to be very difficult. Furthermore, government interventions have failed to recognize the importance of integrating cultivation, livestock, and forestry components of farming systems.[10]

In both arid and semi-arid regions, the introduction of modern transportation and urban services has increased population and the demand for resources. This has placed greater pressure on existing water and wood supplies and has led to environmental degradation around transportation routes and urban settlements.

Displacement of Local Political Authorities

Traditional local political authorities in arid and semi-arid regions once played an important role in establishing and protecting land-use rights in ways that avoided many of the environmental problems that exist today. All this changed during the colonial period and with the centralization by national governments of political authority in the capital or provincial city. This greatly reduced local control of land use rights. As a result, farmers were freer to encroach on arid areas, and herders faced fewer controls and sanctions to prevent them from causing crop damage in farmers' fields before the harvest.

Environmental Problems and their Causes

These forces of change place enormous pressure on the natural resource base of arid and semi-arid areas, sometimes causing severe degradation. Yet population growth, rising demand for livestock and cash crops, and the introduction of new technology are often not the basic causes of these problems. Technically speaking, many arid and semi-arid lands *could* support all these trends, and they do have some positive effects on the natural resource base. Furthermore, there may be some benefits associated with the centralization of political authority—although these are likely to be more than offset by the disadvantages for natural resource management.

To assess the impact of these forces on natural resources and to devise effective policies to improve the management of these resources, both the "proximate" and the "basic" causes of environmental problems in arid and semi-arid areas must be carefully analyzed. The proximate causes are diverse: They include overgrazing, burning of vegetation, cultivation of marginal land, overuse of agricultural soils, gathering of wood for fuel and construction, and destruction of wildlife. Despite this diversity, most of these problems have a single basic cause: natural resources in these regions are usually held in common rather than owned by individuals. One reason for this is that resources in these areas are inadequate to support large populations, especially in the arid tropics, and animals have to be moved over long distances and in patterns that are difficult to predict. This implies that the cost of establishing and enforcing systems of individual land use rights is high. This cost is incurred in industrial countries (despite the fact that population density in their arid and semi-arid regions is even lower than in those of poor countries) only because of the much greater level of capital and intermediate inputs employed per unit of labor. Fencing, transportation and communications equipment, petroleum products, and other inputs in the industrial countries facilitate individual land ownership and control over the use of natural resources.[11]

Within the poorer countries, in contrast, land control has taken traditional "labor-intensive" forms, such as the use of herders rather than fences to guide animal movements, but these have been eroded by many of the changes described earlier. Growing population pressure has severely complicated the maintenance, enforcement, and adjudication of land use rights. Rising animal prices have encouraged an expansion of individual economic activity within the livestock sector and permitted ownership of animals to be transferred to people not subject to traditional forms of control. Increased cash crop opportunities have added further to pressures on cultivable soils. At the same time, technological advances in animal health and water development have increased the pressures on traditional production systems. Finally, both the undermining of local authority by colonial regimes and national governments and the tendency within these governments toward centralized authority have weakened traditional systems for managing the use of natural resources.

Individual exploitation of common resources has led to environmental problems when all the costs to society are not borne by the individual, resulting in overexploitation of the resource. Some of these costs may not be reversible—at least not for many years. Each of the proximate causes of environmental problems in arid and semi-arid regions should be evaluated according to (a) whether it carries social costs not borne by the individual and (b) whether these costs apply only to the current period or also extend into the future.

Overgrazing

The problem of overgrazing has received a great deal of attention. There is a perception that part of the problem lies in the increased orientation toward cattle and sheep, which are less adapted to the environment than goats and camels—though goats also receive their share of blame for environmental degradation.[12] Because cattle need more water, they cannot be grazed more than 15–30 kilometers away from water points, depending on the time of year. Consequently, large concentrations of cattle during the dry season denude the landscape, leading to desertification.

The problem is less one of numbers of animals, however, than of the way water points are owned and organized. Traditional practice in the Sahel is that those who construct a well have the first right to its use. Along with the size of the well, which is determined by the owner, this system permits a measure of control. But colonial and national governments have constructed public wells and boreholes—with unlimited access—all over the Sahel, leading to extensive degradation around these water points. The process is exacerbated by government efforts in a number of countries to sedentarize herders around water sources.

A second issue related to overgrazing is the elimination of perennial grasses and their replacement by annuals. The extent of these losses is not known. The most thorough published study of pasture productivity in the Sahel offers some interesting conclusions. One of these is that water, not soil nutrients, limits the productivity of grasslands throughout the arid region of the Sahel. Perennial grasses are particularly sensitive to drought—and this more than overgrazing accounts for their relative absence in relation to annuals. Furthermore, the advantages of perennial over annual grasses are overestimated. For example, during the rainy season, the concentration of nutrients in the annual grasses of the northern part of the Sahel is greater than that found in perennials further south. This accounts for the importance that herders attach to *transhumance* at that time of year. Finally, overgrazing does not appear to be a significant problem for annual grasses, since their growth is limited by water availability and, except around permanent water points, seeds are almost always in sufficient supply. The growth of trees and shrubs is actually stimulated by intensive exploitation of annual grasses, because this leaves more water in the soil.[13]

The effects of overgrazing may be more important in semi-arid areas, where perennials are more likely to develop than in arid zones. Heavy grazing in this case may cause a deterioration in pasture quality. The spread of nonpalatable species into the sweet *grassveld* of Southern Africa, for example, appears to have been due to heavy concentrations of domesticated animals in stationary locations.[14] Although higher population density in semi-arid areas increases the cost of not regulating the use of common land, it also makes more practicable the development of systems for controlling land use. Furthermore, the availability of agricultural residues, byproducts, and cultivated fodder in this zone provides an alternative to open grazing and possible degradation of semi-arid pastures.

An important overall conclusion is that decreasing the intensity of rangeland exploitation in the arid tropics would probably reduce its productivity in terms of livestock products. The environment would be somewhat more stable, however, because the greater amount of vegetation left on the land at the end of the growing season would help to protect the most sensitive soils against erosion and other forms of degradation. The quantitative production increases that would later result from this greater stability are uncertain, however, and must be measured against the immediate loss of production from less intensive use of the land. In the semi-arid areas, control of common land by individuals, local authorities, or the state would probably increase its productivity, but supplementation of pasture resources with crop residues, byproducts, and cultivated fodder from agriculture becomes increasingly important as the population expands.

Burning

Herders often burn off old vegetation to make tender, green forage readily available to their animals. Pasture research has confirmed the positive effect that burning has on new sprouts and on the productivity of grasses.[15] By volatilizing organic nitrogen compounds, however, fire also depletes soil fertility. This results in excessive leaching during the rainy season and the loss of salts from the ashes of burned grass and animal manure.[16] Burning also destroys the trees and shrubs that provide browse, help to hold the soil in place, and recycle nutrients from deep in the soil.

The use of fire is a classic instance of a technique that benefits the brush burners immediately but exacts social costs from others in the future. Government intervention may be warranted if net social costs resulting from burning exceed the cost of preventing the burning. Government actions to prevent burning therefore require an estimation of these relative costs. Since obtaining these estimates is very difficult, and since enforcement of restrictions on burning is likely to be easier if undertaken by local authorities, regulation of burning should be the responsibility of these authorities.

Cultivation of Marginal Land

The problems associated with rainfed cultivation in arid regions already have been mentioned. Complete land clearance and the turning of light, sandy soils expose the land to erosion by wind and rain. To the extent that the land remains in the hands of the same individual for a number of years, these costs are "internal" and are likely to be taken into account in deciding what, where, and how to plant. The soil may, in this case, be left relatively undisrupted through the use of minimal tillage techniques that result in some loss in immediate yields but preserve the soil for the future. More frequently, however, farmers move onto marginal lands during years of good rainfall only to abandon them in drought years, leaving the soils exposed to degradation. The costs of this degradation are borne not by the individual farmer, but by society.

Overuse of Agricultural Soils

Soils *can* be cultivated in semi-arid areas without depletion or degradation as long as conservation is practiced. Traditionally, this is done by maintaining sufficiently long fallow periods to allow for regeneration after one or more years of cultivation. Other practices involve manuring, erosion control, crop rotation, planting legumes, and brush burning.

Although conserving soils in the face of pressure from growing population and the spread of cash crops is technically feasible, there is evidence that, for complex reasons, this often is not done. In most instances, "externalities" are not the reason, since African farmers generally have usufruct, if not proprietary, rights to their land, and since the first consequence of soil depletion—a decline in yields—does not spill over onto others' land. Rather, it appears that as population density increases, fallow periods are necessarily shortened, but the other techniques to maintain soil fertility are not always employed.

One possible reason is that farmers have a relatively short time horizon because of immediate pressures to assure a subsistence level of food production for their families. Poor farmers do not have the resources to invest in the future and cannot borrow. Evidence from Burkina Faso suggests, however, that farmers with better access to nonagricultural income are *least* likely to invest their time in soil conservation measures.[17] These farmers are also less dependent on the land for their livelihood and food needs, so they do not demand as much from the soil and are able to allow some of it to lie fallow in order to restore its fertility. The outcome for the environment of these two opposing responses is unclear.

Cash crops also present new opportunities to farmers. Unlike off-farm activities, however, the expansion of cash-crop production puts heavier pressure on the land by reducing the area available for food crops. But it also provides cash for the purchase of fertilizer. In addition, some cash crops, such as nitrogen-fixing legumes, may help to enrich the soil.

In summary, clear evidence demonstrates that soil depletion and degradation are occurring in semi-arid areas as a result of overuse of the land. Although much better understanding of the causes is needed, the severe consequences of environmental degradation in this fragile and relatively populated zone demand immediate government intervention to forestall the loss of this land. Recommendations to this effect are presented in the concluding section.

Wood Gathering

Wherever the concentration of poor people is on the rise, demand for wood for cooking, heating, and construction is likewise growing. Despite increases in the costs of firewood and charcoal throughout the world, for most people these sources of energy are still cheaper than kerosene, their major alternative.

The consequences of excessive wood gathering are severe. Intense exploitation leads to the killing of live trees and shrubs rather than the harvesting of dead wood left from the growth and regeneration of trees. This increases rainwater runoff, erosion, and flooding, which reduce the replenishment of groundwater reserves. It also decreases the availability of browse for livestock, prevents the recycling of nutrients from deeper layers of the soil, robs soils of ground cover and organic matter from the leaves, and reduces protection of soils from the wind. In some areas, excessive wood gathering encourages the use of dung for fuel, decreasing this source of nutrients and organic matter for the soil.

Once again, there are social costs not directly incurred by those gathering the wood. To the extent that these costs exceed the cost of preventing excessive exploitation of wood resources, there is a case for government intervention. Unlike burning and subsistence farming, which are only indirectly linked to the market, a substantial amount of wood is gathered for direct sale, especially in and around urban areas. This implies that government intervention might take the form of taxation or regulation of wood marketing rather than controls on wood gathering at its source, which are much more difficult and costly to enforce. The final section discusses this alternative in more detail.

Development Strategy in Dry Areas

The arid and semi-arid tropics are fundamentally poor because of their weak resource base. As long as agriculture and livestock remain the major economic activities, low production potential per unit of land area limits the total income that even advanced techniques can generate. As development proceeds and the opportunity cost of people's time rises, however, herders and farmers leave the land as vehicles, farm machinery, fencing, and other forms of capital arrive. Total income is spread over fewer people until per capita incomes are comparable to those earned elsewhere in the economy.

However, the introduction of these techniques generally is not desirable in poorer countries with fewer and less remunerative employment opportunities outside agriculture and herding. First, these techniques are not economically efficient, given the existing abundance of labor and the scarcity of capital. Second, they worsen the distribution of income by adding herders and farmers to the ranks of the unemployed.

A number of analysts have been concerned about the increasing "marginalization and social differentiation" that characterize pastoral societies in arid and semi-arid regions.[18] In their view, pastoralists are being pushed onto increasingly marginal lands by the advance of cultivation and commercial ranching. They maintain that, at the same time, a small number of livestock owners, both from within and outside pastoral communities, have become increasingly rich and powerful at the expense of the many herders who have become more and more impoverished.

A major culprit, according to this view, is the expansion of cash crops into areas previously used for grazing and food production, which has forced poor farmers to expand food cultivation onto the rangelands. Irrigation is also blamed for reducing pasture reserves for dry-season grazing and the cultivation of cereals on flood recession land. Urbanization has increased the demand for fuelwood, depriving animals of dry-season browse, and pasture has been diverted from communal to private or highly restricted public grazing. All of these developments, according to this scenario, have impoverished herders and small farmers, who have had to accept wage employment to supplement their agricultural and livestock activities.

The problem with this scenario is that it is based on speculation and impressions rather than on hard empirical evidence. There are no reliable data for the Sahel on, for example, the distribution of either income or wealth and how they have changed over time. Nor is there any firm evidence regarding changes in patterns of animal ownership. Irrigation projects have withdrawn land from alternative uses, but the winners and losers remain to be clearly identified.

Economic activity in arid and semi-arid areas has become increasingly diversified with the expansion of cash-crop opportunities, increases in livestock prices, growth of outside wage opportunities, and improvements in transportation and communication. This has decreased the risks confronting herders and small farmers and has strengthened their ability to bounce back after drought years.[19] Outside income has also enabled them to purchase inputs such as fertilizer and veterinary supplies, which have proven critical to maintaining their resource base and increasing their productivity.

The question is not whether poverty exists. Poverty is *very* serious in arid and semi-arid areas because of their poor resource base and their low levels of available capital. Furthermore, the fragility of the environment—together with the fact that most herders and small farmers lack access to capital—implies that the poor suffer disproportionately from low animal prices and high cereal prices in drought years.

Rather, the issue is whether these forces are exacerbated by economic development, leading herders and small farmers toward further impoverishment. If this is the case, the situation in these areas is very serious. Designing development strategies in arid and semi-arid areas is not easy, but devising anti-poverty strategies that are not developmental in nature has proven to be exceedingly difficult. Agricultural projects on marginal lands, for example, have been expensive and ineffective. They have underestimated risks, failed to enlist local participants and institutions, and relied too much on weak central management.[20] They have suffered greatly, too, from the absence of an economically and socially viable technical package. Attempts to extend credit programs to cover herders and small farmers have also been notoriously unsuccessful.

Fortunately, the conflict between development and anti-poverty strategies is not as serious as the writers noted at the beginning of this section have claimed. With economic development has come diversification in sources of income and spreading of the risks associated with subsistence food production. Improved transportation and communications have also increased mobility, which has further helped to protect the poor against drought and other production risks. This reduction in risk is the single most important way of protecting the poor in these regions. The major issue, therefore, is whether the advantages of development and reduced poverty have been outweighed by their adverse impact on the natural resource base and what can be done to minimize these losses.

Recommendations

The problems associated with environment and poverty in the arid and semi-arid tropics cannot be fully overcome without a much better understanding of their causes. A major danger is that donors and governments, pressured to "do something" immediately about the environment or poverty, will take costly action that at best will address the symptoms but not the underlying problems, and at worst will undermine the long-term economic development potential of these regions, especially for the poor. The ecology of these areas is complex, and the mechanisms by which people impinge on this environment are not well understood. Wherever the activities of individuals create costs for society that are not borne by those individuals, there may be a case for intervention by the public sector.[21] Every intervention has costs associated with its administration, enforcement, and adjudication, however, and if these costs exceed net benefits, the intervention is not justified in terms of economic efficiency—although it may indeed be justified on equity or other grounds. As an example, the cost of keeping farmers from cultivating pastoral land might be greater than the losses resulting from that cultivation, but the desire to avoid destroying the pastoralists' only resource could induce governments to undertake strong action to prohibit this practice.

The costs of government intervention in arid and semi-arid regions, however, are often very high. Population densities are low, distances are vast, and people and animals are on the move. In poorer countries, skilled managers and administrators are frequently extremely scarce. These severe limitations on government capacity to manage natural resources by direct intervention to discourage or restrict resource exploitation place a premium on finding *indirect* ways of overcoming environmental problems and alleviating poverty.

The manner in which economic structural adjustment and policy reform influence the natural resource base of poor countries is a current source of concern. Most of this adjustment and reform is not directed specifically toward solving environmental or poverty problems. Indirect effects are, nevertheless, likely to be important. One example is the reduction of government expenditures, which limits the capacity of environmental agencies to enforce public regulation of natural resource use. Another is changes in tax and incentive structures to align domestic prices more closely with world market prices. This usually raises the prices of exports such as groundnuts and livestock products, increasing pressure on the land.

The fact that indirect policies are often less costly and easier to implement than direct interventions suggests the need to pay special attention to unintended side effects. The actual incidence of taxes and subsidies, for example, may be very different from that anticipated, depending on demand and supply conditions. To take one example, the effectiveness of a tax on the transport of firewood into urban areas depends on the elasticity of demand for wood in these areas. If it is not elastic, the main effect will be to reduce the real income of urban dwellers who cannot afford substitutes such as kerosene. Though often difficult to quantify, these unintended effects must be taken into account in choosing from among alternative policies.

The recommendations that follow reflect variations in the current level of understanding of the specific problems discussed above. As a result, some of the recommendations are fairly concrete, while others call for pilot projects and further research to identify interventions that will prove effective.

Control of Water

Control over water is a clear case of existing government policy contributing to land degradation. The notion that water should be made freely available to everyone has no precedent in traditional systems of land control, and its application removes one of the most important public instruments for avoiding overgrazing and land degradation.

The best approach is to turn the control of water back over to the users of the surrounding land, reversing the displacement of local political authority in favor of central governments. Local authorities should be free to tax or otherwise restrict the use of water, and the policy should be applied over the entire range of water points—from small, publicly owned wells to large-capacity boreholes.

Two major dangers are associated with this policy. The first is that local political authorities may abuse their power to gain unfair advantage for themselves. This danger could be reduced if the government that owns the wells or boreholes sold these facilities to local authorities and used the proceeds to benefit the population that pays the water taxes or charges.

The second danger is that the decentralization of authority required for the implementation of this policy may be politically unacceptable to the central government. This is particularly likely to be the case if local authorities are not well integrated into the national political structure. Where authority cannot be delegated, the central government should institute its own water charges or other controls to restrict the use of water and rangeland resources.

The choice between water charges and restrictions on use may be difficult. Charges encourage the purchase of water by the individuals who can use it most productively, but their assessment requires a commitment of administrative and accountability resources unwarranted by the financial and other benefits to be derived. Discretionary restrictions on water use, on the other hand, can give rise to corruption and favoritism. Alternatively, physical constraints could be built into the water delivery system. This might involve restricting the size of wells, capping them when grazing pressure is heavy, or piping water from boreholes to dispersed watering points. Enforcing restrictions and finding ways to prevent local officials from physically altering water delivery systems are critical to effective government efforts to constrain the free flow of water.

Tax on the Transport of Fuelwood

The most effective policy for limiting the cutting of fuelwood is a tax on its transport into urban areas. This is much easier to assess than a tax on cutting. It also differentiates between the commercial sector and individuals who gather firewood primarily for their own use—a distinction that may be desirable for equity reasons. The scope for assessing this tax may be very large. In Niger, for example, during the mid-1980s, a permit for cutting wood cost only 35 CFA Francs per stere, while the urban retail price was about 5,500 CFA Francs per stere.[22] Besides discouraging wood cutting, the tax would (1) encourage efficient use of wood, (2) make wood substitutes such as kerosene more attractive, and (3) generate income for forestry services. The tax might also be used to cross-subsidize efficient cooking stoves or alternative fuels.

Fertilizer Subsidy

The decision to subsidize fertilizers to forestall or reverse the depletion of soils associated with a reduction of fallow periods in semi-arid areas depends in part on (a) whether the government can afford the subsidy, and (b) whether there is adequate foreign exchange to purchase fertilizer imports. If the government budget is severely constrained or foreign exchange is not available, the limited quantities of subsidized fertilizer that are sold are likely to go only to the larger, more influential farmers, leaving smaller farmers on poorer land to fend for themselves. In these circumstances, there is little reason to subsidize fertilizers on either efficiency or equity grounds. If, on the other hand, there is enough fertilizer to satisfy demand at the subsidized price, the subsidy may be justified—provided that private farmers, especially those on marginal lands, are allowing the fertility of their soil to decline. Such neglect results in land degradation and abandonment, increased rural-urban migration, and the negative externalities associated with crowding in the cities.

Industrialization

There is abundant evidence that herders and farmers diversify their productive activities to shield themselves from the effects of periodic drought. An assessment of the pastoral zone of Niger in 1984–85 in fact strongly recommended diversification as the most effective means of coping with drought.[23] Yet relatively little attention has been focused on the development of light industry, the most promising strategy for diversification in arid and semi-arid regions.

Such a strategy might succeed for a number of reasons. First, many pastoralists and agriculturalists have a tradition of handicraft and arti-sanal activity that could be expanded to create the skills required for industry. Second, workers in these zones generally receive relatively low wages, implying a cost advantage for industry. Third, most people in arid and semi-arid areas prefer to maintain their ties with herding and farming, which is easier if industrial activities are located within, rather than outside, these zones. Finally, outmigration is socially disruptive, and migrating workers may run into problems if they are viewed as competing unfairly because of their willingness to work for lower wages than urban-based workers.

Most assessments of the role of industry in arid and semi-arid regions have focused on mining and processing local raw materials. Since the resource base is weak in most of these regions, this strategy does not look feasible. A more promising approach might be to establish footloose industries that use large amounts of semi-skilled labor and produce goods with high value in relation to bulk, to keep transport costs to a minimum. The electronics assembly industry is a good example.

The option of industrialization in poor arid and semi-arid areas may at first appear farfetched, but historically the development of these regions has been associated with the growth of commerce and industry in cities, not with the expansion of output from the land.[24] At the very least, a few pilot projects are warranted to see if the requirements of exterior markets can be profitably matched with the skills of local people. This will require not only knowledge, capital, and organization, but also a policy environment much more conducive to industrial entrepreneurship than exists in many countries today.[25]

Improvement in Livestock Productivity

Environmental degradation is sometimes used as a reason for failing to introduce productivity-enhancing innovations into the livestock sector. Yet animal health interventions could substantially reduce mortality and disease-associated morbidity. This would increase herder productivity and contribute to the growth of income of herders and farmers.[26]

Would this also lead to environmental degradation? Not necessarily. The earlier analysis suggests that overgrazing is not always a problem in arid regions, especially if the rangeland is dominated by annual grasses. Falling animal mortality rates would increase short-run pressure on rangeland resources, but as productivity declined because of the reduced biomass available per animal, herders would be encouraged to sell animals or to move them elsewhere. In the long run, the zone might simply be populated by fewer but more productive animals.

The benefits arising from animal health interventions appear, therefore, to outweigh the consequent losses associated with rangeland degradation. The impact of these interventions should be carefully monitored, however, and alternative courses of action should be undertaken if there is evidence that improved animal health is leading to substantial degradation. It is unlikely, however, that this would involve abandoning the animal health interventions. No one could seriously suggest, for example, that vaccination against rinderpest be abandoned in Africa because there is overgrazing in some areas. Periodic drought appears to be a more than adequate regulator of the number of animals on the rangeland without revival of this devastating disease.

Investment in Transportation Infrastructure

The pressure put on natural resources by the introduction of transportation and urban services into arid and semi-arid regions does not mean that a policy of abandoning investment in infrastructure should be pursued. Like the expansion of industry in cities, improved transportation can act as an important mechanism for diversifying sources of income and reducing pressure on natural resources. During the 1984–85 drought in Niger, for example, the existence of a paved road between the uranium mines in the north and the agricultural zone to the south permitted the trucking of large numbers of cattle out of the arid zone, relieving pressure on the limited range resources. Localized degradation around transportation routes and urban areas therefore must be weighed against the benefits of increased income, greater diversification of income sources, and more flexibility of response during drought.

Reassertion of Local Political Authority

Improved management of natural resources in the arid and semi-arid regions of poor countries clearly requires the reassertion of local political authority. Rules imposed from outside by top-heavy centrist governments without regard for existing regulatory systems are applied too rigidly and may actually frustrate cooperative action at the local level. "Cooperative solutions are most likely to succeed where the locus of decision making is a relatively small, cohesive body."[27]

Outside control, though occasionally necessary, is likely to cost more than regulation of common property by its owners. In addition, the information required for optimal resource management is not easily obtained, and residents of a local area are better placed to acquire it than outsiders. Finally, outside regulation often results in the disruption of socially egalitarian distribution mechanisms and their replacement by situations in which the unearned benefits are captured by those with influence—leaving others impoverished.[28]

Land laws are very important. Most developing countries currently have a complex tangle of laws, decrees, and other forms of legislation that date at least to the beginning of the colonial period. Because much of this legislation ignores local customary law, uncertainty surrounds the security of tenure and impedes the development of local institutions to manage natural resources. Such uncertain circumstances discourage necessary investments in land management because of the likelihood that long-term benefits will not flow to those who made the investments. Land legislation needs to be reviewed, simplified, and brought into conformity with local custom. Particular attention should be paid to women's rights so that formalizing land ownership does not in effect (as has happened in some places) strip them of access to a means of livelihood guaranteed by more informal customary means. Where the state retains the right of eminent domain, unambiguous procedures for expropriation and compensation must be defined.

More broadly, laws and regulations governing social and political organization should be examined to identify barriers they may create to the establishment of local grassroots organizations for natural resource management. These organizations should be empowered to make rules, apply sanctions, raise revenue, and take other actions to exert effective control over scarce natural resources.[29]

Family Planning

Because population growth is a basic source of much of the pressure on the environment, there is an obvious case for family planning. For two reasons, however, this approach may not be successful.

(1) Receptivity to family planning will be low as long as infant and child mortality rates are high. To be sure that a certain number of their children survive to adulthood, parents will hedge against risk by having many children.

(2) Population growth in poor arid and semi-arid regions accelerates as advances in public health lead to a reduction in mortality rates and an increase in live birth rates. These trends will probably more than offset the effects of family planning programs for years

to come, since public health conditions in many arid and semi-arid areas still remain very poor.

Nevertheless, family planning that is closely integrated with programs to improve maternal and child nutrition and health is probably the most effective way of bringing about decline in population growth in the long run. Because of the limited ability of arid and semi-arid regions to absorb further increases in population, family planning programs should be actively pursued and designed to reach both men and women. It is also important that women be involved in the planning as well as the implementation of these programs.

Impact of Commercialization

The impact on the environment and on poverty of the increasingly commercial nature of agricultural and pastoral economies is very poorly understood. What effect, for example, does the transfer of ownership of animals to non-pastoralists have on the management of the rangeland? Do farmers with more diverse sources of income in fact allow their land to degenerate—and if so, why? These are but a few of the many questions that must be answered before effective interventions in this area can be designed.

A series of field studies should be conducted to test a number of hypotheses:

(1) Herders are less careful to conserve rangeland resources when the animals they herd belong to others.

(2) Control of common rangeland by local political authorities is more difficult if the animals are owned by non-pastoralists.

(3) Diversification of economic activities by pastoralists reduces pressure on the rangeland, especially during drought.

(4) Farmers who earn a substantial proportion of their income outside of agriculture do less to conserve their soils.

(5) Farmers and herders who are more diversified have higher levels of income and consumption on average, especially in drought years.

The choice of interventions affecting herders and farmers in arid and semi-arid regions will depend on the validity of these hypotheses and, if they prove true, on the magnitude of the effects involved.

Notes

[1] H. N. Le Houérou, "The Nature and Causes of Desertification," in Michael H. Glantz, ed., *Desertification: Environmental Degradation in and around Arid Lands* (Boulder, Colo.: Westview Press, 1977), pp. 18, 19. The term tropical is used in this paper to refer to both tropical and subtropical areas, where the mean monthly temperature is always above 5C. This corresponds roughly to the latitudes between the Tropics of Cancer and Capricorn.

[2] Ibid., p. 20.

[3] These figures were calculated from table 3.2 in G. M. Higgins, et al., *Potential Population Supporting Capacities of Lands in the Developing World,* Technical Report of Project INT/75/P13 (Rome: Food and Agriculture Organization, 1982). It was assumed that arid and semi-arid areas have growing seasons of 1–90 days and 90–150 days, respectively. This overestimates the land area of arid zones because it includes some deserts, but probably does not change the population figures very much.

[4] World Bank, *World Development Report 1988* (New York: Oxford University Press, 1988), p. 22.

[5] Helen Ware, "Desertification and Population: Sub-Saharan Africa," in Glantz, ed., *Desertification: Environmental Degradation in and Around Arid Lands,* op. cit., p. 168.

[6] Jean Eugene Gorse and David R. Steeds, *Desertification in the Sahelian and Sudanian Zones of West Africa,* World Bank Technical Paper No. 61 (Washington, D.C.: The World Bank, 1987), p. 13. This analysis is based on the assumption that 13 million hectares in this zone are under cultivation, with yields averaging 300 kilograms per hectare. As noted earlier, this is a very dangerous assumption, given the adverse environmental effects that result from clearing and cultivating land in arid regions.

[7] Much of this discussion is based on the author's experience with the Integrated Livestock Project (ILP) in Niger in 1983–88. A large body of related research undertaken by the earlier Niger Range and Livestock (NRL) Project is described in Jeremy Swift, ed., *Pastoral Development in Central Niger: Report of the Niger Range and Livestock Project* (Niamey, Niger: U.S. Agency for International Development, 1984).

[8] L. Bowden, "Development of Present Dryland Farming Systems," in A. E. Hall, G. H. Cannell, and H. W. Lawton, eds., *Agriculture in Semi-Arid Environments* (Berlin: Springer-Verlag, 1979), p. 49.

[9] Ibid.

[10] Gorse and Steeds, *Desertification in the Sahelian and Sudanian Zones,* op. cit., p. 17.

[11] The substitution of fossil fuel energy in richer countries for labor in poorer nations is documented in F. W. T. Penning de Vries and M. A. Djitéye, *La Productivité des Pâturages Sahéliens; Une Étude des Sols, des Vegetations et de l'Exploitation de Cette Ressource Naturelle* (Wageningen: Centre for Agricultural Publishing and Documentation, 1982), p. 467.

[12] Advisory Committee on the Sahel, Board on Science and Technology for International Development, Office of International Affairs, National Research Council, *Resource Management for Arid and Semiarid Regions: Environmental Change in the West African Sahel* (Washington, D.C.: National Academy Press, 1984), pp. 32–37.

[13] De Vries and Djitéye, *La Productivité des Pâturages,* op. cit., pp. 483–502.

[14] Bowden, "Development of Present Dryland Farming Systems," op. cit., p. 55.

[15] De Vries and Djitéye, *La Productivité des Pâturages,* op. cit., p. 500.

[16] Advisory Committee on the Sahel, *Resource Management for Arid and Semiarid Regions,* op. cit., p. 25.

[17] Author's conversation with Thomas Reardon of the International Food Policy Research Institute regarding his research in Burkina Faso.

[18] Michael M. Horowitz and Peter D. Little, "African Pastoralism and Poverty: Some Implications for Drought and Famine," in Michael H. Glantz, ed., *Drought and Hunger in Africa: Denying Famine a Future* (New York: Cambridge University Press, 1987), p. 61.

[19] Recent research in Burkina Faso supports this view. In a sample of households, farmers in the Sahelian region were more diversified and had higher levels of per capita consumption than did those in the Sudanian zone, who produced a larger proportion of their food needs. Overall, the typical household "earned from one-half to only one-quarter of its income in a crisis period in cropping or livestock activities with the rest derived from off-farm businesses, migration remittances, and transfers." Thomas Reardon, Peter Mallon, and Christopher Delgado, "Coping with Household-level Food Insecurity in Drought-affected Areas of Burkina Faso," *World Development,* Vol. 16, No. 9 (1988), p. 1072.

[20] Gorse and Steeds, *Desertification in the Sahelian and Sudanian Zones,* op. cit., pp. 19–20.

[21] This leaves aside the challenging question of whether governments should intervene in instances where all costs are borne by individuals who do not appear to act in either their own or in society's interest.

[22] Gorse and Steeds, *Desertification in the Sahelian and Sudanian Zones,* op. cit., p. 32.

[23] J. Dirck Stryker and Albert Sollod, "The Search for a Pastoral Livestock Production Strategy," Niger Integrated Livestock Project Working Paper, Tufts University, 15 March 1985.

[24] Ware is one of the very few authors to suggest the promotion of industry in arid and semi-arid regions, "Desertification and Population," op. cit., pp. 191–93. She notes that, "the great developments in arid lands in the past have been associated not only frequently but usually with cities." Dudley Stamp, "Some Conclusions," in *A History of Land Use in Arid Regions* (Paris: U.N. Educational, Scientific and Cultural Organization, 1969).

[25] A study of the industrial incentive system in Mali concluded that it is heavily biased against exports, discourages investment in efficient industries, and is very complicated to administer. This statement would apply equally to most other Sahelian countries. J. Dirck Stryker, et al., *Incentive System and Economic Policy Reform in Mali* (Somerville, Mass.: Associates for International Resources and Development, June 1987).

[26] Arguably, the potential for increasing productivity through animal health interventions in arid regions is much greater than for improving crop cultivation in semi-arid regions.

[27] Carlisle Ford Runge, "Common Property Externalities: Isolation, Assurance, and Resource Depletion in a Traditional Grazing Context," *American Journal of Agricultural Economics,* Vol. 63, No. 4 (November 1981), p. 605.

[28] Neal F. Antz, "Must Communal Grazing Lead to Tragedy?" *Proceedings of the International Rangelands Resources Development Symposium,* Salt Lake City, 13–14 February 1985, pp. 146–56.

[29] Gorse and Steeds, *Desertification in the Sahelian and Sudanian Zones,* op. cit., pp. 31–32.

Chapter 3 _____

Development Alternatives for Tropical Rain Forests

John O. Browder

Forests cover over a quarter—or about 40 million square kilometers—of the earth's land surface. Most are located in the tropics--27 per cent in Latin America, 10 per cent in Asia, and 22 per cent in Africa. Of the planet's total tropical forest area of 2.3 million square kilometers, 52 per cent are classified as "closed" forests, 31 per cent as "open" forests and 17 per cent as secondary growth (in both closed and open forest formations).

While many traditional forms of forest cutting, such as that employed in swidden farming under conditions of low population density and relatively long fallow periods, enable tropical forests to recover cleared areas, the large-scale conversion of tropical forests has become one of the most controversial and widely publicized issues of our time. Estimates of the annual rate of tropical forest conversion range from 113,000 square kilometers, an area roughly the size of the state of Oklahoma, to 205,000 square kilometers.[1] Many legitimate concerns are being raised about the long-term environmental impact of extensive tropical forest conversion on biological diversity and species extinction, indigenous human populations, climate, hydrology, and soil conservation. Although the social costs associated with significant human disturbance of tropical forests are by no means precisely understood, there is a rapidly emerging consensus among scientists, economists, and conservationists that present patterns of tropical forest degradation are portentous. Calls for concerted international action to manage an unfolding ecological crisis in the tropics resound in the 1980s. The U.N.

Table 1.   World Distribution of Tropical Forest Formations (millions hectares and percentages)

Forest Type	Total	Latin America	Asia	Africa
Total	2,344	1,071	404	869
Percentage	100	45.7	17.2	37.1
Closed	1,200	684	300	216
Open	734	217	31	486
Falow	410	170	73	167

Source: Based on data drawn from Hans J. Steinlin, "Monitoring the World's Tropical Forest," *Unasylva*, Vol. 34, No. 137 (1982), pp. 2–9.

Food and Agriculture Organization's Tropical Forest Action Plan, for example, is but one attempt to answer these calls.

This chapter explores opportunities for tropical forest management that combine conservation and economic development objectives to meet the needs of poor people. Underlying the ecological crisis of tropical forest destruction is a dense amalgam of troubling social, economic, and political issues: rural poverty in developing countries, rapid population growth, food and energy deficiency, territorial sovereignty, foreign debt, and misguided modernization policies. The structure of the "deforestation problem" is multidimensional and organic; no single component of the problem exists in total isolation from the others. Tropical deforestation is not just an event that sets in motion a chain of devastating ecological consequences; it is also a social process, reflecting a continuum of human responses to diverse and changing economic and political conditions—responses that range from desperate hunger to outright greed.

Responsibility for the deforestation problem, like its consequences, is global in scope, not confined to the tropical countries of the Third World alone. Perhaps most frustrating for technologically advanced countries that can launch human expeditions to the moon and back, there is no single overarching technological solution to the devastation enveloping the world's tropical forests. Effective control of tropical deforestation necessitates confrontation of a host of seemingly intractable social ills and injustices that are both country-specific and global in nature.

The shared task presently facing conservationists and enlightened growth economists is to find long-term human uses of tropical forests that are compatible with the economic development objectives of vastly different countries. This task requires strategies for land development that reconcile the inherent ecological heterogeneity of tropical forests with the relatively homogeneous, but often conflicting, economic demands placed upon them by different groups in society. This chapter examines some of the social and economic implications of three complementary strategies: plantation silviculture, agroforestry, and natural forest management.

Rural Poverty and Tropical Deforestation

Rural poverty is widely acknowledged to be the leading worldwide cause of tropical forest destruction. It is asserted that an estimated 200–250 million subsistence farmers and "land-hungry migrants" living in a state of shifting cultivation and rural poverty destroy some 51,000 square kilometers of tropical forest every year. That is to say, the rural poor have been blamed for at least 45 per cent of the tropical forest area destroyed annually on a worldwide basis. Hence, "attacking the root cause of forest destruction—rural poverty in forest areas—and providing small farmers with a viable alternative to shifting cultivation are the key issues."[2]

There are several problems with any simple or exclusive causal linkage between rural poverty and tropical deforestation, especially in Latin America, where the earth's largest area of rain forest is located. First, some of the people classified as "shifting cultivators" are not always what they appear to be. This category often rolls in a wide variety of forest dwellers—including indigenous agroforesters, traditional forest product extractors, and *mestizo* communities that combine long-fallow swidden farming with natural forest management—who derive a livelihood from sustainable use of relatively small areas of tropical forests. Not all forest dwellers are shifting cultivators—nor are they all poor. Indeed, there is much to learn from such groups about the mechanics and ecology of sustainable tropical forest management.

Second, emphasis on the "poverty factor" should not obscure the fact that important political decisions often contribute to tropical deforestation. "Governments largely determine how forests should be used—and in the Third World over 80 per cent of the closed forest area is public land."[3] Public policies affect individual land use decisions and frequently play a pivotal role in promoting tropical forest conversion. For example, a single Brazilian policy—promoting the development of the Amazon region through a program of corporate tax incentives favoring commercial beef cattle producers—was responsible for an estimated 30 per cent of the total forest area converted in Brazilian Amazonia by 1983. All told, cattle ranching in the region was responsible for about 60 per cent of the 148,000 square kilometers of Amazon forest area converted, whereas small farmers participating in government resettlement schemes accounted for only about 11 per cent of the total reported conversion by 1983.[4] In the Amazon, the world's largest tropical forest region, poor small farmers—whether defined as traditional shifting cultivators, forest product extractors, or modern migrant colonists—are not the principal agents of tropical forest destruction.

Third, the "poverty factor" argument erroneously implies that actions leading to higher national per capita income will reduce pressures on natural tropical forests. Recent research on the causes of deforestation in thirty-nine developing countries in Africa, Asia, and Latin America found that deforestation "is not significantly related to the growth of per capita GNP."[5] Brazil, the world's eighth richest economy, is the most significant deforester among sixty-two developing countries in the tropics, alone responsible for 19 per cent of global tropical forest loss each year. Actions that successfully raise national income offer no guarantee of more sustainable use of tropical forests.

A critical examination of the "poverty factor" approach does not mean that poverty and deforestation are unrelated. If poverty provides only a partial explanation of deforestation, it is clear that tropical forest destruction can exacerbate poverty. While rural poverty and tropical deforestation appear to be synergistic, each alone does not explain the other. Examining either rural poverty or tropical deforestation apart from the structural and institutional issues that in different ways undergird both is unlikely to lead to a more complete understanding of the distinct structures of either problem.

Current Commercial Uses of Tropical Forests

Three major commercial uses of the tropical forest lands of South America—the geographic focus of this chapter—account for most of the forest conversion in the region to date: cattle ranching, government-supported agricultural land settlement projects, and commercial timber extraction. These activities are often sequential stages in a long-term process of land use transition. Each, however, affects forests differently and produces different social costs and benefits. As presently practiced, none of these activities has proven to be either particularly profitable or sustainable—even with various forms of government subsidization.

Beef Cattle Ranching

Cattle ranching is the most significant contributor to deforestation in the South American tropics. As indicated above, pasture development has been responsible for about 60 per cent of the total tropical forest area converted in the Brazilian Amazon. By most accounts, cattle ranching in the region is financially unviable without substantial government subsidies, which recently have been suspended.[6] Between 1966 and 1983, the Brazilian government absorbed about $4.8 billion in costs associated with Amazon livestock promotion, or $4,000 per metric ton of beef produced—an amount four times greater than the average world price for beef during this period.[7] While Brazil has developed the largest beef cattle herd in the Western Hemisphere (some 135 million animals), in twelve of the seventeen years preceding 1984, Brazil was a net importer of foreign beef cattle. Despite lavish subsidies, Amazon livestock production accounted for less than 0.1 per cent of Brazilian gross domestic product (GDP) in 1981 and 0.2 per cent of total gross export earnings between 1975 and 1980, while employing only 1.0 per cent of the Amazonian agricultural labor force. The extremely limited economic benefits of cattle ranching in the Brazilian Amazon, enjoyed mainly by large corporate groups in São Paulo, contrast sharply with the extensive damage to tropical forests associated with this activity.

Agricultural Land Settlement

The 1960s ushered in an era of great interest in tropical land settlement in Latin America. By 1970, the Inter-American Development Bank (IDB) sponsored eight tropical forest colonization projects in six Latin American countries. Between 1969 and 1977, the Brazilian government established sixteen colonization projects in the Amazon, most of which were associated with its audacious National Integration Program (1970–75) to give "land without men to men without land" along the newly constructed and highly controversial Transamazon Highway. During this period, every Amazon nation undertook tropical land settlement schemes, many of which were supported by the major international development lending institutions. Seen as an easy bypass around the tough political issue of agrarian reform, Amazonia's rain forests (like those of Central America and Indonesia), became attractive labor "safety valves" for local politicians and international lenders anxious to defuse social tensions arising from inequitable land tenure or from the pressures of rapid population growth in more fertile agricultural areas.

Despite generally optimistic projections of financial viability (internal rates of return between 10 and 50 per cent), none of these Latin American colonization projects turned out as planned, nor could any be considered successful development models for tropical forests. In addition, most have been severely criticized for their environmental and social impacts.[8]

Probably the most controversial tropical land settlement scheme in Latin America to date is the Polonoroeste Program of regional development in the northwest Brazilian frontier states of Rondonia and (western) Mato Grosso. Cofinanced by the World Bank—which deserves much credit for pressing (albeit belatedly and under pressure) certain environmental protection conditions upon a largely recalcitrant Brazilian bureaucracy—Polonoroeste prompted an unprecedented wave of migration to the Brazilian frontier. Between 1970 and 1988, Rondonia's population soared from 110,000 to 1,500,000 inhabitants (about evenly divided between urban and rural sectors), indicating an annual growth rate of about 16 per cent—more than 7 times Brazil's national average. While initial surveys concluded that 33 per cent of Rondonia's soils were suitable for permanent farming, subsequent studies showed that less than 10 per cent would meet conventional agronomic criteria for commercial tropical agriculture. The combined effects of soil resource degradation and an ever-burgeoning demand for farm land have set in motion a cycle of forest destruction, casual cultivation, and land speculation that by the World Bank's own accounts have resulted in colonist turnover rates of 40 per cent after the first year of settlement in certain areas.[9]

Conventional tropical land settlement projects have had a dismal performance record in Latin America. Yet the question of how colonists can be accommodated in their tropical environment remains a pressing issue.

Timber Extraction

The Brazilian Amazon, with its 48–78 billion cubic meters of living timber representing some 6,000 different tree species, undoubtedly will face new pressures from world timber traders as more accessible South Asian hardwood supplies are depleted. Today, current practices of commercial timber extraction in the region are typically inefficient and rarely accompanied by even rudimentary forms of forest management (e.g., vine removal, replanting, etc.). Yet, as is the case in Central America, timber extraction is not nearly as important a cause of Amazonian deforestation as are cattle-ranching and agricultural settlement.

In 1984 industrial roundwood extracted from the Amazon's natural forests supplied 33 per cent of Brazil's total roundwood consumption and represented about 80 per cent of the total value of production derived from thirty natural forest products extracted from the region.[10] The industrial woods sector in Amazonia, which grew from 89 firms in 1952 to an estimated 3,000 today, employed one-quarter of the Amazonian labor force in 1982. In five of the Amazon's six states and territories, wood products manufacturing is the single largest industrial employer. Capital investment in wood products manufacturing grew (in current dollar terms) from about $4.7 million in 1973[11] to $307 million in 1984, while the value of production increased from $17 million in 1970 to $454 million in 1980.[12]

While its importance to the Amazon's economy is indisputable, lumber production is typically inefficient, wasteful, and not very profitable. Most mills operate at less than 50 per cent of installed capacity, and inappropriate logging and lumber production techniques result in log recovery rates often below 50 per cent. Furthermore, fewer than 10 per cent of all known Amazon timber species are presently extracted in commercial quantities. On a given hectare of *terra firme* tropical rain forest, 30 cubic meters might be extracted as industrial roundwood. As a result, fixed costs of extraction (for example, the costs of road building) must be absorbed by a relatively small quantity of output. Recent financial studies suggest that most selective logging operations on *terra firme* forests are subsidized by lumber producers, many of whom received government export credits.[13] At prevailing levels of exploitation, both costs and revenues of selective logging probably fall within the range of $15–$20 per cubic meter, or $600–$800 per hectare. Not surprisingly, profit margins on lumber production are low. In a survey of twenty-seven lumber mills in Rondonia, the sample average profit rate over a five-year period (1980–84) was just 3 per cent—equivalent to the estimated rate of capital depreciation in the region's lumber industry.[14]

The extent to which selective logging damages residual vegetation varies greatly with type of treatment applied before logging, the intensity of exploitation, the nature of technology involved, and the type of post-removal treatment. In one logging experiment in Suriname, Jonkers and Hendrison found that at a level of exploitation of 15 cubic meters per hectare, about 16 per cent of all remaining trees (greater than 5 centimeters in diameter at breast height) suffered some kind of damage, and 8.7 per cent were destroyed. At a level of exploitation of 46 cubic meters/hectare, about 28 per cent of all remaining trees were damaged, two-thirds of which were destroyed.[15] Under prevailing conditions, where no forest treatments are normally applied, selective logging at the current levels of intensity probably impairs the regenerative capacity of between 25 and 50 per cent of the remaining vegetation; but this estimate is highly speculative.

The inefficiencies and waste characteristic of much of the Amazon's lumber industry impede both long-term economic development and forest conservation. Yet because of its importance to the Amazon's economy, the industrial wood sector will remain a critical component of efforts to develop strategies for sustainable use of tropical forests.

Other commercial uses of tropical forest lands are emerging, e.g., for industrial fuelwood production, mineral extraction, and reservoirs for large hydroelectric facilities. Yet the experience to date indicates that major current uses have failed to promote either equitable economic development or tropical forest conservation. New strategies are needed that blend tropical forest conservation and economic development.

Development Alternatives for Tropical Forests

Three basic strategies for tropical forest land use that might link economic development and conservation objectives have been widely discussed: (1) plantation forestry, (2) tropical agriculture and agroforestry, and (3) natural forest management. This section highlights some of the economic (employment and income) dimensions of these tropical forest land uses and their relative effects on biodiversity.

The Limits of Plantation Forestry

Industrial wood plantations are widely considered to be an essential part of any long-term strategy of sustainable forest resource management in the developing world. The reason is simple: Annual timber production rates range from 10 to 20 cubic meters per hectare (versus commercial production of 1 to 4 cubic meters per hectare in natural forests). Presently there are about 12 to 13 million hectares of plantation forests in the developing world (excluding China), of which 7 million hectares are located in Latin America. It is estimated that by the year 2000 the developing countries will require 50 million hectares of fuelwood plantations, mainly in the arid tropics.[16] Twenty-seven developing countries already face an acute fuelwood crisis, and in another thirty countries fuelwood consumption exceeds sustainable levels of production.[17] As the rate of natural forest conversion outstrips the rate of forest plantation establishment by a ratio of ten to one, the production and long-term supply of wood to meet energy and raw material needs for household and industrial consumption is an issue of strategic concern to both conservationists and development economists. In short, many see the establishment of industrial wood plantations, especially in degraded or secondary forest areas, as a way to diminish the pressure on natural forests while providing essential energy for industry and households.

Plantation forestry alone, however, like other tropical forest development alternatives, is not a panacea for Third World energy inadequacy. Nor is it always an appropriate vehicle for achieving economic development objectives. Forest plantations tend to obtain maximum efficiency at high levels of output over relatively long production cycles (seven to thirty-five years) thereby precluding extensive participation by smallholders.[18] They are relatively expensive to establish (start-up costs range from $250 to $6,000 per hectare) although they do yield moderate to high economic rates of return (roughly 10 to 20 per cent).[19]

Moreover, employment on forest plantations is usually cyclical, being more intensive in the early stages of seedling growth. In sum, the economics of fuelwood plantation forestry tends to favor large enterprises over small producers, often requires government subsidization, and offers little promise of significantly serving household energy needs.

In Latin America, most rural households in tropical forest areas are reasonably self-sufficient in firewood provision. The key issue is whether large-scale industrial development should be based on biomass energy sources—and if so, the extent to which industrial fuelwood production, one important biomass energy source, provides employment and income benefits for local populations. This issue is particularly salient in the case of the Brazilian Amazon. Giant fuelwood plantations that accompany large-scale industrial projects in Amazonia, like the Greater Carajas Program indisputably will have important environmental and social ramifications. The iron ore smelting plants associated with the Greater Carajas Program require extensive conversion of natural forest to fuelwood plantations. In the case of Carajas alone, between 3.6 million and 15 million hectares of natural forest in Amazonia would be turned to fuelwood production.[20] If this one venture alone is not carefully managed (and there is ample evidence to suggest that it will not be), "reforestation," far from relieving pressure on natural forests, could double the natural forest area converted in the Brazilian Amazon region overall by 1995.

The social component of the Greater Carajas Program is as dubious as its environmental implications. According to Fearnside, 83 per cent of the land to be reallocated under the Carajas Program for fuelwood and related agricultural production will go to medium and large properties, which are expected to employ only 39 per cent of the program's projected labor force.[21] In the case of Carajas, plantation forestry, which will significantly transform the natural forest landscape of the Amazon state of Para, may simply reinforce preexisting social inequities that contribute to tropical forest destruction.

Apart from industrial fuelwood, plantation forests for sawlogs, pulpwood, and fuelwood for electrification of small urban areas have been considered or undertaken in various locations in Latin America. These experiences have yet to be systematically studied in a comparative framework. In most cases, however, the hazards facing monocultural tree production—whether achieved by plantations or by the progressive enrichment of natural forests into de facto plantations—include increased probability of fire damage, reduction in biodiversity, depredations of insects and fungi, short-term decline in soil fertility, soil compaction, and weed competition. These environmental dangers combine with high start-up costs, little permanent job creation, and long-term dependency on expensively hybridized or imported planting stock.

Such constraints would seem to relegate monocultural tree farming to a relatively minor role in any extensive strategy for sustainable forest land use in rural areas of the tropics of the Americas.

Tropical Agriculture and Agroforestry

Agricultural development and environmental conservation in moist tropical forest areas converge on three general objectives:

(1) Improving the productivity of agriculture through intensification (higher yields) or increased frequency of cropping;

(2) Diversifying production from monocultures to mixed polycultural farming systems; and

(3) Incorporating a productive tree or forest component into farming.

In most cases, these objectives pertain to small traditional farming systems, which engage the majority of the economically active agricultural population in Latin America and produce most of the region's food supply. For these reasons, conservation-development initiatives should seek to stabilize rather than replace small farms.

Smallholder Agriculture in Amazonia. Presently, between 50 million and 100 million Latin Americans derive their livelihood from farming, a small fraction of whom do so on tropical rain forest lands. The majority of these people live and work on small farms that, in many cases, supply most domestic food consumption. In Colombia and Central America, for instance, about 70 per cent of food consumed is produced on small farms of less than five hectares.[22] Although the experiences of smallholder farming systems in Amazonia are highly varied, they share several general features. First, they tend to be low-input systems, characterized by low capital/output ratios and low-to-moderate utilization of labor and industrial inputs. Intensity of land use varies widely, perhaps in relation to local land availability. Second, production tends to be commercially oriented, especially to national markets. It also tends to be limited to a small number of commercial food crops, and very few forest products are harvested for either sale or consumption. Third, colonist farmers often rely on ecologically inappropriate agronomic knowledge obtained from farming experiences in different ecological zones. To them the retention and utilization of a natural forest component in farming is largely an alien concept. Fourth, these characteristics often reinforce yet another trait: the sensitivity of smallholders to even minimal exposure to risk. Risk aversion, rather than profit maximization, is typically the paramount concern of most smallholders and presents an obvious constraint to the successful diffusion of new agroforestry technologies. Finally, unclear land tenure remains an important determinant of smallholder land use, generally discouraging smallholder investment in long-term perennial tree-cropping systems. It is worth noting that whereas tree *planting* frequently establishes specific land use rights in many parts of Africa where communal land tenure traditions prevail, the reverse—tree *removal*—usually serves the same function in Amazonia and elsewhere in Latin America in cases where property ownership is unclear or contested. In Amazonia, while many recent colonization programs such as Polonoroeste have attempted to overcome tenure problems through land titling, forest clearing for short-term commercial monocultural production continues. This suggests that secure tenure is a necessary but not sufficient condition for the adoption of sustainable forest resource management strategies.

Increasing Smallholder Productivity. Research efforts seeking to increase smallholder productivity have largely focused on soil chemistry constraints to continuous cropping that are estimated to affect about 75 per cent of the Amazon Basin's soils. Research such as that associated with the Yurimaguas experiments demonstrates that soil treatments, particularly the application of low-cost fertilizers, will permit continuous cropping on Amazonia's relatively acidic and infertile soils. In an experimental corn-peanut-corn rotation under traditional management, the annual yield was 5.31 tons per hectare. The Yurimaguas technology (management improvements plus lime and fertilizer inputs) produced 11.4 tons per hectare. Importantly, farmers seemed willing to adopt the technology.[23] While estimates of the net annual financial returns to farmers experimenting with such soil treatments are encouraging (about $1,865 per hectare), they need to be reexamined in light of fluctuating fertilizer prices, increasing fertilizer inputs needed to sustain yields, and labor opportunity costs, which evidently were not considered in this estimate.

While a considerable amount of research support has been devoted to transferring agricultural technology from temperate regions to the tropics, relatively little attention has been given to the techniques employed in indigenous Amazonian soil management strategies. Yet recent research suggests that some of these traditional systems are more productive than conventional smallholder agriculture. In a comparison of crop yields obtained by the indigenous Kayapó with those of smallholder colonists and ranchers in the Brazilian Amazon, Hecht found that after a five-year period the indigenous farming system produced nearly three times the yield of all crops as the colonist farming system and 176 times more output in weight per hectare than the beef cattle ranches surveyed. These substantial differences in output reflect the fact that the Kayapó recognize many more plant products as "crops" than do most colonists.

An important difference between Kayapó and Yurimaguas technologies that may influence sustainability is the type of nutrient inputs applied to fields. Whereas the latter relies largely on artificial chemical fertilizers (nitrogen, potassium, and phosphorus combinations), the Kayapó rely exclusively on natural and locally available inputs (ash, mulch, termite nests, palm fronds, rice and corn stover, banana leaves, and the residue of other crops). Other important differences—in field structure and composition, cultivation practices, and weeding—are also evident.[24] The essential difference is that the colonist system is based on dense sequential monocropping, while the Kayapó strategy is based on simultaneous mixed-cropping or "patch intercropping"—as is the case with the Yakuana of southern Venezuela.[25] More attention needs to be given to exploring the potential for transferring indigenous soil management techniques to small commercial farms in the tropics of the Americas.

Crop Diversification. While the land-extensive production systems of the Kayapó and other indigenous groups may not seem practical on small farm units, the objective of diversifying production is not limited by farm size. In Mexico, for example, traditional home gardens ranging in size from 0.3 to 0.7 hectares are known to produce between 33 and 55 useful species, mostly perennials (including 12 to 30 tree species), of which 30–50 per cent are introduced.[26] Irrigated raised fields (*chinampas* and *cameilones chontales*) of 0.5 hectares are believed sufficient in size to ensure subsistence for one rural Mexican family by providing a variety of food and cash crops.[27] Alcorn has shown that small Huastec farms averaging four hectares in size produce more than two hundred useful species (many cultivated), retain a substantial area in forest land, and generate net returns greater than those obtained from the Yurimaguas experiments.[28]

Thus farm size alone does not determine farm viability. On smaller farms, it is imperative to promote intensive management of a more diverse resource base—something that should be kept in mind in future tropical land settlement schemes. While short-term yields per unit area of any single crop in a monoculture are likely to exceed the yield of that crop in a polycultural setting, the total useful yield over the long term may be significantly greater in the latter. A great deal of research has demonstrated that diversified cropping helps to overcome three important limiting factors to tropical agriculture: soil nutrient depletion, weed competition, and plant diseases.

Incorporating Trees into Farming Systems. Mixed-cropping systems that include a significant arboreal component are essential to many highly diversified small-scale farming systems, simultaneously providing economic and conservation functions. Gliessman's study of home garden agroecosystems in Cupilco (Tabasco, Mexico) showed that 55 useful species of trees provided cover for 96.7 per cent of the garden area (0.7 hectare) in production.[29]

Again, there is much to learn from traditional and indigenous agroforestry. More than 40 per cent of some 300 tree species used by the Chacobo Indians of Peru provide food; 35.1 per cent provide medicine; and 17 per cent are used in construction.[30] On one hectare of forest at Mishana, Peru, 72 species (of a total of 275) produced fruit, latex, and timber for local inhabitants.[31]

Learning from Indigenous Agroecological Systems. The type of farming system most appropriate to any given area depends on topography, soil and hydrologic factors, access to basic physical infrastructure and consumer markets, and policies that affect market prices for different agricultural products. The key conclusion here is that a wide variety of small-scale agroecosystems exist and tend to share the following characteristics:

- They produce a wide range of different useful goods in a relatively small area.
- They retain and utilize a significant area as forest.
- They rely largely on natural and locally available sources of soil nutrient supplements. They are resource-regenerating rather than resource-depleting agroecosystems.
- Cropping is sequenced throughout the year to provide continuity in the supply of food and income.

The key issue for development is that of technology transfer. How can known agroecological technologies that share the above characteristics be successfully transferred to those "modern" small farmers who engage in resource-depleting monocropping on tropical soils?

Natural Forest Management

Natural forest management has come to include a wide range of activities apart from just sustained commercial timber harvesting relying on natural regeneration under various regimes of forest treatment. Natural forest management for so-called "secondary forest products" has not enjoyed a particularly favorable reputation in either the tropical forestry or agronomic literature. Recent research of cultural ecologists, however, suggests that many traditional forms of natural forest management—provided that they are integrated into larger agrosilvicultural land use systems, or complemented by other small-scale agricultural activities—can provide greater financial returns on investment of labor than many strictly silvicultural and agricultural activities. This section presents a few examples that illustrate the financial prospects of traditional natural forest management as a conservation approach.

The Huastec Maya. A relatively small tropical forest area of some 350,000 hectares in northeastern Mexico is currently managed by Huastec Indians and other small farmers. Although these farmers produce a mix of commercial and subsistence crops (sugar, coffee, maize) not unlike peasant farmers elsewhere, a unique component of the Huastec farming system is the natural forest grove *(te'lom)*. In a recent pioneering study, Janis Alcorn indicates that over 300 plant species, representing 90 per cent of the plant species occurring in *te'lom* groves, are used by the Huastec.[32] These managed forest groves are relatively small (from 0.25 to 3 hectares per household) and are maintained indefinitely (80 years or more). While the *te'lom* grove alone could not support a family, its functions within the larger Huastec economy are indispensable. As Alcorn notes, the *te'lom* grove:

- Produces a wide variety of important subsistence goods that would otherwise be expensive or unavailable to the farmer;

- Provides nutritionally important additions to the diet (thus preventing the deterioration of diet quality that tends to accompany the shift to commercial agriculture);

- Produces a variety of marketable goods to supplement farm income;

- Supports the production of farmyard livestock (often an important source of cash for women); and

- Serves important ecological functions that farmers value by protecting the region's genetic diversity for future generations.

The Huastec have developed an agroecosystem that includes natural forest management at low levels of labor input capable of sustaining the average family on about 4 hectares of tropical forest land.

Perhaps the most remarkable finding from Alcorn's research is the potential financial benefits of replicating Huastec production. Applying market prices to both labor inputs and output and shadow prices for nonmonetized production factors, Alcorn's analysis indicates that "the average Huastec household earns a net [cash income and cost savings] benefit equivalent to U.S. $2,459 per year (in 1987 dollars) from farm production excluding ecological benefits."[33] The case of the Huastec poses a striking contrast to (contemporary) smallholder colonization schemes elsewhere in the tropics of South America.

The Cuyabeno Wildlife Production Reserve. As part of Ecuador's tropical forest conservation effort, the Cuyabeno Reserve, encompassing an area of 255,500 hectares in the *Oriente,* was established in 1979. Essential to this conservation initiative is the presence of some four hundred Siona–Secoya Indians, whose tribal lands coincide with the reserve and who thus share a proprietary interest in its defense against intruders. The centerpiece of this project, still in the early stages of development, is the production and management of tropical wildlife of commercial value. Tourism and scientific research complement the project's central focus on natural fauna management. The indigenous inhabitants, acting as "gatekeepers" for the reserve, derive a livelihood from multiple sources.

According to a recent study by James Nations and Flavio Hinojosa, total revenues accrued from scientific research and tourism are expected to be about $54,000 per year, or $135 per local inhabitant.[34] The financial benefits of the principal wildlife production component of the reserve are more difficult to quantify, and such estimates are more problematic. The value of bush meat, obtained from the (presumably sustainable) hunting of natural wildlife (for example, peccaries, deer, tapirs, agoutis, pacas, various fish, birds, and turtles), are believed to exceed $40 per hectare per year. If other reptilians, notably caiman, can be sustainably harvested from the wild, additional gross revenues from skins alone might reach $140 per hectare per year. Production of wildlife, especially turtles, in semicaptivity is expected to generate gross revenues of $20,000 per hectare per year—presumably under the most favorable management conditions. This contrasts with beef cattle production on tropical pastures, which yields gross revenues ranging between $50 and $500 per hectare per year ($148 per hectare according to one estimate).[35]

Floodplain Forest Management in Amazonia. The floodplains of the Amazon comprise several different biotopes that traditional river dwellers *(riberinos)* systematically exploit in different ways.[36] Annually flooded mud flats are frequently cultivated in short-cycle crops like maize, beans, rice, peanuts, and melons. Sugar cane may be cultivated on natural levee slopes. Orchards and garden crops are often planted on levee tops, and so forth. The flood forests supply local inhabitants with various natural products such as fruits, nuts, fiber, timber, and medicinals, as well as providing natural habitats for game.

A recent study by Christine Padoch and Wil de Jong of the *riberino* village of Santa Rosa—located on the lower Ocayali River about 150 kilometers upstream of Iquitos, Peru—examines the agroforestry practices of floodplain farmers on four one-hectare orchard plots, ranging in age from four to twenty-five years. On these plots, fifteen to twenty-three species yielded commercial products—in contrast to fewer than a dozen species harvested by most colonists. Labor requirements for plot maintenance and harvesting ranged from two and a half to twenty-one man-days per hectare per year. The study calculates that if all of the marketable goods produced on the older plot had been sold, the owner would have realized a gross income of $653 per hectare, while the owner of the younger second plot would have earned $635 per hectare. With no urban market nearby, neither farmer actually realized more than 4 per cent of this potential income. The experience of Santa Rosa suggests that while Amazonian agroforesters can produce substantial quantities of commercial crops, they are severely constrained by inadequate transport, marketing, and export facilities. In the absence of such facilities, geographical location of agroforestry sites relative to urban consumer markets or rural processing facilities may be the most critical determinant of their financial productivity.[37]

A more intensive and profitable form of natural forest management has been studied by Anthony Anderson and Mario Jardim on Jaguar Island, located near the major Amazon port city of Belém. Although numerous commercial forest species occur and are exploited on the floodplains (fifty-three species utilized on Jaguar Island), frequently the flood forests of the Amazon estuary are dominated by economically important species of palms. In a series of experimental management treatments of the acai palm *(Eaterpe oleracea)*, from which a variety of commercial products are derived, Anderson and Jardim calculate a minimum net income of $110 per hectare from acai palm management alone. The average labor requirement, mainly associated with site preparation, was ten man-days per hectare. While inhabitants of Jaguar Island obtained income from many other natural forest products, in 1987 the per diem income obtained from acai palm management alone was five times greater than the urban wage rate in Belém in 1987.[38]

Lessons from Traditional Forest Management Practices. These few, but diverse examples of natural forest management in tropical Latin America share, in varying degrees, several common attributes:

(1) They are low-input, highly productive uses that can be practiced on either large or small areas of tropical forest lands.

(2) Although they are associated with low population densities, they often are more land-efficient (that is, use less land per capita) than many conventional land uses.

(3) They have minimal adverse impacts on ecological stability.

(4) They are characterized by a high rate of resource utilization (up to 80 per cent of forest tree species).

(5) They are characterized by a diversity of income sources.

(6) They are often integrated with various complementary productive activities that ensure continuity of income flow over time.

(7) Where such management is a cooperative venture within a large area, the active participation of the local (often indigenous) population is essential.

(8) They are generally found in situations where effective private (or tribal) property rights have been long established and recognized, or where public land use controls have been effectively enforced.

(9) While these production systems involve the extraction or cultivation of a variety of products, they frequently are dominated by at least one important cash crop (sugar by the Huastec, acai palm by the floodplain inhabitants, caiman by the Siona–Secoya, etc.).

(10) The financial viability of these production systems is primarily constrained by market distance, secondarily by market acceptance, emphasizing the importance of geographic location and marketing infrastructure (not necessarily roads).

While the productive potential of several low-impact strategies of natural forest management has been demonstrated, several questions about the possibilities for their widespread application remain unanswered and should be included in any research agenda for natural forest-management-based conservation and development: How can such technologies be successfully transferred, in whole or in part, from one cultural group to another? If such systems are replicable, can they be deployed at scales of production that significantly increase employment opportunities without depending upon costly subsidies, swamping local consumer markets with minor forest products, or endangering local habitats from over-zealous adoption? What are the likely gender implications (household division of labor) associated with transferred technologies? What is the prospective market demand for the commercial goods produced under managed natural forest systems? What support services (credits, marketing, technical extension) and exogenous inputs (fuel, fertilizers, pesticides) would be necessary to ensure stable production of transferred or expanded natural forest management systems? Finally, under what circumstances of land use and tenure are such systems socially acceptable, especially when they entail the restricted use of large areas of forest land?

It is also critical to note that the application of traditional natural forest management strategies relies largely on restrictive land use zoning (i.e., reserves), often in areas where surrounding land uses are incompatible with intended forest management activities. Under such circumstances, reserves must be treated as one component of a larger land use strategy that accommodates the competing land uses surrounding them. Establishing low-use-intensity reserves favorable to one group of people in areas undergoing rapid land use transition may unfairly discriminate against others, resulting in social conflict. "Extractive reserves"—in which lands are set aside especially for the harvesting of tree products (e.g., nuts, rubber) but not for tree cutting— can work, but only if cattle ranchers, landless peasants, and other forest land users pressing at the edges are simultaneously incorporated into complementary solutions to their respective needs for land and forest resources.

Conclusions and Recommendations

Tropical forest destruction in Latin America is largely the consequence of public policies promoting the expansion of commercial agriculture and ranching. As yet, commercial timber harvesting and rural poverty per se are not the leading causes of deforestation in Latin America—as they are, to varying degrees, in Africa and South Asia.

There is no single land use strategy that will successfully harmonize forest conservation and economic development objectives for the Amazon region overall. Different strategies must be adapted to widely divergent local conditions. In all cases, three principles seem most important to the development of such strategies. First, such strategies should be decentralized and their benefits widely distributed. Second, they should be diversified—promoting heterogeneity, not homogeneity, of production. Third, they should focus on activities that can be adapted to small-scale production or low-impact activities on a socially acceptable large scale.

In the Brazilian Amazon, joint conservation and poverty-oriented development strategies should consider three important realities:

1. *Between 500,000 to 700,000 rural households depend for their livelihood mainly on precarious small-scale, short-cycle monocropping.* Most (82 per cent) of these farms occupy less than 100 hectares, and between 20 and 25 per cent are concentrated in a relatively small area, the state of Rondonia (243,000 square kilometers). Successful development strategies must provide these small farmers with the technical and associated technological knowledge base and initial financial backing necessary to incorporate the lessons about continuous cultivation in moist tropical soils that can be derived from traditional Amazonian agroecological systems.

2. *Most of the region's population growth is occurring in urban areas.* Urban population growth rates average 10 per cent per year, in contrast with the overall regional population growth rate of 6 per cent. Joint poverty and environmental development strategies must consider the

implication of growing urban demand for food, energy, and building materials on the region's natural resource base.

3. *Areas of secondary forest growth are becoming increasingly prominent features of the Amazonian landscape.* Between 20 per cent and 40 per cent of the 600,000 square kilometers of natural forest "converted" in the Brazilian Amazon as of 1988 is in some stage of secondary forest recovery. Degraded pastures and abandoned fallows represent an important untapped resource that appropriate strategies should incorporate.

In tropical rain forest regions generally, and especially in the tropical forests of the Americas, this analysis leads to the following conclusions and recommendations.

Small-Scale Farming

Appropriate strategies should promote:

(1) Expanded low-impact extractive utilization of natural forest remnants on existing productive farm lots (such remnants could also be used as laboratories for agroforestry demonstrations).

(2) The planting of trees by farmers in conjunction with ground cropping; the tree should be not just commercial timber, but should include species that preserve vital ecological functions (e.g., fix soil nitrogen, attract game, and provide soil cover).

(3) Diversification of farm production, especially through the planting of "useful" tree species.

(4) Intensification of farm cultivation (continuous cropping with greater utilization of natural rather than artificial fertilizers).

Major impediments to all four of these objectives include:

(a) Insecure land tenure (which frequently creates an incentive to clear forests);

(b) A lack of agroecological knowledge (highlighting the importance of technical agroforestry extension);

(c) Poorly staffed and underfunded extension institutions with parochial work programs (agroforestry, where most help is needed, often falls outside the scope of traditionally separate agricultural and forestry extension agencies);

(d) Inadequate technical and ethnological knowledge (e.g., the financial costs and benefits and culturally distinctive management implications of promising agroforestry technologies are usually unclear in agronomic and forestry research); and

(e) The continued subsidization of monocultural cash cropping and cattle ranching through tax incentives and other government policies that promote large-scale forest destruction often to make way for desultory land uses.

More attention must be given to indigenous agroecological knowledge. Obviously, such knowledge must be blended with modern approaches to tropical agriculture and fit existing sociocultural situations. Hastily mounted reconstructions of pre-Columbian farming practices that fail to consider their vastly different cultural origins are likely to breed disappointing results. Much indigenous knowledge is culturally esoteric and alien to contemporary commercial farming. Nevertheless, many indigenous practices do show the way toward techniques that may be able to overcome ecological and financial constraints facing agriculture in moist tropical forest areas. Indeed, some useful attributes of indigenous agroecology are readily transferable (e.g., mulches for fertilization, manipulated or enhanced fallows, raised nutrient-rich fields). While additional basic research is always necessary, future funding should emphasize the practical management aspects of applying existing indigenous and traditional knowledge at the farm level.

Plantation Forestry

Four potential applications will continue to receive attention:

(1) Electrification of small urban areas;

(2) Urban household firewood production;

(3) Industrial fuelwood production; and

(4) Industrial sawn-wood production.

The high costs of starting and maintaining centralized plantations and the ecological impediments to monocultural timber plantations should be considered in light of the income-spreading and ecologically preferable alternative of decentralized small-scale tree farming by rural inhabitants surrounding small towns. Localized response to urban-driven demand for fuelwood and sawlogs could be an important first step for many farmers toward adopting tree-planting strategies in combination with annual cropping.

Natural Forest Management

A number of promising strategies for traditional forest management and agroforestry have been largely neglected by donors in land use planning for Amazonia. Opportunities to utilize more fully the diverse resources of natural forests in conjunction with agriculture need to be further refined—not only as potential development models for extensive protected forest areas but also for application at the small farm level.

Additional research is needed on the following issues:

(1) The market potential, both local and national, of promising minor forest products and lesser-known timber species.

(2) Technical production aspects of local industrial processing of marketable forest products, especially minor forest products.

(3) Marketing requirements for diverse natural forest products (e.g., grouping by general use characteristics).

(4) Potential uses of different natural forest products as inputs to farm production (e.g., nitrogen-fixing trees, mulches, and vegetable residues as substitutes for artificial chemical fertilizers).

(5) Financial performance and employment impact (by gender and age group) of different management procedures (from home gardens to wildlife and timber production areas) that increase yields and minimize damage to natural forest vegetation.

(6) Financial analysis of forest management at the farm level (e.g., wood lots for urban fuelwood consumption, forest enrichment for local lumber industries), and the use of secondary forest growth areas on farm lots for commercial tree planting and agroforestry demonstrations.

Several important demonstration projects that blend natural forest management and modern development efforts in the tropical Americas have received support from conservation groups and governments and are documented elsewhere.[39]

Secondary Forest Management

Another considerable challenge for tropical forest conservation is the ecological repatriation of degraded secondary forest lands to serve social and economic development objectives. Land use planners in Amazonia should also consider the eventual recolonization of previously settled (deforested) secondary forest lands, which implies, a priori, working with impoverished biological communities at scattered locations. Again, considerable basic research is called for, but research funds should be devoted to management applications of existing fallow enrichment and secondary growth manipulation knowledge guided by social as well as by biological research interests.

Diversification of Production

Diversification of production must become the central and guiding tenet of sustainable tropical forest land use. In one sense, diversity of production runs counter to conventional economic development wisdom advocating specialization around a comparative resource advantage. The

reductive conversion of biotically diverse forest communities, supporting tens of thousands of living species for thousands of years, to
genetic cesspools capable of supporting one or two commercial species
for five to ten years must be rejected as an economic development model.
The comparative advantage of tropical forests is their biodiversity.

In those countries where subsidies play a major role in forest land
use, the shift from (a) subsidies for commodities to (b) subsidies for
biotically diversified land uses should be considered. Instead of rural
credit to convert forest land to upland rice fields, policies could entice
farmers to productively utilize the biodiversity of the natural forest for
financial benefit.

Notes

[1] Norman Myers, *The Primary Source* (New York: W. W. Norton and Co., 1984), p. 2;
and "FAO's Tropical Forestry Action Plan," extracted from *Unasylva,* Vol. 38, No. 152
(1988), p. 40.
[2] John Spears, "Can Farming and Forest Coexist in the Tropics?" *Unasylva,* Vol. 32,
No. 128 (1980), p. 2.
[3] Jean-Paul Lanly, *Tropical Forest Resources,* FAO Forestry Paper No. 30 (Rome:
Food and Agriculture Organization, 1982), cited in R. Repetto, *The Forest for the Trees?
Government Policies and the Misuse of Forest Resources* (Washington, D.C.: World
Resources Institute, 1988), p. 1.
[4] John O. Browder, "Public Policy and Deforestation in the Brazilian Amazon," in R.
Repetto and M. Gillis, eds., *Public Policies and the Misuse of Forest Resources* (Cambridge:
Cambridge University Press, 1988), p. 282.
[5] Julia C. Allen and Douglas F. Barnes, "The Causes of Deforestation in Developing
Countries," *Annals of the Association of American Geographers,* Vol. 5, No. 2 (1985), p. 163.
[6] See, for example, John O. Browder, "The Social Costs of Rain Forest Destruction: A
Critique and Economic Analysis of the 'Hamburger Debate,'" *Interciencia,* Vol. 13, No. 3
(1988); John O. Browder, "Public Policy and Deforestation in the Brazilian Amazon," in
Repetto and Gillis, eds., *Public Policies and the Misuse of Forest Resources,* op.cit.; Philip
M. Fearnside, "Agricultural Plans for Brazil's Grande Carajas: Lost Opportunity for Sustainable Local Development?" *World Development,* Vol. 14, No. 3 (1986), p. 385–409;
Susanna B. Hecht, "Environment, Development and Politics: Capital Accumulation and
the Livestock Sector in Eastern Amazonia," *World Development,* Vol. 13, No. 6 (1985), pp.
663–84; Douglas R. Shane, *Hoofprints on the Rainforest* (Philadelphia, Penn.: Institute for
the Study of Human Issues, 1986).
[7] Browder, "The Social Costs of Rain Forest Destruction", op. cit.
[8] See Part 2, "Colonization and Spontaneous Settlement," in Marianne Schmink and
Charles H. Wood, eds., *Frontier Expansion in Amazonia* (Gainesville, Fla.: University of
Florida Press, 1984).
[9] World Bank, Brazil-Northwest I, II and III. Technical Review. "Final Report"
(Washington, D.C., 1987), p. 4.
[10] John O. Browder, "Lumber Production and Economic Development in the Brazilian
Amazon," *Journal of World Forest Resource Management* (forthcoming).
[11] M. K. Muthoo, *Forestry Development and Research, Brazil: First Forestry Outlook*
(Brasilia: U.N. Development Programme (UNDP), U.N. Food and Agriculture Organization (FAO), and Instituto Brasileiro de Desenvolvimento Florestal (IBDF, 1976) cited in
Browder, "Lumber Production and Economic Development," ibid.
[12] John O. Browder, "Logging the Rain Forest: A Political Economy of Timber Extraction and Unequal Exchange in the Brazilian Amazon," Unpublished dissertation, University of Pennsylvania, 1986, p. 62.
[13] See Browder, "Logging the Rain Forest," ibid.; and John O. Browder, "Brazil's
Export Promotion Policy (1980–1984): Impacts on the Amazon's Industrial Wood Sector,"
The Journal of Developing Areas, Vol. 21 (April 1987), pp. 285–304.
[14] Browder, "Logging the Rain Forest," op. cit.

[15] W. B. J. Jonkers and J. Hendrison, "Prospects for Sustained Yield Management of Tropical Rain Forest in Suriname," in *Management of the Forests of Tropical America: Prospects and Technologies* (Rio Piedras, Puerto Rico: Institute of Tropical Forestry, 1987), p. 168.

[16] John Campbell, "The World's Third Forest," *Commonwealth Forestry Review,* Vol. 59, No. 4 (1980), p. 533.

[17] John Spears, "Deforestation Issues in Developing an Accelerated Investment Program," *Commmonwealth Forestry Review,* Vol. 64, No. 4 (1985), p. 318.

[18] Michael Nelson, *The Development of Tropical Lands* (Baltimore, Md.: Johns Hopkins University Press, 1973), p. 155.

[19] See John Spears, "Replenishing the World's Forests: Tropical Reforestation—An Achievable Goal?" *Commonwealth Forestry Review,* Vol. 62, No. 3 (1983), Table 1, p. 213.

[20] Fearnside, "Agricultural Plans," op. cit, p. 402.

[21] Fearnside, ibid., Table 6, p. 403.

[22] William M. Denevan, "Latin America," in Gary A. Klee, ed., *World Systems of Traditional Resource Management* (New York: Halsted Press, 1980), p. 244, fn. 43.

[23] See J. J. Nicholaides III, D. E. Bandy, P. A. Sanchez, J. R. Benites, J. H. Villachica, A. J. Coutu, and C. S. Valverde, "Agricultural Alternatives for the Amazon Basin," *BioScience,* Vol. 35, No. 5 (1985), pp. 279–85.

[24] Susanna B. Hecht, "Indigenous Soil Management in the Latin American Tropics: Some Implications for the Amazon Basin," in John O. Browder, ed., *Fragile Lands of Latin America: Strategies for Sustainable Management* (Boulder, Colo.: Westview Press, forthcoming, July 1989).

[25] See John Frechione, "Manioc Monozoning in Yakuana Agriculture," *Antropologica,* Vol. 58 (1982), pp. 53–74.

[26] Stephen R. Gleissman, "Local Resource Use Systems in the Tropics: Taking Pressure Off the Forests." Unpublished manuscript, n.d.

[27] H. L. Morales, "Rural Development and the Management of Tropical Integrated Production Units," *Tropical Ecology and Development,* (1980), pp. 429.

[28] Janis B. Alcorn, "An Economic Analysis on Huastec Mayan Forest Management," in Browder, ed., *Fragile Lands of Latin America,* op. cit.

[29] See Gleissman, "Local Resource Use Systems in the Tropics," op. cit., p. 21.

[30] Ghillean T. Prance, W. Balee, B. M. Boom, and R. L. Carneiro, "Quantitative Ethnobotany and the Case for Conservation in Amazonia," *Conservation Biology,* Vol. 2 (1988), pp. 269–310, cited in Ghillean T. Prance, "Economic Prospects from Tropical Rainforest Ethnobotany," in Browder, ed., *Fragile Lands of Latin America,* op. cit.

[31] C. W. Peters, A. G. Gentry, and R. Mendelsohn "Valuation of a Tropical Forest in Peruvian Amazonia," (in press), cited in Ghillean T. Prance, "Economic Prospects from Tropical Rainforest Ethnobotany" in Browder, ed., *Fragile Lands of Latin America,* op. cit.

[32] Alcorn, "An Economic Analysis on Huastec Mayan Forest Management," in Browder, ed., *Fragile Lands of Latin America,* op. cit.

[33] Alcorn, ibid.

[34] James D. Nations and Flavio C. Hinojosa, "Cuyabeno Wildlife Production Reserve," in Browder, ed., *Fragile Lands of Latin America,* op. cit.

[35] Robert J. Buschbacher, "Cattle Productivity and Nutrient Fluxes on an Amazon Pasture," *Biotropica,* Vol. 19, No. 3 (1987), pp. 206.

[36] See William M. Denevan, "Ecological Heterogeneity and Horizontal Zonation of Agriculture in the Amazon Floodplain," in Schminlt and Wood; eds., *Frontier Expansion in Amazonia,* op. cit , pp. 311–36.

[37] Christine Padoch and Wil de Jong, "Production and Profit in Agroforestry: An Example for the Peruvian Amazon," in Browder, ed., *Fragile Lands of Latin America,* op. cit.

[38] See Anthony B. Anderson and Mario Augusto G. Jardim, "Costs and Benefits of Floodplain Forest Management by Rural Inhabitants in the Amazon Estuary: A Case Study of Acai Palm Production," in Browder, ed., *Fragile Lands of Latin America,* op. cit.

[39] See Browder, ed., *Fragile Lands of Latin America,* op. cit.

Chapter 4

Sustainable Approaches to Hillside Agricultural Development

A. John De Boer

This chapter addresses the problems of hillside agriculture in general, with a focus on the Himalayan range—the region with the most severe environmental degradation associated with human impact upon a fragile natural resource base. The analysis and policy recommendations presented here do, however, in large part also apply to hill regions in most developing countries.

The problems discussed here are particularly acute in developing countries because of: the particular nature of poverty-environment relationships found in hill agriculture; the degree and severity of poverty found in these areas, and the pressure that this exerts upon the fragile natural resource base; the pervasive need for subsistence production; and the lack of nonagricultural employment opportunities to partially relieve the pressure on natural resources.

What is the nature of hillside agriculture? Why has it led to such severe environmental impact and such pervasive poverty? Why has widespread concern about these aspects of hillside agriculture had so little impact? Why have *developed*-country approaches encompassing soil conservation, watershed management, controlled grazing, and managed forestry found such limited acceptance in the hills of *developing* countries? Where has public policy gone astray in attempting to solve these problems?

In an attempt to answer these concerns of the development and environment communities, this chapter first examines the nature and extent of constraints facing hill agriculture and then analyzes the relationships between poverty and the environment in this ecological setting. Conventional approaches to the development of hill areas and currently available technologies are briefly examined and found to relate insufficiently to the central problems. Finally, policy issues are discussed, leading to the identification and discussion of the five areas most appropriate for public policy action to reverse current trends of increasing poverty and environmental degradation.

Hillside zones in developing countries are characterized by a number of general traits that make the promotion of environmentally sound, equitable development strategies extremely difficult. These include:

- Widespread poverty;
- Low labor productivity;
- Rapid rates of population growth;
- Dense populations with a high proportion of women, the very old, and the very young;
- Outmigration;
- Off-farm employment;
- Long histories of settlement;
- Highly variable rainfall patterns and soil types;
- Strong interrelationships between agricultural production, livestock production, and forests;
- A subsistence orientation;
- Poor marketing, transportation, and communications infrastructures; and
- Isolation from national political processes.

Highlands occupy about 25 per cent of the earth's land surface and support about 10 per cent of the world's people.[1] Moreover, another 40 per cent of the world's population live in the adjacent lowland areas that are linked to the activities of these uplands. It has been estimated that the hillside zones of the American tropics hold one-fourth to one-third of the 200 million people inhabiting Mexico and the countries of Central America, the Caribbean, and the Andean region.[2] Approximately one-half of the farms in these zones are located on slopes steeper than 20 per cent. Steeply sloping areas cover nearly 50 per cent of the Andean, Central American, and Caribbean region and provide 40 to 80 per cent of the staple foods in each country.

In Nepal, 68 per cent of the total arable land is in the hills, 15 per cent in the mountains, and 17 per cent in the Terai (North Gangetic

Plain). Only 30 per cent of Nepal's total food supply comes from the hills, yet these areas are home to 56 per cent of the population. By 1985, fifty of the fifty-five hilly/mountainous districts were not producing enough food to meet local demand. Rapid population growth (nearly 2.7 per cent or 265,000 new persons per year) seriously exacerbates the increasing problem of inadequate food production.

Other areas that share most, if not all, of the characteristics outlined above include the tropical and subtropical highlands of East and Central Africa and Ethiopia, some of the Caribbean Islands, particularly Haiti and the Dominican Republic, large areas of Central Burma, the Indian Western Himalayas, the extensive non-Hindu Kush Himalayan mountainous regions of China, and the tropical highlands of Indonesia and the Philippines.

The major ecological problems associated with hillside agriculture—notably the thinning of forest cover, deforestation, and soil loss—invariably stem from the interaction of three factors: rural poverty, rapid population growth among subsistence mountain societies, and inadequately controlled commercial exploitation of natural resources. The difficulties associated with land use in these areas can only be understood as a subset of the general problem of rural underdevelopment.[3] Rural poverty is both a direct and an indirect causal factor in environmental degradation. In short, environmental degradation is so widespread in hillside areas because the social and economic factors associated with underdevelopment are there combined with a land resource subject to rapid deterioration under improper human use.

The positive role that improved management of natural resources—especially soil conservation—could play in increasing the productivity of hill agriculture needs greater emphasis. The poorest countries tend to be heavily dependent on their natural resource base, to have relatively high rates of population growth, and to suffer severe shortages of capital and trained manpower—which in turn limits their ability to shift employment to activities that are less dependent on natural resources.[4] The most critical environmental problems relate to the complex interrelationships between overgrazing, fuelwood harvesting, land clearing, deforestation, burning of crop residues and dung, soil erosion, flooding, and sedimentation. Despite many ambitious projects designed to tackle one or more of these relationships, most efforts are failing because of the great difficulty of dealing with vast numbers of small-scale, natural-resource-using activities that, taken collectively, have a massive environmental impact. Governments have often attempted—with little impact—to impose blanket legislation to control these myriad small-scale activities.[5]

The Himalayas: An Overview

The Himalayan region, home to over 45 million people, covers major parts of India, Pakistan, Nepal, Bhutan, and China. It is the source of many of the world's major river systems—including the Ganges, Indus, Brahmaputra, Mekong, Salween, and Yangtze—and thus directly and indirectly affects over one-third of the world's population living in the great river basins. The Himalayas are the world's highest and youngest mountain range, extending 250 kilometers along the East-West axis and covering over 0.5 million square kilometers. The width of the range varies from 325 to 425 kilometers. The combination of high seasonal precipitation and high elevation makes these mountains an energy storehouse of a largely renewable nature, since vast potential for hydroelectric generation remains undeveloped.

Himalayan agriculture is as varied as its topography and peoples. Agricultural practices range from pure pastoralism in the rain-shadow plateaus to slash-and-burn agriculture on lower mountain slopes (where malaria has only recently been eliminated). The predominant form of agriculture, however, is mixed crop-livestock systems in the mid-hills and mountain valleys. As noted later, these systems are also heavily dependent on forests for their viability. Mixed farming systems typically have a major cereal crop (rice or maize), a minor cereal crop (either finger millet, wheat, barley, or buckwheat), oilseeds, grain legumes, vegetable crops, and spices such as cardamon or ginger. Medicinal plants can be locally important. These systems are heavily dependent on livestock, showing some of the highest numbers of livestock per unit of cultivated area in the world. Animals typically provide milk, draft power, and dung as well as occasional sources of cash income. Higher elevation areas are more dependent on potatoes, barley, and buckwheat, and less dependent on forest resources. Yaks, chauries, and high-altitude sheep replace the cattle, water buffalo, goats, chickens, and pigs found at lower elevations.

Environmental Degradation in the Himalayas

The general ecological problems encountered in the hillside agriculture of the Himalayas have been described by many authors as variations of a cycle of environmental degradation that is set in motion by the combination of rapid population growth and the low productivity of agricultural labor. Increased demand for fuelwood, fodder, and food leads to forest clearing for communal pasture and cropping, or for wood needed for household cooking and heating. Where soils and topography are suitable, there is permanent conversion to cropland, but in other areas the cleared land ends up as poor-quality communal pasture or abandoned shrubland. As fuelwood shortages grow, dung is used as fuel, rather than as fertilizer, which causes agricultural yields to fall. And as yields decline, terrace soils deteriorate, and landsliding, gullying, and erosion increase. More and more soil is washed downstream to riverine plains; floods worsen; and groundwater supplies diminish.

Despite the indisputable links between all these factors, the sequence and causal relationships that lead to environmental deterioration in the Himalayas are not always as simple as they may appear. For example, some maintain that pressure to expand cultivated area, not fuelwood use, is the prime cause of deforestation.[6] Others argue just the opposite: that pressure on forest resources in the hills has not been due to the encroachment of cultivation but to rising demand for fuelwood and fodder as inputs in hill farming systems.[7] In either case, however, forest degradation leads to a reduction of the growing stock and reduces future supplies of fodder and fuelwood. A 1987 study by the Water and Energy Commission Secretariat in Nepal found that seventy out of seventy-five districts in Nepal have fuelwood deficits based on current forest yield rates.[8] Domestic use accounts for over 95 per cent of all energy consumed in Nepal, and over 78 per cent of this is fuelwood. In Nepal forest degradation, rather than complete loss of forest cover, seems to be the typical case. There is virtually no forest with a crown cover greater than 70 per cent in the Western, Central, and Eastern Development Regions.

There is also a lack of consensus on the degree to which human exploitation has promoted an increase in landslides in the Himalayas. While deforestation in the Himalayas is often cited as the primary cause of increased landslides, a recent International Center for Integrated Mountain Development (ICIMOD) study indicates that human-induced landslides still comprise only 35 per cent of the total, although the percentage is increasing. Road construction alone accounts for 20 per cent of human-induced landslides.[9] Bedrock geology, soil stability, and steepness of slope are still the primary factors leading to landslides in the Himalayas.

Similarly, the role that increased human and livestock exploitation plays in downstream sedimentation problems is disputed. While on-site soil erosion certainly increases as forest cover is lost and forested land is converted to cropland or common grazing land, there is much less evidence that serious downstream problems are caused by discharges from upstream, overexploited watersheds. Nevertheless, whether carried downstream or deposited in the same watershed, soil erosion on hilly lands poses serious threats to future land productivity and stability.

Overgrazing of common land is the largest contributor to on-site soil erosion.[10] While this practice is most pervasive in the Himalayas, it is also a common contributor to accelerated erosion in the Andean highlands, the Sahel, and in the African highlands.

As noted above, roads have a major adverse environmental impact on the fragile geology of many hill ecosystems. Moreover, it has been estimated that the construction of every kilometer of road generates 40,000–80,000 cubic meters of debris.[11] Each kilometer of roadway also causes another 550 cubic meters of debris due to landslides and rock falls. Yet roads can also help to reduce some of the pressures that lead to excessive exploitation of land in hillside areas. They can, for example, reduce the transport costs of inputs and outputs—allowing specialization in higher-value crops that may be less erosive than subsistence cereal crops—and encourage outmigration (seasonal or permanent) from the hills.

W. M. Fleming has argued that, in the Himalayas: (1) natural geological processes contribute more to sediment loads than do human-induced causes; (2) degraded grazing lands and road construction are the major human-induced sources of soil erosion; (3) deforestation does not appear to be a significant contributor to landslides; and (4) most of the on-site erosion in larger watersheds is not discharged out of the basin. Most experts agree that in regions prone to high rates of natural erosion, like the Himalayas, the inhabitants' contribution to the total levels of sedimentation is marginal. This finding may not hold, however, in many other areas of the world where hill agriculture dominates, and one must be cautious about applying conclusions from the Himalayas to other regions.

Despite the conflicting evidence about the causal factors of environmental destruction in the Himalayas and about how much this contributes to downstream sedimentation and flooding, there is no doubt that increased human pressure on the fragile Himalayan resource base has created major economic difficulties for the region's poor people. The populations most adversely affected are in the mid-to-lower hills, where a combination of steep slopes, shallow soils, and weak geology interacts with increasing levels of human activity.

The conversion of forest land to cropland has reduced the amount of usable forest land and increased pressure on remaining forest land for fuel, timber, and fodder requirements—so that this land is soon degraded as well. Inexorably, cultivation is shifting to steep, poor-quality lands with low productivity, leading to the declining crop yields witnessed throughout the region. Between 1950 and 1972, cultivated land in the hills of the Indian state of Uttar Pradesh increased from 15 to 27 per cent of the total area, with an equivalent decrease in forest and grazing land. Eighty-seven per cent of the cropland in the mountains of this state is classified as having severe erosion problems. As a result, these lands can no longer support the hill populations, making outside sources of income essential. Yet because of the strong cultural and ethnic ties in these areas, outmigration by entire families has been limited and has not served to release much pressure on natural resources.

Poverty and Environment in the Himalayas

The cycle of poverty and environmental degradation in hillside agricultural areas is directly related to low labor productivity. As population expands into areas characterized by a declining marginal productivity of each additional hectare settled, livestock populations increase in proportion to the human population. People clear forests to add to the arable land base and, probably more importantly, to meet the fuelwood and fodder needs of hill farming systems. Household labor is allocated between crops, livestock, non-farm energy supplies, and animal fodder (with the latter two coming primarily from forests). Since land quality is declining at the margin, more labor is required per unit of crop and livestock output. More labor is also needed per unit of noncrop energy gathered for the household and per unit of fodder gathered for animals. Time spent on animal herding also increases as the forest retreats. These factors can lead to a deterioration of soil nutritional status, further contributing to a decline in productivity and a worsening of the cycle of poverty and environmental degradation.

This high dependency on the forests is illustrated in recent studies.[12] Assuring the supply of fuelwood and fodder not only puts tremendous pressure on the forests, but also requires huge amounts of family labor for cutting and hauling, as well as for distributing compost back to the fields. The intensiveness of "production support activities"— defined to include all collection activities (for fuel, fodder, grass, and water for family and livestock needs, as well as food processing, and cooking)—is directly related to deforestation. Evidence of a high propensity to spend additional time on agriculture means that—given the high marginal value of productivity of labor in agriculture—reducing time spent on support activities leads to higher agricultural productivity and output. Increased deforestation forces a greater allocation of labor time for the collection of fuelwood and other forest products, which is the major production support activity and is carried out mainly by women and children. In the poor hill areas of Nepal, women spend almost as much time on this activity as they do on farm labor. Increasing demands upon women's and children's time as a consequence of deforestation have been shown to result in less time devoted to agricultural activities (as well as in an increased overall workload—with probable adverse effects on both agricultural production and child nutrition).[13]

In summary, the low productivity of hill agriculture promotes deforestation as land under cultivation increases in an effort to provide basic food entitlements to an expanding population base and as village demands for fodder, fuelwood, and grasses increases. Deforestation in turn not only leads to adverse effects on the environment, but has been linked to declines in agricultural production, food consumption, and family nutrition because it increases workloads, particularly for women, in production support and collection activities.

The dynamic biological relationships of hill agriculture—nutrient flows between humans, crops, animals, and forests—must also be understood to assess development strategies and policies. Key biological processes that sustain the system operate as follows: Organic matter and plant nutrients are transferred from uncultivated to cultivated land by livestock, which also recycle organic matter and plant nutrients from crop residues to cultivated land. Chemical fertilizers play a limited role—due to the poor quality of soils and limited irrigation as well as to the unavailability or prohibitive cost of fertilizer itself. The flow of nutrients from uncultivated to cultivated land is quantitatively more important—indeed essential. Uncultivated land is called the "support area" precisely because it supports cultivation by supplying organic matter and plant nutrients through the green leaves-dung-compost chain as well as through the dry leaves (bedding)-compost chain. Cultivation is indirectly supported by supplies of fuelwood from these areas, which substitute for dung as fuel, preventing a serious break in the nutrient cycle.[14]

The relationship between the support area and the limits of cultivated agriculture illustrates how food output reaches a plateau through expanded cultivation in a given geographical area. As the cultivated land area is expanded, marginal productivity declines because of: (a) the inherently lower quality of the raw land itself and (b) a shrinking support area left to provide the newly cultivated land with organic matter recycled (through animals) as well as plant nutrients. In other words, food production per unit of cultivated land peaks and then declines as the ratio of cultivated to uncultivated land increases.

The support area concept helps to explain why the more forest cover an area has the more fuel and fodder can be supplied per unit of area. In areas with good forest cover, less labor for production support activities is needed, so that more labor can be devoted to agricultural pursuits.[15] Once the forest cover is lost or becomes too remote, fuel needs must come from crop wastes and animal dung, and the nutrient cycle is broken—with disastrous effects. Even where chemical fertilizer is available and its use is economically attractive to farmers, the recycling of organic matter is essential to the realization of potential yield responses from chemical fertilizers.

The problem of an increasing population living on a declining resource base is exacerbated by the lack of alternative sources of income. In the hill regions of India, manufacturing accounts for only 4.5

per cent of income and 3.7 per cent of employment.[16] As a result, such areas have high migration rates in the male labor force, high ratios of females to males and of children to adults, high participation rates for women in the workforce, and low labor productivity. This lack of employment opportunities in the hills leads to migration and dependence upon remittances. A recent case study shows that about one-third of the total disposable income of rural households in the Indian hill areas comes from cash remittances, which increase the average income of migrant households by about 36 per cent.[17] Loss of production due to this outmigration appears to be minimal, since women and children increase their labor force participation to compensate. In the case-study villages, 21 per cent of the labor force had migrated, and 90 per cent of the migrants were of prime working age (15–35 years, with a mean age of 20). Propensity to migrate increased with educational level. This resulted in a remaining population with a ratio of 1.4 females to 1 male in the 15 to 50 age group. In agriculture and animal husbandry, the ratio was 1.7 to 1.

From 1971 to 1981, the natural increase in the hill populations of Nepal was nearly 30 per cent, while production of major foodgrains increased by about 20 per cent. Outmigration kept per capita supplies about the same—at 140 kilograms per year, or below most estimates of minimal nutritional requirements. Studies on labor constraints and labor productivity in marginal upland agricultural areas maintain that outmigration is not due to an underutilized or unemployed labor force, but to low returns to labor resulting from very low productivity.[18] The latter is a result of the declining support base for agriculture.

The State of Hillside Agricultural Development

Three broad forces of change appear likely to intensify in coming years and to affect significantly the context within which agricultural and rural development efforts in hillside areas take place.

First, improved communications and educational opportunities are being made available—even in the more remote areas. The hills are being opened up to national and international cultural trends. As a result, outmigration is likely to increase and the drain on human capital to accelerate. The more capable, innovative, and educated youth will migrate in disproportionate numbers, leaving even higher percentages of women, the very old, and the very young in the villages. Efforts to reduce poverty, rehabilitate environmental damage, and prevent further deterioration of the environment must focus on these groups as the grassroots agents of change. Extension, communications, and community action and investment programs should target these "clients."

Second, several important trends appear to be intensifying: (a) an upsurge of interest in and support for research on major hill crops and other minor crops of current or potential importance in the hills; (b) a greater focus on high-value crops suitable for specific ecological niches; (c) increased support for animal species or subspecies found at higher elevations; and (d) worldwide concern over the loss of germplasm resulting from the expansion of agriculture in the hills.

Third, there is mounting concern and political support for regional cooperation to mitigate the most visible aspects of environmental degradation in the hills and mountains. The effects of the massive 1988 monsoon floods in Bangladesh and the Sudan focused attention on this need.

The extent to which these trends will stimulate greater attention to the need for grassroots actions to address the problems of hillside agricultural development remains to be seen. But it is already clear that these forces are beginning to affect donor and national government thinking about development objectives for hilly zones. At least at the rhetorical level, much more attention is being paid to the changing nature of the residual labor force (especially, the critical role of women's work), to the importance of special agricultural research to meet the needs of the hill areas, and to the need for direct interventions to reduce environmental degradation in upland regions.

Conventional Approaches to Hill Area Development

In the past, environmental improvement in developing countries has mainly involved projects launched with the primary objective of improving the natural resource base—and consequently the environment. These approaches have focused on curative, piecemeal solutions (reforestation, soil conservation, watershed improvement) rather than on confronting the real issues that led to a degraded resource base in the first place. These issues include:

- How societies cope—or fail to cope—with expanding population pressures on a fragile environment;
- What rules govern the use of communal or common property resources;
- Access to resources by different groups;
- The general climate for investment, trade, and employment generation; and
- Incentives to work in remote areas where problems of environmental degradation are often most acute.

Conventional piecemeal approaches have not been sufficient to significantly alleviate the problems of hill agriculture; more appropriate efforts are needed to integrate natural resource planning and management with economic and social policy and development programs.[19]

Moreover, conventional approaches to natural resource management have focused on the primary resources (soil, water, trees, etc.) without sufficient attention paid to consideration of the people utilizing those resources. This often has led to the nationalization of large areas, putting natural resource management in the hands of the public sector. Higher priority needs to be given to changing the "rules of the game" to achieve the same results through the participation of those who have traditionally used these resources. For example, to reduce externalities imposed on downstream users by hill agriculturists, both donors and governments have generally orchestrated large public investment projects to construct soil- and water-control structures. These have seldom solved the downstream problem or promoted the on-farm actions necessary to reduce the adverse effects of soil erosion. Common problems have been (a) the high cost of terracing by manual methods; (b) the fact that short-term yields often do not show a dramatic impact from terracing (so that farmers are unwilling to devote their own labor to such efforts); and (c) lack of maintenance following the completion of construction. In many cases, terracing of land for upland crops (which require good drainage during periods of heavy monsoon rains) results in more erosion than occurred even in the deforested state.

Promoting Sustainable Hillside Agriculture

Four approaches introduced in recent years as alternatives to conventional strategies seek to integrate development and natural resource management in hilly areas, particularly in areas of limited forest cover and high livestock populations.

The *first* of these approaches is based on rural sources of energy, relying on more efficient cooking stoves, biogas, and solar energy. This strategy has had little impact, except in areas where great effort has been made over a sustained period (and usually at a high cost).

The *second* approach is to increase the contribution of fodder and crop byproducts to the livestock, and thereby to relieve the pressure on labor needed for agricultural support activities. Improvement in the feeding value of low-quality crop byproducts has, however, been constrained by lack of inputs for the process such as small-scale, dispersed units for processing of bulky byproducts and residues. Without clear, demonstrable economic benefits, actual adoption of these new technologies will be negligible. As the primary purpose of the majority of animals is to produce compost and draft animal power, it is difficult to demonstrate the economic viability of fodders and crop byproduct improvements—since these show the clearest economic impact when the final product is meat or milk produced for market, not dung and draft power used for crops.

The *third* approach is agroforestry—more specifically, the better manipulation of multi-purpose tree species to serve the farmers' need for fuel, fodder, litter, and, if possible, soil fertility or soil stabilization. Although agroforestry is widely practiced in the hills, large-scale planting of multipurpose species has been limited because the potential secondary benefits usually are not realized; for example, intense pruning for fuelwood generally reduces the ability of trees to regenerate or to bear fruit.

The key to using agroforestry techniques to improve the productivity of hill agriculture is changing the management of land and animals. Rehabilitation and sustained-use management of the support areas have been shown to be capable of greatly increasing supplies of fuelwood and fodder per unit of area. There is evidence that:

- The same amount of fuelwood and fodder could be supplied on about 50 per cent of the current (degraded) support area;
- Foodgrain productivity would increase by 60 per cent;
- Livestock productivity would increase by 50 per cent;
- Over 40 per cent of the previous support areas could be converted to commercial timber production.[20]

The critical factor is motivating local people to participate in the process of rehabilitation, protection, and sustained-use management of village support areas. Conversion from grazing to stall feeding is a closely related step for viable community forestry in support areas; without this, forest establishment and management is difficult. Greatly increased tree sapling production and training to make optimal use of the saplings are desperately needed. The area under multipurpose tree species must be greatly expanded to relieve pressure on public forests. In most cases, this means that reserved forest land currently being exploited as a common property resource must be made available as private property for tree farming to individuals, groups, or villages.

The *fourth* approach relies on improved agricultural technology to increase farm productivity. In this area, a number of well-organized efforts are now under way. Canada's International Development Research Centre (IDRC) has been very active on the crops side, with good support also from the U.S. Board on Science and Technology for International Development (BOSTID) of the National Research Council. The research base on hill farming systems is now expanding, and indications are that such scientific support will continue in the future. The International Centres of Agricultural Research—under the Consultative Group on International Agricultural Research (CGIAR)—have focused more efforts on crop development for less favored areas. Such areas are usually rainfed—often with problem soils, highly variable climates, and a general lack of the infrastructure needed to support high-input agriculture, mountain farming systems, and mountain development programs. Biological nitrogen fixation (BNF) plays a key role in the resource-poor, low-input systems of hill agriculture. Research support for nitrogen fixation is increasing through projects such as the Nitrogen Fixing Tree Association in Hawaii; the Regional Laboratory in BNF in Bangkok, Thailand; the Rodale Research Center in Pennsylvania; the International Rice Research Institute; and many other organizations.

Support for and interest in research to increase the productivity of agroforestry, a key component of sustainable agriculture, has also increased. The International Council on Research in Agroforestry in Nairobi, Kenya, was formed to help support national and regional efforts. The Forestry/Fuelwood Research and Development Project, sponsored by the U.S. Agency for International Development, is setting up active networks in Asia. Many other international, regional, and national institutions are now working on various aspects of agroforestry research and development.

A recent assessment of the potential of some of these technologies in the context of the problems and constraints of the Himalayan hills recommended increased emphasis on: (1) horticulture, (2) fruit processing, (3) non-resource based light industries, (4) local small-scale production of energy, and (5) well-planned outmigration programs.[21] While this chapter does not focus on the technologies for hill agriculture, a general discussion is useful, if only to indicate the broad range of technologies available for testing in conjunction with overall hill development programs. The technologies available for the rehabilitation of denuded areas often require enclosure of the area followed by soil and water conservation measures; brush control; fertilizer and manuring; choice of multi-purpose tree species appropriate for silvipastoral management; methods for reseeding pastures; conservation horticulture; vegetables, flowers, and seeds of both; aromatics and dry plants; and stall feeding of animals to reduce erosion rates, allow reforestation, and increase yields from managed pasture lands.[22]

Other available technologies include intercropping legumes with upland crops, using tied ridges to hold rainwater more effectively and to reduce erosion; planting Vetivergrass *(Vetiveria zizanioides)* to preserve soil and moisture by establishing permanent grass terraces; off-season vegetable production (which usually requires very good infrastructure and transportation); modified land-clearing methods such as controlled burning; partial retention of natural cover; mechanical systems to reduce the disturbance of upper soil layers; soil cover management to reduce the time during which soil remains unprotected (e.g., conversion of overgrazed common lands to hay fields or managed pastures); crop rotation and use of crop mixes that protect or enhance soil nutrient status; tillage and planting methods to retain soil cover, soil organic matter, and soil nutrients; harvesting methods to maintain crop residues on site and maintain soil cover; and chemical inputs to reduce human labor inputs and limit the need for soil disturbance.

A comprehensive study conducted in the mid-1970s examined the income-generating potential of using improved cereal and vegetable technology in the hills of Uttar Pradesh. With no capital constraints, even on the small landholdings in this area, farm net returns could be increased by 114 per cent, 150 per cent, and 180 per cent, respectively, in low-, middle-, and high-altitude farms.[23] The potential of pasture production to dramatically increase forage yields and quality in the Himalayas is described in another, more recent study.[24] Continuous, uncontrolled grazing results in the loss of perennial grasses, the invasion of tough, noxious weeds, and loss of yield. Under these conditions, legumes make a negligible contribution. Fencing is essential to start the process of rehabilitation and improved pasture production. Experiments conducted in Uttar Pradesh have shown that by enclosure for just two to three years, the yields of fresh grasses could be increased more than fourfold.

Another widely discussed strategy for the development of hill regions is to reduce areas under erosive cereal crops and to specialize in cash crops that are suitable for the multitude of specialized ecosystems found in the hills. The objective should be to optimize *income*—not foodgrain production—since most studies conclude that local production cannot meet the food requirements of dense populations in hilly areas. This strategy would also relieve pressure on the increasingly marginal lands that are being cleared for subsistence cereal production.[25] The strategy does, however, rely on an open, market-oriented economy connected with a good transportation system—in a setting where current limits on the transport system result in subsidies to move grains and fertilizers to the food-deficit hill areas, while exports out of the hills are usually limited to moving high-value cash crops, livestock, and livestock products. Unfortunately, in the past, massive environmental destruction has resulted from building roads to reach these areas, and it is likely that marginal environmental damage would increase more than proportionately with the opening of additional roads along more vulnerable routes. This raises a critical dilemma for development strategy in steep, fragile areas: Any effort to raise productivity and reduce on-farm environmental problems will require more road-building, but road construction itself causes significant adverse environmental impacts.

Barriers That Remain

For poor people in hilly areas, future economic programs will depend heavily on two interrelated developments: (1) migration out of hill areas to better jobs, and (2) the application of more modern, innovative farming methods. Both of these are now severely constrained by poor infrastructure and a lack of amenities. In addition, short-term needs often prevent poor farmers from taking steps that will equip them with job skills or raise their productivity in the long term. For example, the overwhelmingly agricultural nature of hill areas means that individuals (again, especially women) generally confront a direct time conflict between education and the immediate requirements of agricultural work—in addition to the problems of distance from educational facilities and inadequate transport.

Still other barriers relate to current policy interventions that affect hillside agriculture. Land tenure and social relationships can have a pervasive effect on the poverty-environment relationship—not only in the hills but also (even more importantly) in the adjacent lowland areas. Highly concentrated ownership of the more fertile and better situated plains creates pressures for increasing populations to clear and farm more marginal land in the hills. Impoverished farmers resort to large families to help them eke out a living using labor-intensive practices and to provide a margin of social security that the state is unable to supply. In addition, large holdings in the better endowed plains and valleys are often export-oriented and more mechanized than the rest of the agricultural sector, limiting the chances for the absorption of large numbers of hill migrants. The tenure problem is most acute in hill areas of Latin America, where a highly skewed distribution of land ownership and high rates of population growth prevail. Without access to land in the more productive areas, farmers turn to the hills—often with disastrous results. Squatting is common, and the lack of any legal ties to the land makes long-term investments in trees, permanent conservation structures, or fertility-enhancing rotation futile.

A number of other barriers often inhibit effective policy formulation and interventions needed to promote sustainable hill farming systems. The *first* is the perception of hillside areas as economically marginal and as a net drain on the national economy. Residents typically have little political or economic power. Remoteness and weak linkages to the national economy compound the problem. *Second,* deterioration is often misperceived to be a local problem with local solutions—due to poor understanding of the complex interactions that contribute to the degradation of hill areas including land tenure and land allocation, agricultural policy, and the unique problems of hill agriculture in sector-wide investment decisions. A *third* barrier is the frequent failure to take a sufficiently long-term view. Funding and political support are both needed over a long period—usually well beyond the planning and decision-making horizons of political bodies and economic planning agencies. Much of the basic research required will take decades to bring to fruition. High rates of return are well in the future, and the high discount rates faced by the countries with the worst problems make returns in the distant future unattractive. The same holds true for indi-vidual farmers. The *fourth* concern is that there must be political and bureaucratic flexibility to allow for political judgments not anticipated earlier—in order to incorporate inputs from the public into the design of a plan, and to modify bureaucratic structures to meet the requirements of hill people.

Public Policy and the Long-Term Future of Hill Agriculture

The basic issues in public policy for hill agriculture concern:

- The current pattern of resource allocation for the hills,
- The long-term viability of hill agriculture in meeting the basic food needs of hill populations, and
- Alternative patterns of resource flows to address future develop-ment needs.

The arguments regarding the appropriate size and nature of public resource allocation revolve around several questions: Can marginal hill areas ever have the capacity to meet the minimum food requirements of their populations? If so, at what cost? And what are the current and future costs of providing basic services to the burgeoning population of hill agriculturists? Public resource flows to hill areas go predominantly for roads, dams, other utilities (electricity, telecommunications, water supplies, trails, suspension bridges), education, reforestation, and (last but not least) agricultural subsidies. Costs of these subsidies usually include subsidies on the cost of materials supplied to hill communities such as grains, sugar, salt, cooking oil, kerosene, seeds, fertilizers, and transport subsidies. Agricultural subsidies for food-deficit hill areas often exceed the other cost categories mentioned above and seriously detract from the ability of the country to invest in high-payoff inputs such as agricultural research, irrigation systems, input supply systems, and population control programs for the more favored agricultural areas of the country. The effect of such (often high) financial resource flows to the hills is to retain a larger population in those areas than would otherwise remain there. Obviously these high subsidies also represent an opportunity cost for the industrial and service sectors of the country, in that they constrain needed funds for investment in job-creating opportunities, agricultural intensification in plains and delta areas, and the creation of basic industrial infrastructure. A reallocation of public resources might yield a higher payoff by moving low-productivity labor out of the hills to higher-productivity jobs elsewhere—and by making funds available for investment in high-payoff projects for the remaining hill-area residents.

Table 1. Nepal: Food Supply Trends and Population Growth in Selected Hill and Mountain Districts of the Eastern Development Region

District	Food Deficit in Edible Food[a] (metric tons)								Self-Sufficiency in Food Grains, 1986/87 (percentage)	Population Growth 1971–81 (percentages per annum)
	1979/80	1980/81	1981/82	1982/83	1983/84	1984/85	1985/86	1986/87		
Taplejung	3,888	2,427	4,122	5,490	6,992	7,961	8,698	7,372	59	0.34
Solukhumbu	2,653	2,643	2,635	4,168	5,225	4,535	6,013	5,047	47	0.70
Dhankuta	+8,947[a]	+12,981[a]	+18,306[a]	+8,795[a]	+14,567[a]	2,756	2,152	2,919	93	1.53
Bhojpur	7,508	4,947	+937	+712	4,300	349	1,220	48	100	0.81
Khotang	8,273	5,764	8,823	11,392	14,761	13,550	10,695	6,545	68	0.59
Okhaldhunga	7,197	1,860	1,059	4,643	3,704	4,747	5,586	3,531	79	1.00
Udayapur	+3,081	+7,247	+2,120	2,078	2,805	11,633	8,815	12,134	65	3.28

[a] A positive sign indicates a surplus for that year.

Source: Evaluation and Project Analysis Division, Ministry Agriculture, His Majesty's Government of Nepal, District Profile of Agricultural Development (Eastern Development Region) (1987).

Table 2.   Nepal: Food Supply Trends and Population Growth in Selected Hill and Mountain Districts of the Mid-Western Development Region

District	Food Deficit in Edible Food[a] (metric tons)						Self-Sufficiency in Food Grains, 1987/88 (percentage)	Population Growth 1971-81 (%/annum)
	1974/75	1979/80	1984/85	1985/86	1986/87	1987/88[b]		
Dolpa	638	777	947	1,499	933	1,130	74	1.43
Mugu	848	2,805	4,651	4,338	5,274	5,615	40	4.27
Humla	+1,687	1,736	1,195	1,260	+181	+93	105	−2.04
Jumla	3,181	5,020	3,722	4,308	3,202	2,230	72	1.32
Kalikot	2,005	+1,732	8,449	8,132	7,518	4,981	69	1.98
Rukum	5,242	10,307	8,705	10,032	7,332	2,020	91	2.57
Rolpa	7,556	13,732	5,302	5,988	3,749	+2,807	116	0.39
Pyuthan	4,531	8,476	9,029	10,062	5,238	4,346	84	0.078
Salyan	7,434	13,469	9,491	2,380	+1,220	+4,934	117	2.27
Jajarkot	5,849	5,181	8,071	7,741	5,425	4,145	78	1.21
Dailekh	9,796	13,954	13,259	11,275	10,086	9,034	63	1.19
Surkhet	+5,361	+8,477	4,510	+872	+1,607	4,567	87	5.81

[a] A positive sign indicates a surplus for that year.
[b] Preliminary estimate.

Source: Ministry of Agriculture, Evaluation and Project Analysis Division, His Majesty's Government of Nepal. District-Wide Profile of Agricultural Development, Mid-Western Development Region (1988).

Table 3. Nepal Cereal Balance by Household and Land Holding Size

Farm Size *(hectares)*	Household-Expressed Requirements *(kilogram/year)*	Production as Percentage of Expressed Requirements 1977	1978	Household Needs *(kilograms/year)*	Production as Percentage Household Needs
0–0.5	983	37	52	951	54
0.51–1.0	1,261	56	77	1,010	96
1.01 +	1,618	59	86	1,063	130
Average	1,256	51	73	1,008	91

Note: 1977 was a bad year for grain production, while 1978 was a good year.
Source: Adapted from S. Conlin and A. Falk, *Kosi Hills Area Rural Development Programme (KHARDEP), Nepal: A Study of the Socio-Economy of the Kosi Hills Area* (London: Land Resources Development Centre, 1979).

The crux of this issue is the ability of hill agriculture to support itself at a reasonable cost at any foreseeable level of technology. A detailed demand and supply analysis of Nepal showed that increased outmigration from the hills (50 per cent of natural population increase in contrast to the actual outmigration rate of 33 per cent over the 1971–1981 period) to be the only scenario that did not lead to deficits in food, fodder, and fuelwood. The most likely scenario, however, is that per capita food, fodder, and fuelwood deficits will continue to climb in coming years.

The three variables that offer the most hope for a reasonable demand-supply balance for natural resource goods in the hills are: (1) increased outmigration, (2) rapid increases in forest area and forest productivity, and (3) a reduction of overgrazing, with better management of grazing areas to ensure sustained yields. Data from the eastern and western hill districts of Nepal illustrate the slim chance that these hill areas have of ever being able to feed themselves under current projections of population growth and food production. Tables 1 and 2 illustrate the declining levels of food self-sufficiency in virtually every one of these districts—even among those that had substantial food surpluses in the early 1980s. Even in those districts with high outmigration, evidenced by low or negative net population growth rates, food deficits per capita were increasing. A 1979 study of household food deficits in the Kosi hills of eastern Nepal (Table 3) showed that, despite large annual variations, most districts exhibited a trend toward increasing food deficits—even though minimum consumption requirements were placed at very low levels in terms of both foodgrains and calories per capita.[26] Assuming that at most a 25 per cent increase in grain output can be achieved through the application of more fertilizer combined with a greater use of modern varieties, very few districts could attain self-sufficiency even with better technology. As indicated earlier, since labor needed for production support activities will continue to increase, the additional labor needed to achieve significantly higher yields is not likely to be forthcoming.

The review and analysis presented above suggests five major policy thrusts to improve the situation: (1) the promotion of community-based forestry programs, (2) land-use planning and management, (3) active promotion of outmigration from the hills through a reallocation of public expenditures, (4) changing institutional structures and policies to meet poor people's needs in the hills, and (5) widespread promotion of new and adapted technologies.

1. Community-Based Forestry Programs

The interrelationships set out in the preceding sections point to the critical role played by forests in supporting viable, sustainable hill agricultural systems. The specifics of the species, production systems, and uses to be made of the trees will vary, but community-based forestry systems are seen as a key link in reversing unfavorable trends and increasing agricultural productivity. Subsidies for forestry operations—through stumpage rates that do not recover full costs—also encourage overexploitation of forest resources, with little incentive for replanting. Short-term leases can have the same effect.

Formally institutionalizing and supporting traditional forms of community natural resource management is gaining favor. In Nepal, the law distinguishes between village-owned, village-protected (government-owned), and village-leased forests. The infrastructure to support these forests typically includes the establishment of village nurseries, the distribution of seedlings, the demarcation of forest boundaries, and the distribution of free or subsidized efficient woodstoves. Stall feeding of animals is encouraged, and steps are taken to make this practice economical.

Results to date have not, however, been favorable. There is some evidence that the nationalization of forest lands in 1957 greatly accelerated the deforestation process. Lands that were traditionally managed by individual families, family groups, or villages were suddenly government property, and the government's inability to restrict access resulted in a "first come, first served" attitude about these lands. While a rapidly expanding population was bound to intensify pressure on natural resources, there is considerable scope to increase the sustained yield of wood, tree fodder, and grasses from carefully managed forest lands. A gradual recognition of this problem has led to villages being given some management control over nationalized forests. But villagers, lacking a clear title and the ability to levy taxes or fees, have little incentive to invest in these lands. In Nepal, only 61,000 hectares of forest land have been planted or brought under management since 1979, out of a total area of all classes of forest in the middle and high mountains of about 4 million hectares.

2. Land Use Planning and Management

Land use planning for hill agriculture raises numerous questions, including: What is the minimum area within which the proposed system can be applied effectively? Who will decide what land use system to promote and adopt—individual farmers, farmer groups, the community, or the government? What are the mechanisms available to make the decision, put the decision into operation, and manage the consequences? How does the required level of cooperation fit into the established patterns of the community—that is, is the overall strategy to influence individual decisions or to obtain individuals' compliance with decisions reached by the community or government? This is particularly relevant to overgrazing of common lands—a major cause of environmental degradation in hill agriculture.

Requirements for effective land use planning and sustainable resource use in the hills include physical and biological feasibility studies. This calls for a land suitability classification based on the physical characteristics of an area, preferably a watershed or some other physically based unit. This allows planners to identify areas that need revegetation, complete protection, controlled forestry, and various types of agriculture. Also required is a measure of social acceptability. Local cooperation is best obtained by providing a clear explanation of project purposes and benefits at the conception, construction, and maintenance stages. Public participation and a reward system are also needed. Substitutes for the products being provided by the forest land, common grazing land, and erodable cropland must be provided to minimize the potential negative effects of land use changes. Finally, cooperation according to the new "rules of the game" must be unanimous to avoid the phenomenon of non-cooperators exploiting the resources (the "free rider" phenomenon) that cooperators are working to preserve. This is typical of many common property resources that lack strong legal or social sanctions to prevent overuse.

This leads to policies needed for the management of externalities. Despite the need for more reliance on market forces, there are numerous instances where the interests of private individuals and society diverge to such an extent that some public intervention is required. The problem is often aggravated where ownership of a resource is not clearly defined, or where ownership is clearly defined but enforcement of rules associated with ownership is not carried out consistently. Approaches to this problem can include price and subsidy policies to bring public and private costs and benefits closer together, physical restrictions, or the introduction of new property rights and leasing arrangements. Also used are input subsidies on items such as kerosene or efficient cookstoves, which decrease the demand for wood, encourage preservation of forests, and lessen negative effects on downstream residents. Land use planning and management in hill agriculture also require that common property resource management related to grazing and forest lands receive careful consideration. As shown earlier, communally grazed areas have an impact on the environment through accelerated erosion and the preclusion of reforestation programs. Policies and programs to communalize or privatize the use of these lands is relevant to the grazing aspects as well as to the need for a similar set of rules for community forestry programs. The issue of administrative costs also needs consideration; the use of direct and indirect incentives is always preferable because of the impossibility of placing effective administrative controls over the millions of individual users of natural resources.

Political acceptability must also be assured. Popular support at every level is essential, particularly since mountain regions are often isolated and their populations lack the political strength of urban and lowland areas. This support must be generated by the people themselves. Professional training is also needed to complement these efforts. A dedicated core of specialists in soil and water conservation, land use planning, and rural social science is needed. Only the most dedicated and persistent individuals should receive this training. Strong training efforts are also needed at the village level, both in working with village extension programs and in training villagers in managing new systems of land use rights and new technologies needed to support more sustainable land use patterns.

It has been suggested that three elements strongly support the village-oriented component of a strategy aimed at regenerating sustainable agriculture in hill areas.[27] These elements comprise (1) catchment authorities, (2) community budgets, and (3) community forestry as an integral package of administrative reform. These reflect the basic realities of the Himalayas: the nature of the topography and the high proportion of common land. Administrative units should reflect the natural resource areas defined by catchments. The large proportion of common land can then be managed for the good of all hill people.

Hazard-zone mapping, another useful technique for land planning in hill areas, is used to assess the magnitude, severity, and extent of environmental hazards and their possible consequences and to identify the population exposed to risk. Mapping involves in-depth investigation of many factors related to the land resource base as well as information relating to current land use patterns.[28] Once zones are identified as currently or potentially hazardous, public policy can come into play by banning or restricting specific activities within the zone. This idea has been taken one step further, with a strong case made for defining a minimum data set needed to make decisions for specific purposes.[29]

3. Promotion of Outmigration

Since rural-urban and hills-plains linkages exist even in the most remote hill areas, sustainable approaches to agricultural technology must not be confined solely to the agricultural sector. The Tennessee Valley Authority experience in the United States is an early example of a design that recognized this reality. Heavy emphasis was placed on more sustainable agricultural practices such as terracing, crop-pasture rotation, farm woodlots, contour farming, and permanent pastures. This emphasis was reinforced by industrialization in the area, which created alternative employment opportunities, relieved pressure on marginal lands to produce erosive cash crops such as cotton and corn, prompted off-farm migration and farm consolidation, and created other sources of income that part-time farmers could reinvest in their farms.

As the marginal product of labor in off-farm activities rises, labor tends to be attracted out of rural areas, where its marginal product in agriculture is the lowest. In the context of hill agriculture, this movement tends to be away from those areas where the marginal cost of cultivating additional areas is the highest, where labor inputs in production support activities are highest, where the productivity of support areas is lowest, and where ecological conditions have led to the lowest yields. The creation of employment opportunities in rural areas or in urban areas can have a major impact on taking fragile, marginal lands out of agricultural production—or at least putting them under longer-term enterprises such as tree crops or permanent pastures.

The role of public expenditures in creating *long-term* solutions to the problems of poverty and environment in the hills needs careful consideration. This includes assessment of: the cost per job created in the hills versus areas more favorable for industrial development; the use of public subsidies on consumable items for hill residents versus the number of productive jobs that could be created with these funds elsewhere in the economy; the effect of these subsidies on keeping too many people in the hills and the impact this has on the environment; and the use of public funds for programs whose higher rates of return have been amply demonstrated, such as population programs, basic-skills education, public health, and agricultural research.

Outmigration is a necessary but by itself insufficient condition to improve living levels and to stem environmental degradation in the hills. It must be effectively linked to the four other major policy thrusts discussed in this section and to the specific development programs that flow from those policy thrusts.

4. Institutional Structure and Public Policies to Meet Poor People's Needs

A number of public policies can help lead to a more sustainable environment. The first is agricultural pricing policy, with the most common pattern being subsidization of food prices for urban consumers. This tends to lower producer incomes. Short-term needs consequently dominate decisionmaking—since producers have little time or capital to invest in conservation measures, land improvement, or longer-term investments such as the planting of trees or perennial fodders. Input subsidies have the additional effects of encouraging expansion of cultivation into more marginal areas, leading to pesticide abuse, and prompting the establishment of uneconomic grazing operations in fragile areas.[30]

Land distribution and land tenure also are key issues of public policy that need to be considered in promoting sustainable agriculture in hill areas. The relationship between access to land resources and poverty has been examined in many studies. Links to environmental degradation, however, are less obvious. Large landholders often push small farmers or landless laborers into regions of low agricultural potential and areas that are ecologically sensitive. Farmers without well-defined land tenure have less incentive either to conserve the land or to make long-term decisions that could enhance the sustainability of their agriculture (tree crops, agroforestry, soil conservation measures, fencing, technological improvements). They are also less likely to gain access to capital without having a secure land title to pledge as security.

Another issue concerns the impact of economic policy on natural resource utilization. The traditional piecemeal, project-by-project approach to patch up damage already done must be supported and supplemented by long-range programs that integrate environmental concerns and natural resource management directly into economic and social policy.[31] This integration can be achieved through investment programs supporting environmental objectives and through the promotion of economic, social, and institutional policies and incentives that influence positively the behavior of public agencies, major resource users, and the myriad small producers who utilize natural resources. Economic incentives—backed up by strong local organization and support as well as technical assistance—must replace the "administrative fiat" approach that has been unsuccessful in changing patterns of resource use motivated by self-interest and survival.

On the issue of appropriate institutional structures, current political and administrative structures are seldom able to cope with the complex set of problems arising from accelerated use of natural resources or large public investments in dams, forests, roads, and irrigation systems. Another common problem is that the parameters of watersheds (often the most appropriate unit for managing natural resources) never coincide with administrative or political boundaries and often cross national borders as well. Coordination and control of natural resource use to address externalities and to implement incentive systems that affect several sectors will require powerful public authorities within the functional, regional, or national ministries.

One major issue in the area of institutional structures concerns the role of nongovernmental organizations (NGOs) in the implementation process. Implementation of comprehensive plans will cut across many government agencies and political boundaries, making smooth implementation via normal bureaucratic channels difficult if not impossible.

Therefore it is recommended that specific implementation activities be carried out by qualified NGOs with line technical agencies operating only in the areas of technical guidance, setting objectives, and coordinating resources at the national level. Specific areas where NGOs may have a comparative advantage are in village-based programs that require a lot of decentralized decisionmaking, good links to outside sources of assistance, group organizations, and self-help programs. Of the main policy areas mentioned above, reforestation and improved management of communal lands stand out as good potential candidates for NGO involvement. Possibilities also exist for doing a better job of implementing locally based watershed management plans and in planning village use of, and investment in, natural resources.

Perhaps the most important of needed changes in institutional structures concerns the role of women in agriculture and natural resource utilization in the hills. In the Himalayas, women are usually responsible for decisions about: livestock management; collection of fuelwood, fodder, and leaf litter from the forest; preparation and application of compost; collection and consumption of water; and consumption of fuel. These are the key decisions regarding natural resource use. Ignoring this fact in formulating policies and programs for hill agriculture and natural resource management is irresponsible.

Women must be assured access to the incentive systems necessary to lessen environmental degradation and poverty, and they must be a target group for promoting new practices and new technologies. Improvements in technology that demand more labor will be problematic, however, unless the amount of time demanded for support activities can be reduced—most probably through reforestation on a managed basis. A high payoff would be obtained by introducing labor-saving technologies for women in conjunction with technologies that raise productivity. Technologies that benefit women would also improve nutrition among children of pre-school age, as food production would increase, and more time could be devoted to caring for children.

The following points illustrate the more appropriately women-oriented agenda to be addressed by those who design and implement policy:

- Focus existing and new development efforts more specifically on the productive activities carried out by women and ensure their participation at all stages;
- Introduce improvements to ensure that women get sufficient information through existing channels;
- Ascertain that programs focused on community forestry, community grasslands—and even fuel-efficient cooking stoves—in fact reach women;
- In designing and implementing programs, take into account the constraints on women's time imposed by the multitude of their productive and other household responsibilities, as well as social constraints on their participation in programs whose format ignores cultural considerations.

5. Promotion of New and Adapted Technologies

This section synthesizes the numerous references made throughout the chapter to potential technologies that can help promote more sustainable agriculture in the hills and help overcome some of the constraints facing farm families.

A major policy thrust is needed to promote labor-saving technologies oriented toward women. These must be considered on a household basis and include: rural water supplies, improved food processing and food preparation technologies, agroforestry to reduce collection time for fuelwood and fodder, labor-saving management practices for livestock raising, improved cooking devices, and simple agricultural tools to reduce drudgery in the fields. Along the same lines, mini-hydroelectric plants should be fully exploited so that low-cost power can assist with cooking, heating, and food processing. Rapid advances in solar power and photovoltaic cell technologies can have potential impact in remote areas and greatly reduce pressures on forest resources as well as reduce household labor requirements.

Rapid advances in communication technologies and cost reductions for communication equipment is also helping remote hill areas in many ways as well as improving mobility and the efficiency of public services to remote areas.

In the more traditional areas of agricultural research, clonal propagation techniques are showing great promise to carry out mass propagation of superior multi-purpose tree species that are difficult to multiply under farmer conditions of heavy lopping. Low labor costs in developing countries help keep the cost per tree cloned to reasonable levels. Biological nitrogen-fixation must receive more emphasis—particularly on ways to incorporate green manure crops into traditional cropping patterns.

Improved seed storage in remote areas is also possible through the use of low-cost metal bins that can be transported to remote areas. The production of quality seed is a key link to fully utilize the superior varieties of plants being bred for hill conditions.

More emphasis is also needed on conventional agricultural research for hill crops, livestock and livestock feeding systems, high value crops, and non-traditional crops that can be introduced into hill areas from other continents.

Conclusions

Hillside agriculture represents tremendous diversity as well as the common features of pervasive poverty, a declining resource base, and increasing degradation of the environment upon which hill communities exist in a fragile web. The relationships between the rapid growth of both human and animal populations, the pressure that this exerts upon the limited natural resource base, and the increasing poverty that results have been amply described in this chapter. The historical response to these trends has been outmigration by the male workforce and the repatriation of earnings to supplement household incomes. This response, however, has been inadequate to reverse the current unfavorable trends, and various public policy responses are needed to create a more favorable climate for improving hill agriculture, increasing resource productivity, and stabilizing returns.

The focal point of environment- and equity-minded policies must be the improvement of the low labor productivity—and, consequently, the low incomes—of the people who live in the developing world's hillside areas. Specific efforts outlined above in relation to five major recommended policy thrusts to improve the long-term future of hill populations and the resources base of these areas include: (a) promotion of continued outmigration to regions where labor productivity is higher, (b) allocation of capital away from subsidies and toward productive investments with strong employment-creating effects, (c) careful balancing of job creation costs in the hills vs. more favored areas, (d) increased efforts to promote higher-value agricultural products along with better marketing infrastructure, (e) more and better-focused research for the hills that considers constraints and opportunities at the village and household level, (f) increased emphasis on forestry to raise overall household productivity and reduce environmental stresses, (g) more work on alternative institutional structures and management practices to promote village-based forestry and agro-forestry and drastically reduce overgrazing, (h) development of new sources of energy for remote areas and more efficient utilization of existing sources of energy, and (i) appropriate public policies that provide secure land tenure and promote long-term investments in trees, conservation structures, and improved livestock.

Notes

[1] E. P. Eckholm, *Losing Ground: Environmental Stress and World Food Prospects* (New York: W. W. Norton, 1976), p. 74.
[2] Andrés R. Novoa, and J. L. Posner, eds., *International Seminar on Agricultural and Forestry Research in the Highlands of the American Tropics Americas,* Technical Report No. 11 (Turrialba, Costa Rica: Centro Agronomico Tropical de Investigacion y Ensenánza 1981), p. 14.
[3] Development Alternatives, Inc. (DAI), *Fragile Lands: A Theme Paper on Problems, Issues and Approaches for the Development of Humid Tropical Lowlands and Steep Slopes in the Latin American Region* (Washington, D.C.: Development Alternatives, Inc., 1984).
[4] J. J. Warford, "Natural Resources and Economic Policy in Developing Countries," *Annals of Regional Science,* Vol. 21 (1984), pp. 3–17.
[5] Ibid.
[6] Deepak Bajracharya, "Fuel, Food or Forest? Dilemmas in a Nepali Village," *World Development,* Vol. 11, No. 12 (1983), pp. 1070–71.
[7] T. B. S. Mahat, D. M. Griffin, and K. R. Shepherd, "Human Impacts on Some Forests of the Middle Hills of Nepal—Part I: Forestry in the Context of the Traditional

Resources of the State," *Mountain Research and Development,* Vol. 6, No. 3 (1986), p. 228; and D. M. Griffin, K. R. Shepherd, and T. B. S. Mahat, "Human Impacts on Some Forests of the Middle Hills of Nepal—Part 5: Comparisons, Concepts and Some Policy Implications," *Mountain Research and Development,* Vol. 8, No. 1 (1988), pp. 48–50.

[8] Water and Energy Commission Secretariat, *Fuelwood Supply in the Districts of Nepal* (Kathmandu: Water and Energy Commission Secretariat, 1987).

[9] Brian Carson, "Erosion and Sedimentation Processes in the Nepalese Himalaya," ICIMOD Occasional Paper No. 1 (Kathmandu, Nepal: International Centre for Integrated Mountain Development, August, 1985), p. 11.

[10] See W. M. Fleming, "Phewa Tal Catchment Management Program: Benefits and Costs of Forestry and Soil Conservation in Nepal," in L. S. Hamilton, ed., *Forest and Watershed Development and Conservation in Asia and the Pacific* (Boulder, Colo.: Westview Press, 1983).

[11] K. S. Valdiya, "Accelerated Erosion and Landslide Prone Zones in the Central Himalaya Region," in J. S. Singh, ed., *Environmental Regeneration in the Himalaya: Concepts and Strategies* (Dehli: Kay-Kay Printers, 1985), pp. 24–26.

[12] S. K. Kumar and D. Hotchkiss, "Consequences of Deforestation for Women's Time Allocation, Agricultural Production, and Nutrition in Hill Areas of Nepal," *Research Report 69* (Washington, D.C.: International Food Policy Research Institute, October 1988) pp. 24–37; and U. Pandey and J. S. Singh, "Energy Flow Relationship Between Agro- and Forest Ecosystems in the Central Himalaya," *Environmental Conservation,* Vol. 11, No. 1 (1984), pp. 50–52.

[13] Kumar and Hotchkiss, "Consequences of Deforestation," ibid., pp. 46–60.

[14] M. G. Jackson, "A Strategy for Improving the Productivity of Livestock in the Hills of Uttar Pradesh," in Singh, ed., *Environmental Regeneration in the Himalaya,* op. cit., pp. 137–41; and R. R. Harwood, *Small Farm Development,* (Boulder, Colo.: Westview Press, 1979), pp. 93–100.

[15] Kumar and Hotchkiss, "Consequences of Deforestation," op. cit., pp. 24–37.

[16] T. S. Papola and B. K. Joshi, "Demography, Economy and Environment in the Development of Hill Areas of Uttar Pradesh," in Singh, ed., *Environmental Regeneration in the Himalaya,* op. cit., p. 189–95.

[17] S. S. Khanka, "Labour Migration and Its Effects in a Low Developed Region of Uttar Pradesh," in Singh, ed., *Environmental Regeneration in the Himalaya,* op. cit., p. 210.

[18] See, for example, Kumar and Hotchkiss, "Consequences of Deforestation," op. cit., pp. 42–45.

[19] For a fuller discussion of these issues, see C. P. Rees, "The Asian Development Bank's Approach to Environmental Planning and Management: Focus on Economic-cum-Environmental Studies," *Regional Development Dialogue,* Vol. 8, No. 3 (1987), pp. 1–11.

[20] Jackson, "A Strategy for Improving the Productivity of Livestock," op. cit., pp. 146–48.

[21] Papola and Joshi, "Demography, Economy and Environment" op. cit., pp. 194–95.

[22] R. K. Gupta and Y. K. Arora, "Technology for the Rejuvenation of Degraded Lands in the Himalaya," in Singh, ed., *Environmental Regeneration in the Himalaya,* op. cit., pp. 173–83.

[23] L. R. Singh and S. P. R. Chaurasia, "Role of Cereal and Vegetable Technology in Regeneration of Hill Region of Uttar Pradesh," in Singh, ed., *Environmental Regeneration in the Himalaya,* op. cit., pp. 214–26.

[24] N. P. Melkania and J. P. Tandon, "Dry Matter Yield and Strategies for Regeneration of Pastures in Central Himalaya," in Singh, ed., *Environmental Regeneration in the Himalaya,* op. cit., pp. 405–8.

[25] See Singh and Chaurasia, "Role of Cereal and Vegetable Technology" op. cit.

[26] S. Conlin and A. Falk, *Kosi Hills Area Rural Development Programme (KHARDEP), Nepal: A Study of the Socio-Economy of the Kosi Hills Area* (London: Land Resources Development Centre, 1979).

[27] N. Reynolds. "The Himalaya: Crisis in the Evolution of Policy and Programmes," in J. S. Lall, ed., *The Himalayas: Aspects of Change* (Delhi: Oxford University Press, 1981), pp. 461–473.

[28] See Valdiya, in Singh, ed., *Environmental Regeneration in the Himalaya,* op. cit., p. 33.

[29] Jack D. Ives, "Himalayan Environmental Regeneration: An Overview—What Are the Problems and How Can They Be Tackled?," in Singh, ed., *Environmental Regeneration in the Himalaya,* op. cit., pp. 1–11.

[30] Warford, "Natural Resources and Economic Policy," op. cit.

[31] Warford, ibid., p. 5.

Chapter 5

Environmental Dilemmas and the Urban Poor

Tim Campbell

Issues and Trade-Offs

Environmentalists familiar with urban development in the Third World
often see the large cities there as symptomatic of environmental decay:
They are overcrowded, bulging with the disordered growth of shanties,
congested with traffic, and poisoned by acrid air pollution and a lack of
sanitary facilities. Large cities in particular have grown rapidly out of
proportion with their ecological settings. This chapter examines in
detail some of the assumptions related to environmental decay and
addresses several key questions: Can development policy redress the
problems of urban gigantism causing imbalance between human and
natural systems? Can the rapid flow of rural migrants that fuels city
growth be slowed to a manageable pace? Can the imperatives of social
and economic well-being be made to fit within the constraints of the
natural environment in cities? Is it too late to save the poor in the cities
of the Third World?

   The discussion that follows answers all of these questions wholly or
in part in the negative. Gigantism per se is not the problem; indeed, to
the extent that the poor can take advantage of special informational
resources found only in the city, very large cities may be part of the solution to the environmental and economic problems confronting the urban
poor. While rural-to-urban migration still fuels city growth in Asia and
Africa and where agricultural productivity is low and good land is

scarce, the rapid growth of the very largest cities in Latin America is now due mainly to natural increase, not migration. Besides, as several other chapters in this volume argue, migration away from the working of fragile lands may be part of the solution to massive rural environmental destruction. Not all of the basic needs for human well-being can be met in cities in a harmonious way, but large improvements can be made without major environmental or technological breakthroughs. Finally, it is not too late to "save" the cities, but this form of the question, posed (like the others) mainly for rhetorical purposes, misses the point that environmental improvements—especially those often desired by urban elites—are costly, and capital for economic development is scarce. In this context, efforts to address environmental decay in large cities must make room for the rights of the poor to be informed about environmental dangers, to define their own priorities, and to live with the environmental consequences of their decisions.

This does not, however, mean that international donors, governments, and nongovernmental organizations (NGOs) cannot do more on the scientific, technological, and educational fronts to develop and disseminate new knowledge and new tools to meet the needs of the urban poor in developing nations; they *should*—and important changes are already visible as a result of such efforts in many parts of the world. But scientific, educational, and technological objectives must be focused in the right direction, and the policy debate so far regarding urban development, like the questions raised above, often misses the point.

Recasting the Debate

This chapter invokes the notion of an "urban ecosystem" to examine the environment-development trade-offs affecting the well-being of the poor in large Third World cities. The urban ecosystem idea makes it possible to visualize the city as a place in which a wide variety of resources—natural, human, and social—are intertwined, some created, some consumed, still others left as wastes.[1] Among the most important environmental resources for the urban poor are informational resources in the form of social ties and networks that help sustain the survival strategies of low-income populations. In light of this view, the widely observed "costs" of giant cities must be weighed against the environmental benefits that form much of the attraction of cities for the poor. Yet this is only one of many environment-development trade-offs in Third World cities. Resource consumption and degradation has taken a serious toll on the health and safety of all residents, as well as on the future development prospects for urbanized Third World countries.

This chapter is divided into three parts: The first will demonstrate the magnitude of the urban environmental challenge in terms of the scale of urbanization and the degree of poverty in Third World cities. The second section is the heart of the matter: the forms of environmental trade-offs facing policymakers into the next century, subdivided by scale. A discussion of environment-development trade-offs at the household level will be followed by consideration of the environmental problems of the city writ large. Policy prescriptions and suggested areas for action form the third part of the chapter. Policy recommendations made in the course of the chapter will be recapitulated and recast in terms of priority.

Urban Development and Poverty: The Magnitude of the Problem

Urbanization in the Third World

Urbanization is perhaps the most dramatic social transformation taking place in the Third World since World War II, and despite the decades of rapidly growing cities, from a demographic standpoint, the process has only just begun. The urban population of the Third World increased by 450 million between 1975 and 1985. The rural population increased by only 300 million during this period, and most of this increase took place in China.[2] By 2010, another 1.2 billion people will be living in cities, and according to United Nations projections, just 7 per cent of this Third World population increase will be rural. Table 1 shows the distribution of this population growth by the principal regions.

Cities are growing everywhere at more than twice the rate of rural populations, but there are distinct regional differences. African cities are growing at an annual rate of over 6 per cent; even more dazzling urbanization rates took place several decades ago in Latin America, when oil was still cheap. Latin America is by far the most urbanized area, even though it accounts for less than a quarter of the total urban population of the Third World. With a "head start" of several decades, Latin America may also be the most likely forerunner of demographic shifts and environmental problems that will arise in other regions over the next few decades.

By the turn of the century, the Third World will have thirty-seven cities with populations of over five million; six of them are already that size in Latin America, and three more will join their ranks during the next ten years. The growth of very large cities (those with populations of over five million) was pushed initially by migration. This expansion, however, is no longer primarily a consequence of people leaving the land to seek their fortunes in the cities. Migration ceased being the driving

Table 1: Urban Population Estimates and Projections, 1985 and 2010 (millions and percentages)

Region	1985				2010			
	Total	Rural	Urban	Urban as % of Total	Total	Rural	Urban	Urban as % of Total
Africa	453.5	336.2	117.3	25.9	988.6	566.7	421.9	42.7
Asia	1,669.7	1,191.9	477.8	28.6	2,563.9	1,408.9	1,154.9	45.0
Latin America	331.4	112.6	218.8	66.0	536.9	116.4	420.4	78.3
Total	2,454.6	1,640.7	813.9	33.2	4,089.4	2,092.2	1,997.2	48.8

Sources: U.N. projections, and A. van Huyck, "Urbanization in the Developing Countries" (unpublished paper prepared for U.S. Agency for International Development).

force behind urban growth more than ten years ago, at least in Latin America. Furthermore, most experts now agree that attempts to slow rural-to-urban growth have been futile, for today the urban poor in Latin America are born to urban parents. Finding ways to survive in this setting is increasingly difficult.

Urban Poverty

The poor form the largest single economic grouping of urban residents in the Third World. By relative measures—that is, based on the distribution of income—nearly three times more rural than urban households lived in poverty in 1975, according to World Bank estimates. Because of the rapid rate of urbanization, however, this relationship will be reversed by the turn of the century: More poor households will be located in cities than in rural areas. Many of the largest cities are comprised of households living under the "poverty line"—that is, having less income than that needed to buy the minimum requirement of calories and proteins, shelter, clothing, and other necessities. In Latin American cities, the proportion of poor inhabitants ranges from 25 per cent to over 50 per cent of total city populations. Thus cities are the principal locus of trade-offs in environment and poverty alleviation.

But statistical measures of poverty are not very useful for understanding the environmental concomitants of being poor in Third World cities. In this setting, poverty means not only that elemental necessities are often out of reach, but that progress in one area often comes at the expense of advances elsewhere. For instance, Turner showed twenty years ago that low-income families living in squatter conditions gradually expand their shelter and secure a property title, first giving up good location for a foothold, and then, as resources and opportunities permit, improving amenities and increasing their shelter's size.[3] Similar trade-offs are seen in other areas. The largest fractions of peoples' daily lives are consumed in obtaining bare necessities such as water and cooking fuel. These chores often require many hours of hauling and rob many, especially young females, of the opportunity to obtain an elementary education. Compared to urban populations as a whole, the urban poor also have larger families, lower life expectancies by years or decades (especially for females), and mortality and morbidity rates that on a daily basis reflect the deaths of hundreds of thousands of children under five years of age. Moreover, in this decade most Third World countries have experienced economic decline; heavy indebtedness combined with other factors such as low commodity prices signifies a deterioration of environmental conditions for the poor in the medium term. The worsening of nutritional and child mortality levels in a sample of countries struggling to make the economic adjustments needed to improve growth has been documented in a major UNICEF study.[4]

Dilemmas in Environmental Policy

These severe resource limitations underscore the imperative of addressing poverty when formulating environmental strategies for the Third World. Narrowly conceived environmental policy can adversely affect the economic circumstances of the poor, just as small changes in the macroeconomic context have had a negative environmental impact. This chapter does not attempt to catalog all of the dilemmas for policymakers regarding the poor. Rather, it focuses on a few selected issues that are common to many regions, concern basic needs, are closely associated with the health or survival of the poor, and affect the most people. Using these criteria—and for purposes of simplicity of presentation and convenience in policy formulation—urban environmental problems affecting the poor can be divided into two main categories: (1) dilemmas in the microenvironmental setting—the shelter and its immediate environs, and (2) those of the larger physical and social setting, described and largely managed at the level of urban, regional, and national policy.

A number of important issues are omitted: food security, tobacco, lead in gasoline and formaldehyde in alternative vehicular fuels, industrial safety, and nuclear energy. Food security, the sure and daily provision of adequate calories and proteins, is a rural as well as an urban problem of major proportions and deserves separate treatment. Other issues—the taking of productive agricultural land to accommodate urbanization and the pollution of air and water—also deserve more detailed treatment, but are subsumed in the discussion of topics of more immediate relevance to the survival of the poor.

The Environment of Human Shelter

Cooking and Fuel Substitution

Energy specialists often point out that the quality of urban cooking fuels is frequently higher than that of fuels used by rural households. However, not all cooking in urban households makes use of high-quality, "clean" cooking fuels. Many low-income households still depend on traditional biomass fuels. Urban households in Pakistan, for instance, consumed about 18 per cent of the country's fuelwood in 1979 and may have accounted for as much as half the fuelwood consumed in the country over the past ten years.[5] Dung and fuelwood form a significant fraction of fuel stocks in Karachi, as do charcoal and fuelwood on the outskirts of Mexico City. Relatively high urban incomes, even within the low-income ranges, outbid the rural poor for wood and other fuels and help drive deforestation. Vyasulu and Reddy report that fuelwood for Bangalore comes from as far away as 140 kilometers.[6] Thus a critical element for the survival of the poor contributes to lasting environmental imbalances that can have repercussions on both the city and soil conditions in distant watersheds.

The harvesting of biomass energy sources, erosion, and the consequent flooding are not the only problems created by the demand for biomass fuels. Indoor cooking with low-temperature fossil fuels leads to respiratory ailments that are barely understood; indeed, they are as yet poorly measured. Survey evidence shows, however, that indoor environmental contamination may be related to a range of respiratory disorders, tuberculosis, and cancer. These problems probably affect women and children more seriously than men, making it more difficult to gauge the economic impact (for instance, in lost work time). Health problems appear to arise from two sources: First is the prolonged exposure to the products of combustion of biomass and possibly lignin burned at relatively low temperatures; second is the problem of poor ventilation, irrespective of fuel type.[7]

Proponents of alternative technologies advocate "soft" (that is, environmentally benign) pathways to providing cooking fuels for the poor—solar stoves, for instance. The first experiences with solar stoves, in southern Mexico and Guatemala, quickly fell prey to the many pitfalls of extraneous technologies not linked to the cultural and social milieu of the intended users. These problems, outlined concisely by Jequier, are now relatively well understood but far from solved.[8] Even the Lorena and other high-efficiency cookstoves, which have proven promising in many environments, run against the tide of experience, which shows that modifications of indigenous designs and technologies are best.

Bulky, immovable, and inflexible, often-untried Lorena stoves, for instance, like "clean" fuel substitutes, also cost more in terms of initial capital and recurrent expenditures than the traditional open fires or brick stoves and fuelwood. In addition there are the costs of uncertainty: the risk of loss of capital or social station if the stoves fail to perform for some reason. Again, these are risks borne mostly by the poor, not by the proponents of alternative technologies.

Nevertheless, these stoves, and numerous other ideas like densified biomass and producer gas, offer some promise and require a lot more resources and support. A 10-per cent increase in the efficiency of cook-stoves could save millions of tons of fuelwood per year in the Third World. The solution to the health problem lies with increasing the thermodynamic efficiency of the cooking process: Contain the heat, vent the exhausts. Human and capital resources in this area would produce multiple benefits. Research and development must follow several tacks. First, invent more efficient forms of traditional fuels; second, perfect stoves; and third and most difficult, reduce initial and recurrent costs for the poor as well as offset the inherent risks of new ventures. One promising example is the "packaging" of fuels, as in densified, or compressed, biomass suitable for withstanding long periods of storage, rough transport, marketing in small and large quantities, and burning in modules in high-efficiency, ventilated, indoor stoves. World Bank experiences document that the social acceptance and commercial viability of low-cost, locally made cookstoves are prerequisites for their success.[9] These need to be complemented by marketing systems for renewable fuels such as densified biomass, which reduces the volume per unit of energy and makes feasible the harvesting of slash-and-mill wastes.

Environmental Sanitation

Waterborne diseases traceable to poor environmental health conditions account for many hundreds of thousands of deaths per year among the poor in the Third World, and a growing proportion of those at risk will be urban. Ironically, while the media and international environmental groups have focused increased world attention on the destruction of rain forests in developing countries, they have distracted international development assistance organizations from an important problem. Household sanitation, which affects many millions of poor people, generally has not been the target of educational and action campaigns on the environment in Third World countries. Water supply and sewerage have never accounted for more than 6 per cent of World Bank annual lending, and this figure includes both rural and urban projects. If the costs and benefits of investments in environmental improvement are weighed in light of their significance to the poor, urban sanitation improvements are among the most effective of any short-term measures. Since there is sufficient capital neither for the elimination of risks of child death and illness due to waterborne disease nor for the creation of environmentally viable options to slash-and-burn techniques in the rain forest, policymakers in donor agencies, borrowing countries, and nongovernmental organizations alike face a trade-off.

A full-scale attack on urban sanitation problems in developing countries would require huge increases in investment. For example, at least a *threefold* increase in historical levels of annual investment would be needed to reach World Health Organization goals for water and sanitation services in urban Latin America by the turn of the century.[10] This would entail the expenditure of approximately $50 billion to catch up by the year 2000. These are gross estimates that probably undercount the effects of rapid household formation. In Brazil for example, household formation is presently occurring 20 per cent faster than the growth of the urban population as a whole. The youth bulge in Brazil's population pyramid is moving into the age range of marriage, and this combination is generating a demand for 800,000 connections to water and sanitation per year—just to keep up with present levels of service.

The stakes in this competition for capital are dramatic. Although no hard correlations have been drawn to isolate the health benefits per dollar invested in water and sanitation, it is obvious from the evidence that morbidity and mortality go down in rough proportion to the volume of water, good or bad, flowing through households. Again in Brazil, child mortality among the urban poor in the Northeast is 50 per cent higher than among the poor with water in the larger cities of the Center and Center-South. In the same way, the children of poor families in São Paulo face many times greater risks from waterborne diseases than do middle-income children living only several city blocks away. In a country like Brazil, child mortality indices translate into tens of thousands of deaths annually. The prevention of child mortality is a function of many variables: wealth, education, health care, and the level of knowledge and awareness of young mothers. But water, drainage, and sanitation are key factors in keeping environmental pathogens from finding human hosts.

Despite the high cost of sanitation, the problem is not insoluble, nor do solutions involve major technological breakthroughs. The basic formula for improving local environmental conditions was invented by grassroots groups concerned with housing in the 1950s and 1960s, the period of most rapid urbanization in Latin America. The formula involves the social organization of low-income groups and their exertion of political pressure on local and national officials, coupled with "sweat equity" and capital channeled into the construction of household and community facilities. The solution also involves low-cost, locally manufactured hardware (plumbing, sanitary sheds, concrete caps for pit latrines) that can be upgraded and installed using labor-intensive techniques.

Both the social and technological factors have been tested in urban and rural settings in Africa and in large cities in Asia and Latin America. The central technologies range from improved ventilated pit latrines, which cut costs per served household by two-thirds, to improved microdrainage at the neighborhood level, to simple modifications of standard sewerage designs that reduce diameters, excavation, inspection chambers, and other standard specifications—all of which can result in reductions of between 25 per cent and 50 per cent in the costs of conventional sewerage systems. More than 40,000 urban Brazilians and tens of thousands of rural Africans and Asians are benefiting from on-site or simplified waste disposal systems. The most rapidly changing factor in this equation is the socio-political context created by democratization and decentralization, at least in Latin America. In countries like Brazil, Mexico, and Colombia, freely elected mayors with new powers granted by constitutional and other reforms have dramatically shifted political alliances between local governments and community groups. In dozens of cities in these and other countries, local alliances are carrying out community projects unthinkable ten years ago.

Environmental groups and donors can contribute a great deal to this process, and the timing for work in this area is propitious. The international development assistance community has been much more active in rural areas and in basic research. Now the focus must be placed on (1) redefining the environmental problem to incorporate sanitation more explicitly into the environment-development agenda for action, (2) educating the poor about household environmental sanitation, and (3) translating the knowledge developed in rural settings to the urban poor.

Conclusions: Engaging an Old Environmental Front

It is in some sense ironic that the immediate, household-level environmental problems of indoor air quality and sanitation are often ignored or given slight treatment by activist environmental groups, international agencies, governments, and even national groups concerned with the environment. Most of the international attention over the past ten years has been focused on issues of "the commons," or those that threaten global tragedy. But the adverse effects of household airborne and water-carried wastes on child mortality and female life expectancy are of no less global proportions than, say, the destruction of tropical forests, and in immediate human terms they may be the most urgent of all worldwide environmental problems. Certainly, the immediate threats to the urban poor of hazardous indoor air quality and inadequate sanitation exceed the adverse effects of global warming, or even vehicular pollution. Of course the world needs action on both these and other fronts. And much can be done to improve the hygienic conditions of the poor to save lives, create jobs, and assure the welfare of children.

The challenge for development assistance agencies, developing-country governments, and nongovernmental organizations is to redirect their considerable intellectual, communications, educational, and capital resources to address the "front line" environmental battles on behalf of the Third World urban poor. For development assistance agencies, this is a tall order. A first step must be to begin to redefine the dimensions of global environmental and urban problems. One of the basic philosophical issues concerns the need to adopt an environmental ethos that takes into account the threat of immediate loss of life related directly to components of basic processes such as cooking, water, and wastes—as well as the threat of losing unrecorded biota that may be crucial for the welfare of future generations. Another problem has to do with the practical matter of donor organization and policy. Despite the debate that has raged over the past few decades about rural versus urban bias in development assistance, the truth is that the "urban sector" has always been fundamentally at odds with the economic and programmatic dimensions of development assistance agencies, simply because of the multidimensionality of things urban. "Urban sector" interests are now experiencing a renaissance in the U.S. Agency for International Development (USAID) after nearly twenty years of emphasis on agricultural and rural development. Environmental matters are mentioned in USAID's most recent report to Congress. But urban issues are not nearly so prominent in USAID's environmental policy. The World Bank is even further from a synthesis. What urban focus the World Bank had before 1987 has been blurred by the internal reorganization of that institution. To this policy no man's land, urban environmental matters must be added.

Despite this disarray, donor agencies can still help borrowers develop the socio-technical strategies that are needed to improve the environment of household shelter. There is much to build on from past experience with housing and alternative technologies to improve cooking efficiency and waste disposal. Research and development is needed to improve stoves and fuels and to elaborate on waste disposal hardware such as pour flush toilets, small and maneuverable vacuum pumps for latrine systems, inspection boxes in sewer lines, and the like. Most important, donors and NGOs can expand their expertise in the socio-cultural dimensions of cooking and waste disposal in order to understand how the short-term gains in health may come to be valued by the poor as much as or more than the loss of status they perceive for having a second-class—that is, less than standard—system for cooking and waste disposal. Work is also needed to invent ways for these new values to be converted into tangible contributions of cash and labor by intended beneficiaries. Finally, the approach needs economic and technical evaluations to measure results and find ways to cut costs.

Environmental Trade-Offs in the Cityscape

Giant Cities and Environmental Resources

1. *Informational Resources.* The continued growth of cities, even the giant cities of the Third World, generates its own momentum for reasons that are advantageous to the poor. One of the emerging qualities of cities is that they produce their own kind of environmental resources that cannot be found in the countryside. Cities are filled with information-intensive resources—interpersonal networks of exchange, chance encounters on the street, various forms of printed and electronic media—much of which comes at little or no monetary cost to the poor. Tips about employment opportunities, locations of "squattable" land, or the identity of someone who can clandestinely tap a water main to provide an indoor source of water are examples of informational resources that lead to concrete improvements in the quality of life and the environment of the urban poor. Informational resources constitute what Larissa Lomnitz once thought of in metaphorical terms as "hunting and gathering" grounds for the poor.[11] Despite more than three decades of ethnographic literature on urban settings, we still need to strengthen our understanding of how the poor gain access to these and other kinds of resources and transform them into tangible improvements or a means of making a living.

Informational resources in cities are closely analogous to economic infrastructure; both are necessary inputs into productive enterprises. It is now known that the so-called informal sector—an inadequate term to describe a wide assortment of industries, commerce, and trade operating at various scales, with differing forms of and access to capital, and subject to different degrees of government knowledge and control—constitutes a growing fraction of employment and an unknown proportion of domestic product. Yet in contrast to the importance development assistance strategies give to "productive infrastructure" for industry, and to the "social infrastructure" of water and sanitation, there is no concept of a "communications or informational infrastructure" that supports and advances the informal or subterranean productive activities of urban households and commerce. On the contrary, the economic and environmental literature scarcely mentions the resource inputs from the urban environment. Moreover, the rich environmental resource base, like the biological wealth found in tropical forests, is a function of large-scale systems and ceases to exist below a minimum city size. Therefore, there is more than a little irony in the policy approach—for instance of USAID and the Inter-American Development Bank (IDB), which for many years was phrased in terms of retaining migrants in the countryside or otherwise preventing the growth of large cities. Such policies may be seen as roughly analogous to arbitrarily limiting the richness of biotic resources in the humid tropics by keeping forestry reserves small.

This is not to argue for "megacities" or to minimize the special environmental drawbacks of urban areas, which are real, detrimental to human health and other life forms, and far from solved. But it is important to recognize the positive, potentially decisive impact that informational resources in large city environments can have in improving the quality of life of the poor. This means first that policymakers in donor agencies and countries alike must give explicit recognition to the potential benefits of large city size and structure technical and financial assistance accordingly. Second, more research is needed on the kinds of knowledge concerning the environment that circulates in cities and about the mechanisms of informal learning. Very little international attention has been focused on organizational and institutional structures such as kinship networks, workers' groups, cooperatives, social clubs, and the like—components of the informational infrastructure—that are used to spread news and learning and to recruit participation in neighborhood improvement. NGOs and local environmental groups have already demonstrated many times—through confederations, housing cooperatives, women's groups, NGO networks, political associations, and other grassroots organizations—that a communications apparatus can function effectively both locally and internationally. More needs to be done to turn this effort inward, to strengthen the sociological dimension, and to focus on the problems of fuels, cooking, sanitation, and other aspects of the urban environment.[12]

Third, donor agencies must step up efforts to incorporate community involvement and participation in projects to improve the urban environment. This policy approach has been tried only sparingly in Latin America. One good example is in a World Bank loan to Brazil to finance low-cost sanitation technology for the urban poor. This technology yields benefits for both the poor and for lenders. For the poor, it means more direct attention to local environmental problems. For lenders, it means having the benefit of local knowledge about specific conditions in the project area. Also, the direct involvement of beneficiaries means increased local counterpart contributions. But to generate community participation, donors need to upgrade the sociological skills of their own professional staffs and address problems of weak local governments.

2. *Land Capability.* Another quite distinct aspect of large city size is settlement on steep, swampy, or otherwise unsuitable land on the periphery of cities. High land prices and the limited availability of land force the poor (and in many cases the middle classes) to settle on marginal land. During the periods of most rapid city growth in the 1960s and 1970s, settlements sprang up in marsh and lake bed preserves in Mexico City; shallow bays and inlets in Salvador, Bahia (Brazil), and Manila; estuaries in Dacca; steep hillsides in La Paz; and polluted lagoons in Cartagena. Many such communities today are large and consolidated. Perhaps Netzahuacoyotl is the most dramatic example. By the early 1980s, this community in the state of Mexico, perched on the outside edge of the Federal District but integrated functionally and visually into the general fabric of Mexico City, numbered nearly two million residents and was the second or third largest city in the country. Netzahuacoyotl is subject to adverse conditions of aridity or flooding— just as over-water settlements in Salvador and Manila are vulnerable to contamination by human wastes, and hillside settlements of tens of thousands of residents in La Paz and Rio de Janeiro are subject to sudden earth movements and flooding. Heavy rains in La Paz, Rio de Janeiro, and Dacca have left thousands dead and tens of thousands homeless in just the past few years.

These cases illustrate a conflict between environmental safety and the need for affordable housing. Similar conflicts arise in relation to the location of industry in many Third World cities. The gas facility explosion in Mexico City and the Union Carbide disaster in Bhopal are vivid illustrations of these dangers. But there are thousands of other examples that do not make front-page news. Before the Brazilian government took drastic clean-up actions, the industrial city of Cubatao near São Paulo was contaminated with airborne lead and mercury, along with numerous organic compounds that were suspected of playing a role in the high local incidence of cancers and birth defects. Many more not-so-striking examples of inappropriate or incompatible land use in large cities have led to long-run environmental problems such as the depletion of groundwater, the cooptation of agricultural lands, erosion, and the disruption or interference with estuaries or wetlands.

Controls over land use and urban development have been weak in Third World cities, and most of the tools and techniques customarily employed in developed countries—land use planning and master plans, zoning, land and building permits, and property taxation—are overwhelmed in developing countries by the power of demand, administrative burdens, special interests, and graft. During the periods of most rapid city growth, many governments undertook wholesale resettlement of low-income populations as a solution to inappropriate—usually meaning politically inconvenient or embarrassing—settlements. Resettlement and the low-income housing projects built to accommodate the poor were rarely satisfactory solutions from the social, economic, or architectural standpoints. As much as a third of urban settlement in the 1970s in Latin America was organized and sponsored by quasi-legal circumstances. Some of the legal requisites for settlement—registration of land title, installation of infrastructure, and acquisition of building permits—were properly completed, but illegal payments were made at some point in the process, eroding the integrity of the land control mechanism. Not even large-scale projects sponsored by the public sector can be counted on to follow the environmental or other criteria adopted to guide land use in Third World cities.

Donors and governments must focus on several fundamentals in city and regional planning in order to tackle the problems of incompatible land use. First, donors and governments are beginning to turn attention to strengthening local governments and, in particular, to gaining control of land registration and taxation. Many countries are undergoing a process of political, administrative, and financial decentralization that devolves new powers, and usually new resources, to municipal governments. International lending agencies have already begun to focus on local governments as the new locus of lending activity in Latin America. More attention needs to be given to exploring the possibilities of approaches suggested by a handful of experiments in large-scale urban development over the past several decades. One is the cooperation of the public and private sectors in facilities development—such as private financing of shopping, business, and residential facilities in rail stations and transfer points. Another is the reclamation of urban land through careful management of solid waste landfills. NGOs can play an important supportive role in the areas of environmental information and planning techniques, among others. One area of great need is to develop low-cost solutions to land registration and the strengthening of information systems, such as those used to control land title transfers. Other areas that require strengthening are impact analysis, land capability studies, and land use management tools. In the industrialized world, this group of analytical tools is fairly well developed, some of them to the point of expert systems. Some of these methods could be adapted to relieve specific bottlenecks in Third World cities, namely the problems of limited hardware support, intermittent backup of technical expertise, and the scant resources available to develop the data bases required to make such techniques useful.

Food, Water, and Energy

Since the populations of most Third World cities are growing faster than the supporting infrastructure and institutional apparatus, it is not uncommon to see mismatches and disproportions in the major supply and circulation systems. Food, water, and energy are among the most basic of these systems and are fundamental for low-income populations. Because these needs are basic, governments sometimes exert herculean efforts to maintain minimum flows of water and food. The supply of water is a major problem for most of the largest cities in the Third World—either because the natural resource is not available or because it is expensive to import. In a few instances, such as the water system for Mexico City, where detailed data have been collected, it is possible to see the extent to which water shortages are overcome by the brute force of capital- and energy-intensive technologies such as massive water basin transfer systems. The consequences for the natural environment are marked, and the beneficiaries of this expensive water system in Mexico City are, because of geographical circumstances, rich and poor alike. Therefore, supply system reforms that achieve greater environmental balance will have a heavy impact on the poor.

Although each system for supplying food, water, and energy in Mexico City is separate in terms of supply lines, markets, ministries, and geographic incidence, each is in fact tightly intertwined functionally with the others. In Mexico City, as in many Third World cities, major components of the water and power infrastructure were built two to four decades ago, during times of relatively cheap energy. The food and water systems are still heavily energy dependent, as any outsider might suspect. But it is not so obvious that the energy and food systems also depend on water, and that the water and energy systems are dependent on food production technology and export policy.[13] To illustrate, to meet water supply needs in the Valley of Mexico by the mid-1990s, large interbasin transfer systems have been built that pump today nearly a fifth of the city's water, about 12 cubic meters per second (cms) from the Cutzamala reservoir—100 kilometers to the west and nearly 1,000 meters below the level of the Valley rim. Several larger catchment basins—Tecolutla, 200 kilometers to the east and nearly 2,000 meters below the Valley rim, and Amacuzac, a rich agricultural basin—are slated to be tapped for another 20 cubic meters. The capital costs of these projects are very large, but the energy requirements are so great that they dramatically transform the pattern of energy use in the city. A similar, if less dramatic pattern holds for food supply: Large volumes of food are imported by truck, often from great distances, into the Valley of Mexico.

The fail-safe functioning of the energy system depends on a small fraction of the power generated by hydro sources. In times of drought, the loss of these units in the national grid can be enough to trigger brownouts and blackouts, which have a significant impact on industrial output. In the same way, food production around the Valley of Mexico has gradually diminished over the past several decades, in part because water—even partially treated wastewater—is not available for irrigation of food crops. Completing this triad, the food-for-export strategy over the past several decades has sought to transform labor-intensive, rainfed agriculture into mechanized, irrigated production of fodder to support livestock exports. This strategy put water for power and domestic consumption in direct competition with agriculture in important areas around the Valley of Mexico.

Two major institutional controls have failed to prevent these environmental and infrastructural imbalances: First, the pricing system has been circumvented, and second, environmentally sound development strategies for supplying basic needs have not been available. The pricing system should have signaled the inviability of these energy-intensive schemes, but prices have been bypassed for political reasons—in part to keep the costs of bread, milk, corn, water, and gasoline at levels affordable to the poor. This affordability of course is artificially supported, the environmental resource base is decapitalized, and in the long run the people of Mexico will suffer. Second, as regards alternative strategies, it is not inconceivable that a different course of development could have been followed, with lasting environmental benefits, if a strategy had been defined and present in the decisionmaking arenas of Mexico City. There, as in an increasing number of Third World urban centers, a growing constituency of policymakers, officials, and interest groups is disposed to new developmental pathways. In the particular case of Mexico City, this would mean much less energy support for water and food systems, more locally produced and marketed perishables, and the organization of water conservation and re-use programs to reduce or delay the need for energy-intensive interbasin transfer projects.

For donors, governments, and environmental groups, the policy agenda for the next several decades should include the development of analytical techniques to incorporate a broader range of environmental factors to complement the monetary measures typically used in assessing project viability. Donors need not focus only on adjusting prices so that environmental resources are managed with greater care. Resource-conserving strategies for urban development are also needed to reduce domestic water and power consumption and avoid the need for new projects. To illustrate, a 25-per cent reduction in the large losses (estimated at 40 per cent to 50 per cent) in water produced by the Mexico City system could postpone hundred-million-dollar investments for a decade. Environmental groups can contribute a great deal by demonstrating through specific instances the feasibility of secondary water markets and urban food production. Education is also needed to sensitize consumers to the need for and advantages of resource conservation at the household level. Many officials in Third World governments are cognizant of the need for reforms in the water, food, and energy regimes. In Mexico, alternative strategies can be propelled by the knowledge that each unit of energy saved in domestic consumption is a unit for potential sale on the international market, earning foreign exchange with which to pay debts and make investments.

Materials Recycling

No issue affects the urban poor with such direct irony as that of solid waste, which is simultaneously a source of income and of endangerment in Third World cities. Urban parts of the Third World produce nearly 700 grams of solid waste per person per day. By the turn of the century, urban areas in Latin America will produce 370,000 tons per day— almost an 80 per cent increase over present levels. Only about 60 per cent of this total is collected, and less than half of the collected amount is disposed of in an environmentally sound manner. Because so many other problems press local governments, solid waste disposal has been given low priority on the list of needed public service improvements. Health conditions are much more dramatically affected by the provision of pure water and the sanitary disposal of human wastes. Public sector neglect of solid waste disposal gives private, informal sector operations greater scope to collect, sort, recycle, and sell solid waste recovered in large cities.

Large numbers of families depend for their subsistence on urban waste. Workers are highly organized, stratified by their position on the dumps and by the materials they seek to recycle. Others work in the streets, gathering materials ahead of or alongside city trucks. The waste business is harsh and is controlled in Mexico, the Philippines, and Colombia by organized bulk materials buyers who shape the work and the income opportunities of the poor.

In undertaking this work, low-income fathers and mothers expose themselves and their children to a wide variety of health hazards. The problem is not just that dump sites, waste lots, and dump bins in the city are replete with bacteria and disease. If this were the only problem, rather fundamental public hygiene measures would suffice to solve it. The more serious problem is that solid waste in Third World cities includes a host of hazardous and toxic wastes; wastes from industries, hospitals, utilities (including polychlorinated biphenols, or PCBs, in discarded transformers), and from many other sectors of society end up in municipal dumps. Tropical wastes are heavy with water, and in dumps, this water gradually seeps into the groundwater, carrying a multitude of chemical and toxic substances. No one knows the types and quantities of hazardous substances reaching the groundwater or contaminating the poor who work at dump sites. The $5 billion spent since 1980 on Superfund efforts to clean up hazardous and toxic wastes in the United States provides some indication of the magnitude of this problem.[14] Protecting urban environments and low-income families from contamination by solid waste materials also involves trade-offs, because the livelihoods of tens of thousands of families depend on their access to the dumps. In Mexico City, the dump site workers, known as "pepinadores," stoutly resisted efforts to move them from their collection areas when government authorities attempted to close down one of the several city dumps with chronic problems of spontaneous combustion.

Environmentally sound waste strategies cannot ignore the social (employment) dimensions of the problem, so conventional waste collection and disposal methods used in developed countries have to be modified in several ways. In the first place, donors have yet to discover whether the relationship between capital costs and operational expenses warrants programmatic lending for solid waste, or whether assistance in this area should best be handled as part of municipal improvement projects of state and local governments. Second, assistance agencies have to help design modifications in recycling strategies, as they have done in Manila and Cairo, by making labor-intensive recycling a part of the solution. Only a handful of experimental projects have been implemented, and the role of the poor is still marginal. Still another challenge is to educate the public about waste separation and recycling. Educational materials and technical assistance is needed in hundreds of cities to diagnose problems and design hazardous waste disposal strategies. Environmental groups can make a contribution to both branches of this work.

Conclusions: Environmental Actions Needed in Large Cities

The poor are directly involved with and affected by many of the most basic dynamics of the urban environment on the macro scale. With this perspective, it is possible to see that some of the trade-offs surrounding environmental and developmental objectives are more subtle and complex than those seen at the household level. For one thing, the costs and benefits of city-wide environmental change are less amenable to clear distinctions between the rich and poor. For another, the relative importances of technology and information are reversed in comparison to environmental problems of the household. More important, the close linkages of the poor with environmental resource flows—informational, energy, food, and wastes—demonstrate the extent to which addressing environmental problems in cities over the next several decades will be as much a social as an environmental task. The solutions to some of the problems identified in this section, such as land use control and the handling of wastes, require no great technological breakthroughs. Rather, the application of relatively well-known technologies and administrative practices can lead to great improvements as long as the interests of the poor are taken into account. But the application of policies and the implementation of programs in land use control and waste management over the past several decades have not been promising. New responsibilities are now being devolved to local governments in many Third World countries, and this decentralization increases the complexity of making progress in the areas of the environment and poverty. The focus of attention on the local level opens new, largely unexplored fronts for donors, governments, and nongovernmental groups alike.

"Informational" resource flows and the interdependence of food, water, and energy are more subtle, and taking these into account challenges the conventional wisdom on developmental and environmental approaches to urban growth. In the face of this intersectoral complexity, progress depends to some extent on having a more complete and robust paradigm within which to ground policies and actions. With this in mind, the notion of the urban ecosystem has been invoked. This model helps to show the tight connections between waste and resource, environment and development, and it more easily accommodates measures of value in economics and ecology. Donors are not structured to make much progress in this arena. Nongovernmental groups—academic, environmental, and policy-oriented organizations—are better equipped to develop theory and conduct research. But the work should be collaborative and applied—as opposed to basic research—and this implies the need for stronger ties between development assistance organizations and nongovernmental groups.

Dealing with the Dilemmas: Social and Economic Dimensions in Strategies for Environment and Development

Conclusions and Recommendations

Since the U.N.-sponsored Stockholm and Vancouver conferences of the 1970s, a lot has been learned about environment and development in human settlements.[15] Although the environmental problems of the urban poor were a major theme at the Stockholm meeting, very little talk was heard then about indoor air pollution due to poor combustion, urban on-site waste disposal, the complexities of informational and other resource interdependencies, the possibilities of urban food production, or the dependence of the poor on solid waste. Our awareness and knowledge have increased, but the scope of environmental policy and action over the past fifteen years has been focused more on large-scale matters of natural resource management than on the environmental conditions facing the urban poor. Over the same period, a wide range of environmental problems has been intensifying in Third World cities, leading to serious adverse effects on large numbers of the poor. The environmental problems of large cities will grow more intense both because much of Third World urbanization is still to come and because of the rapid pace of household formation expected over the next several generations. Consequently, the environmental agenda of the future must consider new, large-scale, and somewhat more complex social dimensions than those characterizing most problems of the past.

Policymakers, bilateral and multilateral technical and financial assistance organizations, as well as groups active in environmental and urban arenas must give increasing attention to, and expand their knowledge about, the social and economic dimensions of environmental policy as well as the environmental dimensions of urban development. The poor have limited channels to articulate their concerns and limited means to amplify their message. Few outsiders have gained the attention of the world concerning the long-term environmental dangers and short-term harm faced by the urban poor. This urban social dimension brings new political color to environmental affairs. As with issues of tribal peoples and relocated groups, the subject of the environment and the urban poor encroaches on sensitive political territory where the interests of minorities and the disenfranchised often are not in concert with those of the established order. Past work in the area of family planning—strongly social, quasi-environmental, mostly educational, and highly political—most closely approximates the political challenge of future environmental actions. Environmental groups in the developed and developing parts of the world have a strong intellectual and operational grounding based on past research and experience to advance the state of knowledge, develop policy options, and create fora for discussions with national policymakers and nongovernmental organizations.

Development assistance organizations have long addressed many of the technical and financial issues raised in this discussion—including the problems of poverty and the environment—but not with the focus nor the kind of conceptual orientation taken in this discussion. For the past two decades, development assistance organizations have been struggling with the organizational and institutional arrangements necessary to deal separately with environmental issues and urban development challenges. The World Bank still emphasizes poverty, but it has not given this subject the kind of systematic scrutiny and policy focus it had under Robert McNamara ten years ago. In general, the major development institutions are increasing their emphasis on environmental matters but have found no compelling reason to stress urban issues. On the contrary, the focus on urban dimensions has been narrowed in the reorganization of the World Bank. Perhaps the most promising locus for organizational change in large multilateral assistance organizations is in the areas of water and basic sanitation. No great policy or conceptual leap is required to address problems of solid waste disposal and land management, and this kind of intersectoral coordination may well prove easier to accomplish with the reorganized World Bank. However, raising the *priority* assigned to these areas and implementing actions is more difficult. Accommodating the broad vision of an urban resource base for the poor, and the interdependencies of food, water, and energy, for instance, goes far beyond the present institutional capabilities of most of the assistance agencies. It is possible, however, to give a stronger environmental emphasis to urban affairs and bring a much sharper urban focus to environmental policy through the formation of special teams or working groups with a mandate to address policy perspectives and devise effective intersectoral operations. In the short term, development assistance agencies will do well to highlight the institutional capacity of local governments, as this is likely to be an important part of the battleground over issues of the urban environment and poverty over the course of the next several decades.

This analysis has attempted to be selective in the kinds of problems discussed in order to highlight common issues that are susceptible to environmental action. These problems have been divided into two major groups: (1) those concerning the immediate household environment, and (2) those related to the sheer magnitude of cities themselves. The following action agenda is recommended:

1. Highest priority should be given to the immediate risks posed to low-income families lacking adequate protection from their own household wastes. A fair amount of experience has already been gained in the design and implementation of stoves and systems for water supply and waste disposal. More work needs to be done in the areas of cost analysis, social organization techniques for recruiting community participation in projects, the social and cultural dimensions of user-technology interaction, and education campaigns as to real self-interest—including opportunities for market-related incentives, cooking efficiently with wood fuels, and taking advantage of low-cost water and waste services.

2. Although fewer families are affected by the problems of solid waste than those of waterborne wastes, it is important to address the long-term hazards of inadequate urban solid waste disposal in a way that protects related employment opportunities developed by the urban poor. The social dimension of livelihoods and control over resources

requires the promotion of nontraditional strategies of waste removal, such as labor-intensive recycling. The risks of hazardous wastes require research and education, first as to the dimension of the hazards and later into the development of affordable techniques and technologies for disposal.

3. Conceptual approaches, techniques, and methodological tools are all "on the shelf" and ready to be adapted for strengthening the soundness of land settlement patterns in Third World cities. The challenge lies in the adaptation and diffusion of these approaches and in the inculcation of stronger skills of policy analysis—an unfamiliar and underemphasized area of the social and environmental sciences. Adaptation of tools and techniques, however, is a complement to, not a substitute for, basic institution-building in the capacities of local governments to acquire information about land uses and to collect property taxes.

4. The management of the environment and of resources depends fundamentally on demand and technology. Both of these dimensions are magnified in the urban setting and both have been left out of the development strategies of the major assistance agencies. A major structural change in concepts—something akin to a paradigm shift—is needed, and development, environment, and policy research groups working in collaboration with development agencies have much to contribute to a new vision that puts the values of the natural environment on a more equal footing with the goals of social and economic development.

Notes

[1] For origins and applications of the ecosystems model, see Amos H. Hawley, *Human Ecology: A Theory of Community Structure* (New York: Ronald Press, 1950); I. Sachs, "Population, Technology, Natural Resources, and the Environment," *Economic Bulletin for Latin America*, Vol. 18, Nos. 1–2 (1973), pp. 125–36; R. L. Meier, *Planning for an Urban World* (Cambridge: MIT Press, 1974); and S. Boyden, S. Millar, K. Newcombe, and B. O'Neill, *An Ecology of a City and Its People: The Case of Hong Kong* (Canberra: Australian National University, 1979). Boyden and his colleagues have developed a thorough analysis of Hong Kong seen from the urban ecosystems perspective.

[2] Robert Fox and his colleagues have projected urban and rural populations for the major regions of the world and have published handsome graphics depicting these demographic changes; see Fox, *Population Images* (New York: U.N. Fund for Population Activities, 1987).

[3] J. F. C. Turner, "Housing Priorities, Settlement Patterns, and Urban Development in Modernizing Countries," *Journal of the American Institute of Planners* (November 1968), pp. 354–63.

[4] Giovanni Andrea Cornia, Richard Jolly, and Frances Stewart, eds., *Adjustment with a Human Face: Protecting the Vulnerable and Promoting Growth* (Oxford, England: Clarendon Press, 1987).

[5] See Tim Campbell, "Socio-Economic Factors in an Alternative Densified Fuel Strategy for Pakistan," Report prepared for the U.N. Inter-Regional Energy Advisor, New York, 1985).

[6] Vinod Vyasulu, and A. N. K. Reddy, *Essays in Bangalore*, four vols. (Bangalore: Karnataka State Council for Science and Technology, 1985).

[7] See K. Smith, *Biofuels, Air Pollution, and Health: A Global Review,* (New York: Plenum Publishing Corp., 1987).

[8] Nicolas Jequier, *Appropriate Technology* (Paris: Organisation for Economic Co-operation and Development, 1976).

[9] G. Leach, and M. Gowan, *Household Energy Handbook: An Interim Guide and Reference Manual,* World Bank Technical Paper, No. 67 (Washington, D.C.: The World Bank, 1987).

[10] Tim Campbell, "Applying Lessons from Housing to Meeting the Challenge of Water and Sanitation for the Urban Poor," in *APA Journal* (Spring 1987), pp. 186–92.

[11] See Larissa Lomnitz, "The Social and Economic Organization of a Mexican Shantytown," in W. Cornelius and F. Trueblood, eds., *Latin American Urban Research,* Vol. 4 (Beverly Hills: Sage Publications, 1974), pp. 135–56.

[12] Still another approach to improving the informational infrastructure has been investigated at the University of California at Berkeley. The economic and financial feasibility of using cellular phones was calculated for specific applications in Bogotá, Colombia. Because of the high price and long waiting period for conventional telephone service, cellular telephones, which can be obtained immediately, can be sold to businesses in sufficient quantities to subsidize service for low-income *barrios.*

[13] Tim Campbell, *Resource Flows in the Urban Ecosystem: Fuel, Water, and Food in Mexico City,* Working Paper No. 360 (Berkeley: Institute of Urban and Regional Development, University of California, 1981).

[14] As reported in "Superfund Program Under Fire," *Science,* No. 240 (June 1988), p. 1725.

[15] The Stockholm Conference on the Human Environment was organized in 1972 by Maurice Strong at the request of the U.N. General Assembly. The Stockholm Conference addressed the subjects of resources, contamination, cultural and educational factors, institutional arrangements, and human settlements. One of the decisions taken at Stockholm was to reorganize the U.N.'s effort regarding human settlements and to create a new program—the U.N. Committee on Human Settlements and the U.N. Environmental Programme—and to hold a follow-up conference to deal with the environmental problems of human settlements in greater detail. This was done at the 1978 Vancouver Conference. The Stockholm Conference also produced a seminal paper—known as the Founex Report—on the problems of environment and poverty. See *The Founex Report on Environment and Development. A Discussion Document* for the U.N. Conference on the Human Environment (New York: U.N. Committee on Human Settlements, 1972).

Chapter 6

The Madagascar Challenge: Human Needs and Fragile Ecosystems

Alison Jolly

Imagine an area where strange and beautiful animal species, as well as the big shady trees that surround them, are protected from human exploitation. Teachers and school children, scientists, and tourists all come to visit, and the income they produce helps to offset the costs of maintaining the park. Let us call that park the Bronx Zoo. The surrounding region, however, is one of extreme human poverty. Children are malnourished, adults have lost hope of finding gainful employment, innocent victims die in local shooting wars and turf battles, and the physical environment stinks of decay. Call this region the South Bronx.

Now imagine that these two adjoining areas are both part of one small country, and that the destinies of the park and the impoverished population are therefore inextricably linked. The poor people, and even the government, may come to see the park as a luxury they cannot afford and wish to open it for human habitation and exploitation. A few local groups and a bevy of international conservation organizations insist on the necessity of keeping the park's boundaries inviolate, arguing that extinction is forever and, besides, that opening up the park will only extend the zone of poverty—not deal with the underlying causes of poor people's misery.

The debate may be academic anyway, since without a growing army of park guards, human encroachment grows inexorably. As social, economic, and environmental conditions outside the park deteriorate, it becomes harder and harder to maintain the physical boundaries between the two areas. Homeless people invade the park for shelter, destroying the animals' habitat in the process. Hungry people take birds and game species for their meat. And unemployed people discover that the pelts, shells, and tusks of many of the park's animals bring very high prices.

How accurate is the metaphor of the inevitable clash between the Bronx Zoo and the economic needs of the South Bronx? Unfortunately, it is all too real for many parts of the tropics, where local human needs are increasingly impinging upon wildlife survival. This chapter examines the dilemmas raised by this reality in one country, Madagascar, which has the natural diversity of a continent, not a zoo, and where poverty is much harsher and more widespread than in the South Bronx.

First, even though the vast majority of the world's wild plants and animals still live outside protected areas, the image of the zoo is all too close at hand. Even Kenya, whose remaining great wild herds are the remnants of the animals that earlier surrounded evolving humankind, and whose game parks are the symbol of national profit from tourism, is now considering fencing in those parks, as the only defense against elephant poachers. In the future, most remaining wild species will survive only by the active choice of human beings. They may not all be in inviolate protected zones, and most will not survive if that is all the remains. In or out of protected ares, however, they can only exist if people choose to let them grow.

Second, the conservation of wild species depends on macroeconomic policy, not just on a separate "environmental sector," or on a national parks department which is somehow set apart from human needs. And third, the value of the park has an element that is not measured by any economics. It can be valued as a watershed, or a climate regulator, a pool of untapped genes, or a source of tourist income—all of which are too often left out of the calculations. And not even such an innovative economics can measure the wonder in the children's eyes, or the pride of local people who learn that their country's animals are unique in all the world.

The twentieth century has seen inexorable decline in the world's plant and animal species. This decline has three primary causes: (1) expanding numbers of poor people living in ecological areas that house many of the world's unique species—for example, the African savannahs, or jungles in Latin America, Asia, and Africa; (2) growing demand in the industrial world for the products that can be extracted from these habitats, such as tropical timber and cattle ranching; and (3) the poaching of such high-value species as elephants, tropical birds, turtles, and furred creatures. Of these threats, habitat destruction is far more final and larger in scale than the poaching of species one by one.

In the face of this onslaught, conservationists have increasingly focused on identifying the world's greatest remaining wilderness areas, which are the richest in species. These areas are overwhelmingly in the tropics and heavily concentrated in a small number of countries. In fact, just seven "megadiversity" countries include some 50–60 per cent of the known species of the globe, and probably far more—if we could count the insects of the rain forest canopy. These seven (all developing countries except for Australia) are Mexico, Colombia, Brazil, Zaire, Indonesia, Australia, and Madagascar.[1] Three of them—Brazil, Zaire, and Indonesia—have the earth's remaining huge tracts of continuous rain forest: the Amazon, the Zaire Basin, and the towering dipterocarp forest of Southeast Asia. Conservationists have long focused on the most threatened reserves, as they have on the most endangered species, but they are realizing that even the largest tracts are now vulnerable. These last large wildernesses are the very first priority. It will take global political will to save them. Such a political decision is required if our descendants are to know what wilderness is.

All of the megadiversity countries except Zaire also have extraordinary internal diversity: rain forest and desert, mountains and lowland. Mexico and Colombia are bridges between continents. Australia and Madagascar, in contrast, are isolates, separated for many millions of years, most of whose species exist nowhere else. This is not to say that other countries are unimportant, or lack endemic species. Concentrating on the megadiversity countries first will, however, give us the highest return in species diversity. Again, this marks a shift in the mentality of conservationists.

As biologists and economists jointly realize that the world is finite, we are both changing our ways. We are slowly recognizing that humanity cannot infinitely increase demand on the world, whether through population growth of the poor, or unlimited greed of the rich. Population checks are a shock to some cultures; checks on energy use in the face of nuclear pollution and the greenhouse effect will shock many more. The actual integration of economic planning with environmental planning is, however, different in each case. So far there are few cases that show how human needs and aspirations can be met while preserving the fragile web of the biosphere.

Madagascar's government and a currently enthusiastic consortium of donors and scientists all hope that Madagascar will be one such case. This article analyzes the ways that hope may, or may not, be fulfilled.

Madagascar's Diverse Vegetation: Remaining Forested Areas

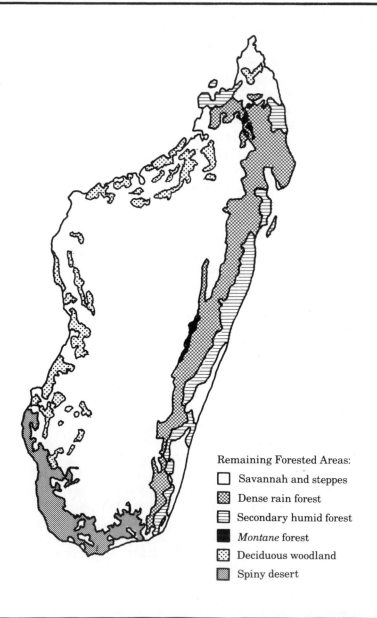

Remaining Forested Areas:

- ☐ Savannah and steppes
- ▨ Dense rain forest
- ▤ Secondary humid forest
- ■ *Montane* forest
- ▦ Deciduous woodland
- ▨ Spiny desert

Sources: Remaining forested areas data from *Eaux-et-Forets* survey, 1949-58—after Humbert and Cours Darne 1965 and Tatersall 1981. Map adapted, with permission, from Alison Jolly, *A World Like Our Own* (New Haven, Conn.: Yale University Press, 1980), p. xii.

Madagascar: A Unique Ecosystem Under Siege

Madagascar is a country of extremes. It has one of the world's great riches of biodiversity: More than 80 per cent of its flora and fauna species are unique to the island-continent, including the wide-eyed lemurs, the nearest living representatives of our distant, pre-monkey ancestor.[2] With a per capita income of $225 in 1988, it is also, in cash terms, one of the world's poorest countries. Madagascar is a relatively pure case of small farmers working against their environment; the threats come from slash-and-burn clearing and from deliberately set brush fires— not from large ranchers or international lumber companies. Since 1960, Malagasy income has been declining. The economic crisis of the 1980s has vastly accelerated both human poverty and environmental degradation.

The World Bank and other international donors have chosen Madagascar for the implementation of a coordinated Environmental Action Plan (EAP), a model that may be followed in many other countries.[3] This is an effort both to ameliorate the human environment and to preserve natural biodiversity. The Bank focused on Madagascar for three reasons. First, in 1984, the government of Madagascar declared its commitment to a national Strategy for Conservation and Sustainable Development.[4] In 1985, the government held an international conference announcing the new policy and inviting donors to contribute. It is now transforming the Bank's plan into its own National Environmental Charter *(Charte Nationale de l'Environnement)*. Second, the World Wildlife Fund calls Madagascar one of the world's highest conservation priorities. There are perhaps more unique species in more immediate dan-

Table 1. Madagascar's Biodiversity

Type of Organism	Species on Record	Percentage Endemic to Island
Flowering plants	8,000–10,000	80 +
Amphibians	150 +	99
Reptiles	235	96
Birds	238	50
Bats	26	50
Terrestrial mammals	69	97

Source: Modified from Alison Jolly, *A World Like Our Own* (New Haven, Conn.: Yale University Press, 1980) pp. 15–20.

ger of extinction in Madagascar than anywhere else. Third, the country is not only poor but has also been a "good pupil" of the International Monetary Fund (IMF). It has followed the IMF's precepts (however painful) on structural adjustment and has paid back fifty cents on the dollar of its debt service—payments amounting to half its yearly export earnings. The IMF and the World Bank thus have an ideological stake in Madagascar's eventual success.

A Brief History from Human Settlement to the Closing Frontier

Madagascar is one of the last habitable regions settled by human beings. Perhaps 1,500 years ago, colonists came across the Indian Ocean from Indonesia—bringing paddy rice cultivation, a close-knit family structure, and reverence for their ancestors and ancestral land. Others came from Africa, bringing humped zebu cattle and perceptions of livestock as the only noble form of wealth. Later, Arabs traded with the northern regions, which accounts for the very Malagasy version of Islam that now coexists with equally Malagasy Christian churches.

The early settlers found an island-continent of 587,000 square kilometers—stretching 1,600 kilometers from northern to southern tip, the distance from London to Naples or from Boston to Orlando. Madagascar is both tropical and temperate, with rain forest on the eastern escarpment, dry deciduous woodlands in the northwest, and the semi-arid "spiny desert" in the south.

Biologically, it is more like an archipelago than a continent. Each forest in the remaining ring of natural habitat is like an island: Travel a hundred kilometers to the next, and you will find different trees, lizards, and lemurs. One nature reserve does not substitute for another. To preserve the island's biodiversity, we need a whole ring of reserves in the remaining forest—the "necklace of pearls," with each "pearl" a different center of species evolution.

The island is fragmented not only biologically, but also in human terms. The infrastructure of roads was always minimal, and several of the major port towns still have no all-weather link to the capital. To travel from one pearl in the necklace to another you need to return to the capital and start over.

What lies within the necklace of forest is the settled land of the central plateau. When people first came, the central region was a mosaic of wooded valleys and tree-savannah. The highland fauna could boast lemurs the size of modern great apes, tortoises with shells like babies' bathtubs, and *Aepyornis,* the elephant-bird, whose five-liter eggs can still be found intact. These animals became extinct about 1,000 years ago. The central plateaus are now rice paddies in the valleys, and dry,

The Species-Rich Countries

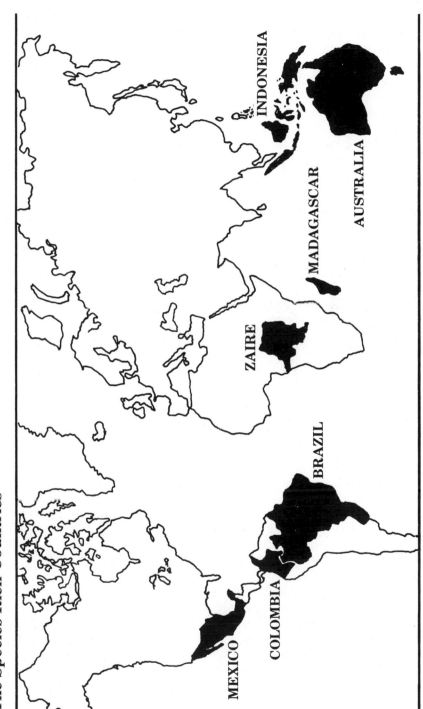

INDONESIA

AUSTRALIA

MADAGASCAR

ZAIRE

BRAZIL

MEXICO

COLOMBIA

rainfed fields or bare savannah on the adjacent hillsides. Only about 5 per cent of Madagascar is now cultivated, and only some 10 per cent more is considered cultivable; the rest is mainly arid, windswept grassland.

Every year, people set fires to clear the hillsides, burning between one and three million hectares annually. Herders set fires because the perennial bunch grass (Aristidia) produces green shoots after burning. This "green bite" tides cattle over the worst of the dry season. Rice farmers burn the land because bare hills allow increased rainwater runoff; this means that the first rains flood the paddy fields, facilitating early planting and an early harvest. The third reason for setting fires is political protest. Madagascar has one of the world's highest erosion rates. Government after government has forbidden burning because each year the pastures degrade, the soil bakes harder, and erosion increases. Indeed, most foreign donors or scientists form their first impressions of the country by flying in over the Betsiboka River, which hemorrhages red soil into the blue sea. Setting fire to the grass has become a form of protest aimed at governments that seek to substitute their new values for peasant traditions. The fires also burn into the remaining vulnerable stands of natural forest and into tree plantations—unless someone has the incentive to keep them out and can muster the wherewithal to do so.

Along the coast, natural forest does persist as separate patches. Coastal people farm rice or maize in the valleys and flatlands. They also make slash-and-burn clearings, called tavy, in the remaining woods. Traditionally the woods regrew as second growth before being cleared again, but there is considerable doubt whether tavy cultivation was ever in ecological balance. Malagasy forests apparently have been retreating throughout history, and the retreat is now a rout. The Malagasy—like Americans—are frontier people who use up their forests instead of sustaining them.

Madagascar has now reached the point of the closing frontier. The rain forest has diminished by 50 per cent in the past thirty years. An estimated 77,000–101,000 square kilometers of natural forest remain, but forest land is disappearing at a rate of some 2–4 per cent, or 1,500–3,000 square kilometers, each year.[5] The higher-percentage scenario suggests total destruction in twenty-five years and the lower one in fifty years. The worst scenario is the more cautious one for preventive action, given the growth in population and need for land and for fuel, and the vulnerability of remnant forest fragments to fire and human invasion. If Madagascar's forests are to be preserved for their biodiversity or for any other reason, decisions are needed now. If the frontier is not closed by active choice, it will inevitably close when no more natural habitat remains.

Debt and Adjustment

Madagascar is currently considered a showpiece of structural adjustment. Since 1982, the government—following the philosophy of the World Bank and the IMF—has restricted imports, reduced its budget, and devalued its currency. These policy steps have not been easy, and the poor, particularly the urban poor, have suffered. In a recent interview, Pascal Rakotomaro, Madagascar's Minister of Finance, commented: "I was going to say you can't make an omelet without breaking eggs. But socially speaking, that would be a rather cynical way of putting it. We genuinely deplore the social effects of the measures we have had to take to right the economy."[6]

In 1975, when the present government took power, there was an attempt to combine traditional Malagasy structures with socialist principles. Malagasy socialism was very different from the Soviet or Chinese varieties. The government was restructured to allow more, not less, provincial and local autonomy. The *fokon'olona,* the village council since pre-colonial times, is now generally translated "village commune." But it is still the same group of elders, arguing toward consensus in the same oratorical style, under the same baobab tree where they have always met—only now they have a place in the hierarchy. Madagascar has turned to the Soviet Union and China for aid, but also to everyone else, in a policy called "All compass points." As a result, while the Chinese were rebuilding the highway eastward from the capital to the main port, West German aid rebuilt the highway toward the south and west.

Attempts to nationalize crop marketing failed due to the predictable bureaucratic inefficiencies and small-scale corruption in this fragmented country, whose road structure barely links climatically and culturally disparate regions. Food production plummeted, and black markets grew as alternatives to the inadequate public rations. In 1978, the government attempted to break out of the country's poverty through a crash program of investment. The great dam at Andekaleka was built at a cost of $40 million with World Bank funding—to be repaid with interest (Madagascar has surplus electricity for the next decade, at least). Textile factories were improved and now produce most of the nation's clothing. Many other projects, however, were ill-chosen and unviable—including, for example a fertilizer plant that imported its raw materials and a soy oil plant for a nation that does not grow soybeans. The projects were financed by external borrowing.

By 1981, debt service had built up to the point where constant rescheduling was required. Assistance from the IMF helped to reduce the fiscal deficit from 15 per cent to 4 per cent of gross domestic product (GDP), and the current account deficit was cut by half. In the period 1982–86, imports dropped by more than half, while exports stagnated.

By 1988, Madagascar's national debt stood at $3.3 billion. Madagascar has regularly paid 50 per cent of its debt service, registering one of the highest payback rates for a poor country: It repaid $120 million dollars in 1986, when its total export earnings were $300 million and its loans and grants from abroad were $164 million.

The social cost has been heavy. By 1988, per capita income was only $225—about 20 per cent lower than in 1980, or about one-third lower than in 1975. Civil service *real* wages fell by 25 per cent in five years. Malaria, considered eradicated from the high plateau in 1970, has now reached epidemic proportions, as people who were once protected and have no natural immunity are infected and die. There has been no cash to import drugs, and rural health systems have disintegrated. Even if drugs had been available, there would have been almost no cash to buy them. Malnourishment has also risen steeply, especially among children.[7]

Since 1986, under World Bank and IMF pressure, rice and most other commodities have been returned to free market status. This, along with good weather, has greatly increased production, and the country is again self-sufficient in rice, though with an imported buffer stock that the government could use to counter price increases. Urban food prices rose sharply as "buffer stocks" in fact magnified price swings, but by 1988 began to fall again as supplies increased.[8]

In 1987, the government moved toward a market-dominated foreign trade regime. It devalued the Franc Malagasy by 46 per cent. In January 1988, import licensing gave way to imports under a simple tariff and free access to foreign exchange. There are even plans for an eight-year tax holiday for foreign investors and the establishment of a free-trade zone in Antananarivo. The licensing system had encouraged hoarding, monopolies, and theft—to the point where the sellers of table-cloths in the market would join together to pay someone's airfare to the island of Réunion to buy embroidery thread rather than trust the open system. Import liberalization means that buses and bush-taxis are being put back together, which should revitalize the economy at all levels in a country strangled by lack of transport. The foreign investment that is supposed to justify this change may be ill-adapted to the needs of the poor, but the country's goal has clearly changed to having a bigger "pie," however it may be apportioned in the future—as Jean Robiarivony, Director-General of Planning, has emphasized.[9]

Exports, as they stand now, will not provide this larger pie; the country must turn to foreign investment and another injection of lending. Madagascar's chief exports are coffee, cloves, and vanilla. In 1987, export earnings fell by 15 per cent—because of lower world coffee prices—despite increased coffee production. (Vanilla may soon be replaced by tissue culture biotechnology and wiped out altogether as an agricultural cash crop for an estimated 70,000 Malagasy farmers.) Madagascar can tighten its belt on imports, or woo foreign exchange as investment, but it cannot control or even much influence its export markets. The World Bank and the consultative group of major donors calculate that Madagascar will receive $700 million a year in foreign grants and loans in 1989–91. This sum is not as generous as it might appear, since it includes renegotiated debt on the order of $200 million per year. The remaining $500 million does, however, still exceed total export earnings by at least $100 million. Some of this foreign assistance is aimed at small-scale agriculture and forestry, particularly aid from Switzerland and the United States. The main thrust of the economic program, however, is not to support rural needs or develop internal markets, but to further push Malagasy exports toward an unwilling world.

Although the specific approaches to hoped-for economic growth have changed, the major focus continues to be on the cash economy and the export-import balance. For the past few years, the government's and the donors' plan was to right the balance by cutting down on imports; now thinking has swung around again to encouraging exports. The prevailing dogma, however, continues to assert that Madagascar should try to grow rich—to become a newly industrializing country—and that the distribution of such new wealth will eventually sort itself out.

The Environmental Toll

While economists have been concentrating on the cash economy, the environmental basis of life has further disintegrated for both humans and other species. The second wave of extinction in Madagascar has begun. In the first, a thousand years ago, we lost the elephant-birds and the giant lemurs that lived in the ecological niches of great apes and baboons—and might have given us a separate insight into the evolution of primate society. Now the fragments of forest are closing in around the remaining lemurs, Malagasy carnivores, and forest birds. We do not know which vertebrate species have recently become extinct, but this is in part a measure of ignorance. No one has seen the Madagascar serpent-eagle in fifty years. When scientists go to look, sometimes they do not find what they hoped to see, and sometimes they find a whole new creature—like the golden bamboo lemur discovered in 1986. Forests that still hold undescribed primate species are disappearing before they are even explored. In 1989, yet another new primate has been recognized—the golden-crowned or silky sifaka. This enchanting animal may set a world record for speed from discovery to extinction—perhaps a hundred remain in scattered forest patches.

The effects on the human environment are even clearer. The World Bank's Environmental Action Plan attempts to quantify the cost of burning and erosion (Table 2).[10] It estimates the country is losing

Table 2. Estimated Annual Value of Losses through Burning and Erosion in Madagascar

A. Effect of Burning: **($ millions)**
    Low Estimate (1 million hectares burned)

600,000 hectares pasture	3
5 per cent becomes useless	
95 per cent loses 5 per cent productivity	0.25
300,000 hectares *Tanety* (rainfed farmland)	6
5 per cent becomes useless	
95 per cent loses 10 per cent productivity	1
100,000 hectares natural forest, 50 per cent	12
good quality and 50 per cent degraded	
10 per cent becomes useless	
90 per cent become *tavy* (shifting fields)	72
Low Estimate Total	94

B. Effect of Burning: **($ millions)**
    High Estimate (3 million hectares burned)

1,800,000 hectares pasture	
900,000 hectares *Tanety*	
300,000 hectares natural forest	
High Estimate Total	283

C. Direct Effect of Erosion on Infrastructure   **($ millions)**

Irrigated field damage	7–8
Road destruction	1.5
Port siltation	1
Total	10

TOTAL A, B, and C:	**Low Estimate $104**
	High Estimate $294

Source: The World Bank, U.S. Agency for International Development (USAID), Cooperation Suisse, U.N. Educational, Scientific, and Cultural Organization (UNESCO), U.N. Development Programme (UNDP), and the World Wildlife Fund, *Madagascar: Plan d'Action Environnemental* (Washington, D.C.: The World Bank, 1988), Vol. I (2-1 to 2-5).

$100–300 million per year in productivity of agricultural and forest land. Only about $10 million of this is direct effect on infrastructure such as roads and harbors. Oddly, the visibility of erosion effects to government and foreign donors is almost in inverse ratio to their importance. The silting of the estuary at Mahajunga, the country's second largest port, blocks a major trade route, but it is estimated to represent only a $1-million annual loss. Erosion damage to roads is estimated to be slightly higher, and to irrigation works, higher still—but these modern-sector costs are minor compared to the loss of forest, farmland, and pasture productivity to the population at large.

The economic crisis that has denied market prosperity to the country has intensified the pressures on land. In the towns, the effects of the crisis are measured in the wild eyes and clutching hands of street children. In the country, the results are apparent in the potbellies of children who drink wormy water and eat a measure of rice that is smaller every year.

World Bank Policies for Development and Environment in Madagascar

Is Development Sustainable?

What does "sustainable development" mean? "Sustainable" must mean that the population does not degrade its life-support systems, at least not irretrievably, but rather conserves or even improves them. People may take a little here and there, or sacrifice some capability in the present if it can be restored by other means in the future. This definition of sustainability does not prejudge the social system in place. If a feudal society can keep its watersheds as royal hunting parks and its topsoil in fallowed fields, it may be environmentally sustainable no matter how wretched the life of the serfs.

"Development" is different. It demands that human life somehow improve. The narrow definition of economic development as rising per capita income has been rightly attacked. Seeking to meet "basic needs" is a more humane goal for development planning—yet it, too, is only a partial goal, since it provides no guidance as to priorities once the poorest segment of the population has attained a bearable standard of living. Perhaps the simple definition of "a continuously improving quality of life" is best, since it allows for cultural gains as well as material ones and for a future of increasing hope.

To attain such sustainable development, however, the cycle of poverty and degradation must first be broken.[11] In Madagascar, where traditional land use has been progressively eroding and deforesting the country for a thousand years, sustainable development cannot be achieved simply by restoring some idealized traditional equilibrium with the land; a whole new rationale of peasant agriculture must be explored.

What are the dimensions of the problem? The population is currently growing at a rate of 3 per cent a year. The World Bank's *Population and Health Sector Review* gives the staggering projections shown in Table 3.[12] The Report's high projection is 28.1 million in 2015 (assuming that population growth continues unchecked at the present rate of 6.6 live births per woman). The low scenario assumes a fall in population growth that has been achieved by very few countries. This fall is unthinkable with present cultural values and heavy dependence on child labor, so it is included only to show a lower theoretical limit. The Report states that, for Madagascar to feed itself,

> domestic food production would, without fertility decline, need to increase by 4.6 per cent annually up to the year 2000 and 3.5 per cent thereafter. It must be noted that only a few countries have ever been able to sustain agricultural growth of more than 3.5 per cent per annum over more than two decades (e.g., Mexico, Thailand and the Philippines).[13]

The specifics, however, are not so daunting. If, for the sake of argument, all the extra calories were to come from rice (close to the ideal for most

Table 3. Madagascar's Demographics

	1950–60	1985	2015 (high)	2015 (medium)	2015 (low)
Population (millions)	5	10.3	28.1	22.2	19.8
Population growth rate (percentage)	2.3	3.0	3.5	2.2	1.5
Doubling time (years)		24	20	36	46
Fertility (live births per woman)		6.6	6.6	4.0	2.8
Density/square kilometers	9	18	48	38	34
Density/cultivated land	229	381	1,041	822	733
Density/cultivable land	26	53	493	415	347
Per cent urban population		19	30	24	30
Urban population (millions)		2.0	8.5	6.7	6.0

Source: World Bank, *Population and Health Sector Review,* Report 6446, (Washington, D.C.: May 1987), pp. 8–9.

Malagasy), this would mean tripling rice production over the next thirty years on the high population growth scenario—or doubling it on the low projection. Smallholder paddy fields now produce only 1.8 tons per hectare; more advanced projects with fertilizer and careful water control yield 4 tons—even in Madagascar—and up to 8 tons in places like Japan. There is, moreover, an estimated 5.5 or 5.7 million hectares of arable but uncultivated land. If Madagascar could invest in the agricultural productivity of its smallholders, it might produce and distribute enough rice to feed even three times its present population.

But how will people cook their rice? If the supply of fuelwood remains constant, and if population continues to grow at present rates, the deficit in 2015 will reach two and one-half times the current sustainable annual production. As natural forest decreases, the supply of fuelwood will fall, increasing the deficit. In the highland provinces of Antananarivo and Fianarantsoa, where the fuelwood supply is shortest, this translates into 1.3 million hectares of fuelwood-tree plantations needed on the high population scenario, and 0.86 million hectares on the low scenario. That means adding 25–45 thousand hectares of productive fuelwood plantations per year. None of the programs envisaged, even within the scope of the Environmental Action Plan, approaches even 10 per cent of this goal.

The conclusion that seems to emerge from all four of these considerations—erosion, population, food, and fuel—is that the Malagasy people must face a massive change in their way of life. To some extent it may be possible to fiddle about at the margins with industrial development and tourism, or even to hope for a major technological fix like a breakthrough in solar energy, which would transform places like Madagascar into energy-rich countries. According to present projections, however, Madagascar is rapidly heading toward a confrontation between the human population and its supply of food and fuel, with fuel running out first.

In these circumstances, it may be urgent to think in terms of alternative development approaches—ones that differ from the standard "economistic" prescription. That is:

- Massive support for small-scale tree plantations, beginning with the recognition of land rights to the bare hillsides. As Robert Chambers explains, peasants need full rights to own, cut, and sell trees at times of personal economic need if they are to be interested in planting and maintaining trees.[14]

- These peasant tree plantations need agricultural extension advice and possibly initial subsidies. Meanwhile, natural forests must be policed, for as long as natural wood is free, the charcoal burners undercut tree-farmers' prices while further degrading soil and watersheds.

- Rural electrification, possibly using solar power.
- Intensification of yield on small farms. This will importantly involve land registration and tenure for small farmers, so they can invest in irrigation and long-term soil improvement.
- Improved rural feeder roads to link producers with markets.
- Integrated family and national child health planning programs as a national priority.

The PASAGE Program and Population

The World Bank is beginning to address *some* of these concerns in the Program of Social Action and Support for Public Management (*Projet d'Actions Sociales et d'Appui a la Gestion Economique*).[15] PASAGE is a social stop-gap, uncorrelated either to what economists consider "real" hard core economic planning, or to what ecologists consider "real" physical planning of the Environmental Action Plan. PASAGE is meant to be a transitory response to Madagascar's current financial problems with a credit of $24 million over three to five years. In his "letter of development policy" that introduces the PASAGE document, Prime Minister Victor Ramahatra stated:

> In general, the Government feels that the financing of [these efforts] should be regarded as *additional* to the public expenditure project to be established within the framework of its macroeconomic policy. . . . Actions taken in favor of vulnerable groups should not *jeopardize* what has already been achieved through the adjustment process. All actions . . . will accordingly be guided by the following clearly defined criteria:
>
> —Mechanisms for targeting the beneficiary groups
>
> —Cost minimization . . . implying that the activities would be limited in time.[16]

PASAGE encompasses a social action program, a research program, and a public management component. The two largest efforts are (1) an attack on the malaria epidemic at a cost of $8.75 million, and (2) a program, costing $7.34 million, to re-employ civil servants due to be laid off when the government closes uneconomic public-sector enterprises. Five milion dollars go for targeting employment and building roads in drought-stricken areas, and $2 million for children's food security. Finally, $0.83 million is included in support of family planning.

The family planning component is small compared to other parts of the program, but it is nevertheless huge by Malagasy standards. The government has just begun to make announcements about the possibility of family planning, and it is removing a law on the books since the 1930s that forbids the sale of contraceptives. The contraceptive demand of women who even now would prefer to have fewer children can be calculated, as can the savings in maternal and child mortality. It may be summed up, though, by one Malagasy friend's remark: "It is all so easy for you Western women to have a baby. You know you won't die."

The new family planning funds will be channeled through a Malagasy nongovernmental organization, FISA, established twenty-five years ago. FISA will produce educational films and pamphlets as well as set up branches in the four largest provincial towns. The PASAGE report, however, speaks of "a financial plan to ensure sustainability when outside financing has ended," rather than proposing family planning aid as a pilot step in meeting one of Madagascar's greatest economic as well as personal needs.

The Environmental Action Plan

The Environmental Action Plan for Madagascar (EAP) is the pilot model of what may grow to be thirty or more country-focused programs. Having originated as a Malagasy government request, and then an action plan put forward by the World Wildlife Fund to preserve biodiversity in Madagascar, it now represents a combined effort by the Bank, USAID, Cooperation Suisse, the U.N. Educational, Scientific, and Cultural Organization (UNESCO), the U.N. Development Programme (UNDP), and the World Wildlife Fund with potential input by many other donors. The donors' document has included input by some 150 Malagasy officials and experts who now (early 1989) are reworking the document to express official government policy. That final stage will be published as Madagascar's National Charter for the Environment.

The EAP's clear and thoughtful introduction emphasizes the urgency of the problem and outlines some local examples of the spirals of increasing poverty with increased environmental degradation. It also emphasizes, however, that Madagascar is not a hopeless country, but one with potential wealth of both land and resources—provided that these are used to best advantage.

The EAP attempts to estimate the annual cost of environmental degradation in Madagascar. The low hypothesis posits this figure to be about $100 million; the high, about $300 million—that is, 5–15 per cent of GNP. The total proposed input of aid from the Plan's foreign backers for the EAP is around $300–400 million over fifteen to twenty years. The authors of the EAP stress that although this cost may seem high, it is equal to their higher estimate of the *annual* cost to Madagascar of environmental degradation.

The five priority areas of the EAP are: (1) protection of biodiversity, (2) improving urban and rural environments, (3) land registry and mapping, (4) environmental education, and (5) institutional support for the EAP.

The direct improvement of the human environment may absorb 30–40 per cent (or $50–75 million) of the EAP over the first five years. This would involve small-scale reforestation, irrigation, and other land improvements. In the capital, it would address water supply and refuse collection needs. The EAP stresses the importance of *scale* of inputs— small and responsive to people's needs—and that the Bank must work through local government extension agents and foreign NGOs to encourage locally adapted schemes and local private initiative. The EAP proposes a National Environment Fund administered within the country, which would serve as a "microscope" for identifying projects too small for the Bank's normal mega-visions. Such a country-based fund could work from a few "miniprojects" as models, and could then decide on "microprojects" at a level very close to the communities concerned.

As part of this community environment aspect, the National Environment Fund would be able to give technical help to existing field workers of the ministries of agriculture, livestock, and forestry, though the EAP does not quite propose program funding. The Fund might also cooperate with the existing banking system to improve small-scale credit availability.

This broad proposal differs from the Bank's earlier (and sometimes unfortunate) ventures into integrated rural development in several ways: first, in its emphasis on micro scale and local decisionmaking; second, in the delinking of various aspects of community development; and, above all, in its emphasis on soil conservation and forestry projects for the future.

The third priority area highlighted by the Plan is mapping and land registration. This has a detailed proposed budget, which is expected to amount to about 25 per cent of the EAP's total funding. It is, however, the most controversial component—and the one most likely to change as the EAP becomes the Malagasy government's Environmental Charter. Mapping would be done by air and satellite photos, giving Madagascar its first accurate picture since the air survey done in the late 1940s of the amount of forest and cultivated land that the island actually encompasses. The EAP then proposes a national attempt at land registry, beginning in areas around the national reserves, where it is urgent to stabilize land use. The argument is that, without some rationalization of land tenure and a firm promise of land rights, farmers have no incentive to plant trees or invest in long-term irrigation. A counter-argument is that land registry is an invitation to bureaucratic confusion and corruption, imposing yet more burdens on the peasants. It is, at minimum, an attempt to deal with the problem of land degradation at the right level to give people a clear indication that the future of their property is their own future.

The fourth aspect is environmental education, due to receive some 10–20 per cent of EAP funding. This includes money for training professionals—recognized to be one of the major prerequisites for any further progress in sustainable development. Madagascar has a high literacy rate for Africa (74 per cent men, 62 per cent women),[17] but the schools, like everything else, are scarcely functioning for lack of funds. Major Bank support for public education is now under negotiation, and the Ministry of Education has already produced little reading books of poetry on environmental themes, funded by the World Wildlife Fund. The educational section of the EAP points out frankly that in Madagascar peasants usually regard government extension officers as enemies who propose abandoning traditional ways without understanding them. But peasants understand erosion firsthand, and they, like everyone else, are fascinated to learn that even the common animals and plants of their nation are unique.

The final priority is to establish institutional structures that facilitate rather than block the program. In particular, a high-level directorate formed under the auspices of the president, the prime minister, or the Planning Office could cut through some of the interministerial boundaries. The EAP could then take its rightful place among the country's other economic programs—and not be submerged by them.

The final National Charter for the Environment will represent one of the most comprehensive national commitments to sustainable development. But what is still left out? Basically, the EAP is both too large and too small; it cannot be absorbed by the country in its present state. The National Environment Fund for small-scale projects and mediation by NGOs thus become crucial to the early stages of implementation, and the EAP's inception must be handled with great care. For later years, however, the EAP is still too small. To increase productivity in balance with population growth, Madagascar must mobilize still larger sums of money and effort. Hundred-million-dollar flows of money now exist as aid for "structural adjustment" and as debt service paid by Madagascar in return for such aid. If the nation's goal is really sustainable development, then investment in the human environment and in "the human capital" of health and education must have a high priority in the general macroeconomic picture.

The EAP is now essentially an addition to the existing macroeconomic pattern of "development," although what is needed is a fundamental change in that pattern toward a long-term path of sustainable development. In this, the EAP suffers from the same weaknesses as PASAGE: inadequate funding, additionality, and top-down planning. The EAP will probably need to be greatly revised in five years' time. Perhaps by then it will be more generally recognized that environmental planning is central to the national economy.

National and NGO Accomplishments

Madagascar's pre-colonial monarchy had already promulgated laws against felling mature forests in the nineteenth century. Then in this century, in 1927, French scientists who recognized Madagascar's worldwide scientific importance, urged the colonial government to set aside pure wilderness reserves—the first nature reserves in Africa. They established twelve "integral" reserves designed to preserve the endemic flora and fauna (accessible only to research scientists) as well as two national parks open for general enjoyment. No infrastructure or upkeep was planned, since the reserves were chosen as remote, untouched areas, protected by their isolation. After independence in 1960, the Department of Water and Forests was increasingly unable to defend them. At present, 10,347 square kilometers—or 10–13 per cent of the remaining forest—are designated as national parks, integral reserves, or special reserves. "Forêts classés" designated by the government for future exploitation, constitute a further 26,710 square kilometers. Under the EAP, fourteen new reserves are planned, adding about 5,400 square kilometers. The World Wildlife Fund has supported the study, which identifies new reserves and sets priorities among them for protection, ecodevelopment, and promoting foreign tourism.

Each of these reserves in the "necklace of pearls" contains different species, and each abuts different human populations with different agricultural traditions. Madagascar's minimial, radially arranged road system means that a field worker rarely passes by one research site en route to the next—each is a separate venture or journey. Scientists and NGOs have therefore been able to focus local efforts in isolation from each others' concerns. This also means that foreign conservationists become passionately attached to particular regions, people, and wild species. The necklace of pearls is not only a biological description, but a political one; it emphasizes that each site is as precious as the next. Eventually this concept may translate into local pride, as the different regions realize each has a separate natural wonder—and that each can claim a share of wildlife tourism because of its differences from the others.

A variety of current projects support reserves through cooperative action of NGOs and foreign development agencies. The oldest and most established is the Beza Mahafaly Project, a joint effort of the agronomy school of the University of Madagascar, Yale University, and Washington University (St. Louis), supported by the World Wildlife Fund-U.S. since 1977. Recently USAID has collaborated with these university researchers to make U.S. Public Law 480 funds available for road and agricultural development in the villages bordering the Beza reserve, which originally donated their sacred forest for university research and protection. The Beza reserve is tiny—only 600 hectares—and the project so far extends to only about ten villages. It is clearly a success in research, in training Malagasy students, and in assuring input by the villages. Yet it has a high input of expatriate time, energy, and funds, and it indicates how long and hard outsiders must work to count real achievements at the local level.

The achievements at Beza have encouraged the same team to take on a much larger region, the National Reserve at Andohahela in the southwest, which comprises some 75,000 hectares and presents both the biological and human diversity found from rain forest to spiny desert. Success at Andohahela will show that the Beza initiative can be generalized to "real-life" scale. Similarly, World Wildlife Fund-U.S. supports a team from Duke University that is creating a reserve at Ranomafana around the "flagship species" of the newly discovered golden bamboo lemur. The Water and Forest Department enthusiastically supports designating Ranomafana as Madagascar's third National Park, protecting not only the forest, but also the watershed of a downstream electricity plant. The reserve, which is already receiving partial ecodevelopment support from USAID and UNICEF, will include some 40,000 hectares of rain forest. French researchers from the Musée d'Histoire Naturelle in Paris are working with UNESCO to establish a biosphere reserve—an area of untouched forest surrounded by a buffer zone of sustainable agriculture—in the east coast rain forest of Mananara, and a World Heritage Reserve including the limestone pinnacles of Bemaraha in the west. World Wildlife Fund-International is concentrating its efforts on the Montagne d'Ambre and Marojejy.[18]

However, each of these projects will predictably face the dilemma of the buffer zone. If an earnest conservationist pulls in money to develop a local region, this is likely to attract more people to live in that region and to prompt the building of more roads and more development "point centers" such as schools and clinics. It is all very well to extract promises that people will not cut the forested hillsides for slash-and-burn fields, or graze cattle in the woods, or set fires. If these are the traditions—and a little development makes it easier to live near the forest— such promises cannot be kept. The solution seems to be *more* development—irrigation as an alternative to slash-and-burn strategies, and the encouragement of tourism—to bring in hard cash. But if such activities are carried out within the buffer zones, these zones may well be degraded past serving their purpose. Eventually the conservationist becomes responsible for an ever-widening region that spreads well beyond the finances of conservation NGOs or their welcome in the country. This means that small conservation projects now need to turn to large development agencies, which in turn can use the NGOs' expertise to help focus down to the local needs.

Biodiversity and the Environmental Action Plan

The advent of the Environmental Action Plan (EAP) suddenly shifts the scale of available funding. Three years ago, the budget for Madagascar's national reserves amounted to $1,000, or about $25 a year for each of the protected areas. Now there is a prospect of $130 million over the next twenty years. In the early stages, the part for biodiversity would rise from about $3 million to about $6 million per year, divided between the protection of reserves per se and buffer-zone aid. This is still low— more like the budget for single national parks in Africa—but it represents a huge gain for Madagascar.

The portion going directly to the protection of biodiversity will presumably come from grants from other international agencies, not from loans—since the funding cannot be expected to generate income directly, however important it may be for watersheds, tourism, or for science. The World Bank is now inviting a consortium of donors to underwrite the preservation of the native forests of Madagascar.

The EAP will greatly reinforce protection, upkeep, and research in the 1,034,782 hectares of designated reserves, which comprise only 1.76 per cent of Madagascar's land area. It will also add another fourteen sites, totaling some 540,000 additional hectares. The whole "necklace of pearls" may be sufficient to encompass the diverse local fauna, although most sites should be larger for long-term viability. It will be a race against time, however, even for these nuclei, since the forest is disappearing at 150,000 to 300,000 hectares a year.

A separate section of the EAP explores the prospects of "nature tourism." The Malagasy tourist office had previously drawn up ambitious plans for 100,000 tourists a year, but Air Madagascar would need to buy two more jumbo jets to admit such numbers, and there is nowhere near the infrastructure of hotels or internal transport to compete with established mass sunbaths like the Seychelles or the Costa del Sol. The Plan estimates that an alternative approach of small-scale, elite "exploration" tour routes, based on simple, locally crafted accommodations, could offer a high rate of return. The initial draw must be Madagascar's birds, lemurs, landscapes, and local culture—all like nowhere else. One suggestion is that each party should view a local education show in a reserve education center before entering the reserve, and then walk with a local guide, which would increase both local employment and understanding. Then even earnest birdwatchers can succumb to a final week on a beach, extending their stay. There is a challenge to make accommodations sympathetic to local mores—both to preserve the country's special character, which attracts tourists in the first place, and to make foreign visitors not overly resented by the Malagasy.

The World Bank is ready both to contribute to any part of ecodevelopment that justifies the government contracting further loans and to urge other donors to support the reserves. It recognizes biodiversity both as a good in itself and as a source of further goods. The Bank does not, however, have a solution for the buffer-zone problem. Projects administered under the EAP will naturally cluster in buffer zones. "Development" projects administered as part of "normal" aid may not be coordinated with the buffer zones—and so may not serve their proper function of pulling people away from the forest, not pushing them into the forest.

Collaboration between the World Bank and environmental groups such as the World Wildlife Fund is just beginning. The achievement of raising the number of reserves to fifty, paying their guardians' salaries, and providing transport and biological inventories will be only a starting point. Furthermore, the provision of tourist revenue, the registering of land around the parks, and modest irrigation schemes in the valleys will still be only a beginning. Any "development" that thinks only of buffer zones will fail—just as any "conservation" that thinks only of parks will fail. It is necessary to marry the defense of the wild with advance for humanity, which means that the conservationists—and even the lemurs—have a stake in the well-being of the country as a whole.

Madagascar is now a country to monitor closely. The success or failure of the collaboration between donors, NGOs, the national government, and local people will show much about the possibilities elsewhere, as well as mean life or death for Madagascar's wild species.

Policies to Preserve Biodiversity with Sustainable Development

The argument of this article suggests several policy recommendations that go well beyond the macroeconomic framework now urged upon Madagascar, though most are integral to the EAP itself. As Chambers and Leach have pointed out, what is good for the environment may not be immediately good for the poor, but what is good for the poor is usually good for their environment.[19]

First, wilderness areas really must be defined and defended as wilderness—in both rich and poor countries—or they will be invaded by both rich and poor. Long-term defense depends on conservation education and a conservation ethic among professionals and people at large.

Second, people who live partly from and within the forest deserve long-term, sensitive encouragement and sometimes support. Depending on the people, such encouragement often requires recognizing the sustainability of their own traditional land use. It will often also require micro-irrigation, or other agricultural changes, combined with long local discussions and *local* agreements on how and why to maintain wild land around the micro-improvements. It may even mean providing people with support to move away to a more fertile and less vulnerable habitat, or to jobs in manufacturing and services.

Such local interventions are relatively cheap in terms of cash but very expensive in terms of the time and wisdom of ecodevelopment personnel. Madagascar clearly will need major international investment—not just in cement and all-terrain vehicles, but in training and salary support for its conservation cadres.

This is a complete reversal of the usual economic development priorities. People living beside the forest have long been considered "marginal" in the strategies of governments and agencies. They usually seem to have access to enough natural resources to sustain themselves; unlike people living near deserts, they are not generally famine victims that claim international aid. They contribute little to the country's formal economy and are seldom vocal in domestic politics, so they are neglected by their own governments.

Now, with foreign aid and tourism focusing on biodiversity, these "marginal" people suddenly become crucial. It is on the marginal land and in the buffer zones that the battle for species preservation will be won or lost.

Yet the removal of poverty as the driving force in ecological destruction does not assure the protection of biologically valuable areas. In fact, when it comes to extractive use, it is far more important to keep the rich rather than the poor out of wild lands. The remaining tropical wilderness is there because people have taken relatively little away by their "small-scale" traditional uses. It is the rich who clear, fell, and strip mine.

What steps can the governments of poor countries take to ensure that the international community provides the help they need to protect their most valuable ecosystems? First, they should press for an international fund for biodiversity. If they are to set aside land and use their scarce personnel to preserve a global heritage, they should expect contributions from richer countries, which will also benefit.

Developing countries should use the current concern with the environment to increase their claims on the rich countries. The debate is now polarizing in a negative fashion—with environmental concerns being branded as yet another form of "conditionality" that seems designed to slow or stop the disbursement of funds. Instead of resenting and blocking such conditional clauses, the less developed countries can use them to increase the amount of grants or to attract new ones by claiming funds for biodiversity preservation. If the rich countries refuse to pay, the poor countries should address public opinion, through scientists and journalists, to tell the rich how much they stand to lose.

International lending agencies and donor governments also have a major role to play in this shift from negative to positive. Too often, their environmental guidelines take the form of the Ten Commandments: "Thou shalt not lend for projects that . . ." Instead, they need guidelines beginning with "Thou shalt" lend or give aid to increase biodiversity, train conservation professionals, improve ecological education, search for sustainable use or non-use of buffer zones, and learn from local elders, healers, and women what their needs may be. In the course of this learning, more funds may be spent for local salaries and small-scale infrastructure than for large development projects, but this is often socially as well as ecologically appropriate. As discussed in this chapter, such spending is usually best accomplished through foreign or local NGOs and through program support for local government. Simply dropping millions of dollars on the local scene can overwhelm the absorptive capacity of the recipients.

The World Bank's Task Force on Biodiversity, in conjunction with the World Wildlife Fund and the World Resources Institute, is now drawing up guidelines for multinational aid to the biosphere. Many aid agencies, like the Canadian International Development Agency (CIDA), for example, have drawn up their own environmental manifestos. It remains to implement these hopes—and to make them integral to entire development efforts and priorities, not simply an addition to more traditional economic patterns of development and support.

What are the conclusions for the World Wildlife Fund and other conservation organizations? For them, this is a period of fundamental change. In one way they have succeeded in conveying their message. The powerful of the international community have now heard of the crisis in species survival, and new funds are available for ecodevelopment. Countries like Madagascar have realized there is money in their wilderness, as well as a source of national pride, so they are increasingly politically open to new proposals. In this new climate, what is the proper role for conservation groups? Should they put their limited financial resources into guarding reserves? Or into ecodevelopment around the reserves? Probably into both—but they can do more by drawing on the far larger funds of USAID or the World Bank. The enormous importance of NGOs lies in their expertise. It is they who know scientists, both foreign and local. It is their people who have slept in the woods, birdwatched at dawn, negotiated at noon with the provincial politician, and exchanged oratorical speeches of friendship with the local chief under the moon, washed down in local beer. This style may not cut much ice in Washington, but people who link diverse worlds, and who know and work with the local conservation professionals as friends and colleagues, not clients, are the ones who will in the end be respected.

In short, NGOs now have a unique opportunity to guide the new international funds where they can best help their local colleagues. If they can help those funds reach people—university scientists, national park officers, villages with a tiny scheme for self-improvement, forest guards—the NGOs will be fulfilling their task.

It will take *local* wisdom to solve the dilemma of the "buffer zones." The general problem is the same, but the solution will be different in each case. To live in harmony with nature, people will need to understand how to husband the resources of nature and to use them sustainably. This means that when extra cash is needed, people must be able to look outward to the rest of the economy. They should not be forced to exploit their own ecosystem more harshly or to move on and invade a previously inviolate reserve.

That wisdom must come from the people, aided by their own national government. Their needs, may, if required, be met at least in part by international donors. Fairly often, it may be the conservation organizations that link the two.

Finally, what are the conclusions for public opinion and for the media, which both shapes and follows public opinion? An informed constituency that knows the dangers ahead, and knows that a sustainable world is possible, is the strongest force for environmental sanity. A generous impulse makes people want to believe that the preservation of nature should be compatible with the lessening of poverty. This analysis of the Madagascar challenge indicates how lessening poverty is fundamental to saving the wilderness environment, and that wise use of the environment is one of the strongest means to combat poverty. Young people who demand to live in a world of natural riches and beauty, and old people who wish such a world for their grandchildren, may turn the crisis of the biosphere into a world of sustainable hope.

Notes

Note: I would like to thank Richard Jolly for advice, insights, and vehement arguments. Eleanor Sterling contributed valuable information on environmental initiatives in Madagascar. I should also like to thank many people at the World Bank for their openness, their time, and their help, in particular Francois Falloux, Director of the EAP. Opinions and omissions remain my own.

[1] R. Mittermeier, "megadiversity concept," quoted in *The Economist,* 4 June 1988, pp. 73–74.

[2] See Alison Jolly, *A World Like Our Own* (New Haven, Conn.: Yale University Press, 1980); and Alison Jolly, P. Oberlé, and R. Albignac, eds., *Madagascar* (Oxford, England: Pergamon Press, 1984).

[3] World Bank, U.S. Agency for International Development, (USAID), Cooperation Suisse, U.N. Educational, Scientific, and Cultural Organization (UNESCO), U.N. Development Programme (UNDP), and the World Wildlife Fund, *Madagascar: Plan d'Action Environnemental,* Vol. 1, *Document de Synthèse Générale et Propositions d'Orientations;* and Vol. 2, *Synthèses Specifiques et Recommendations* (Washington, D. C.: The World Bank, 1988).

[4] Democratic Republic of Madagascar, "Stratégie Malgache pour la Conservation et le Dévéloppement Durable," Presidential Decree, pp. 84–116, 4 April 1984.

[5] World Bank, et al., *Madagascar: Plan d'Action Environnemental,* Vol. I (2-1 to 2-5).

[6] A. Oyowe, Interview with Pascal Rakotomaro, Minister of Financial and Economic Affairs, *The Courier, E.E.C.* (September–October 1988), pp. 32–34.

[7] The World Bank, *Projet d'Actions Sociales et d'Appui a la Gestion Economique (PASAGE),* Report 7410-MAG (Washington, D.C., 1988); and W. Leonard, "Social Effects of Structural Adjustment in Madagascar," (Madagascar: UNICEF Office, 1987).

[8] Graham Shuttleworth, "Policies in Transition: Lessons from Madagascar," *World Development,* Vol. 17, No. 3 (March 1989), pp. 397–408.

[9] A. Oyowe, Interview with Jean Robiarivony, Director-General of Planning, *The Courier, E.E.C.* (September–October 1988), pp. 34–37.

[10] World Bank, et al., *Madagascar: Plan d'Action Environnemental,* op. cit., Vol. I (2-1 to 2-5).

[11] Robert J. H. Chambers, "Poverty, the Environment and The World Bank: The Opportunity for a New Professionalism." Unpublished paper prepared for the Strategic Planning and Review Department of the World Bank (Washington, D.C., 1987).

[12] The World Bank, *Madagascar: Population and Health Sector Review,* unpublished report, 6446-MAG (Washington, D.C. 1987), p. iv.

[13] Ibid., p. 15.

[14] Robert J. H. Chambers and M. Leach, "Trees as Savings and Security for the Rural Poor," *World Development,* Vol. 17, No. 3 (March 1989), pp. 329–42.

[15] World Bank, *PASAGE,* op. cit.

[16] Ibid.

[17] United Nations Childrens Fund (UNICEF), *The State of the World's Children* (Oxford, England; Oxford University Press, 1989), p. 100.

[18] M. Wells, *Report to USAID on Small-scale Environment and Development Projects in Madagascar,* (Washington, D.C.: U.S. Agency for International Development; 1988); Alison Jolly, "Man Against Nature: Time for a Truce in Madagascar," *National Geographic,* Vol. 171, No. 2 (1987), pp. 160–83; and Alison Jolly, "Madagascar's Lemurs on the Edge of Survival," *National Geographic,* Vol. 174, No. 2 (1988), pp. 132–61.

[19] Chambers and Leach, "Trees as Savings and Security," op. cit.

About the Overseas Development Council

The Overseas Development Council is a private, non-profit organization established in 1969 for the purpose of increasing American understanding of the economic and social problems confronting the developing countries and of how their development progress is related to U.S. interests. Toward this end, the Council functions as a center for policy research and analysis, a forum for the exchange of ideas, and a resource for public education. The Council's current program of work encompasses four major issue areas: trade and industrial policy, international finance and investment, development strategies and development cooperation, and U.S. foreign policy and the developing countries. ODC's work is used by policy makers in the Executive Branch and the Congress, journalists, and those concerned about U.S.-Third World relations in corporate and bank management, international and non-governmental organizations, universities, and educational and action groups focusing on specific development issues. ODC's program is funded by foundations, corporations, and private individuals; its policies are determined by a governing Board and Council. In selecting issues and shaping its work program, ODC is also assisted by a standing Program Advisory Committee.

Victor H. Palmieri is Chairman of the ODC, and Wayne Fredericks is Vice Chairman. The Council's President is John W. Sewell.

Overseas Development Council
1717 Massachusetts Ave., N.W.
Washington, D.C. 20036
Tel. (202) 234-8701

Overseas Development Council
Program Advisory Committee

The Editors

Environment and the Poor: Development Strategies for a Common Agenda is the eleventh volume in the Overseas Development Council's series of policy books, U.S.-Third World Policy Perspectives. The co-editors of this series—often collaborating with guest editors contributing to the series—are Richard E. Feinberg and Valeriana Kallab.

H. Jeffrey Leonard, guest editor of this volume, is a Vice President of the World Wildlife Fund and The Conservation Foundation and the Director of the Fairfield Osborn Center for Economic Development, a new joint venture of The Conservation Foundation and the World Wildlife Fund. Dr. Leonard has been at The Foundation since 1976. During that time, he has worked on projects relating to land use in the United States and several European nations, to the international location of industry, and to environmental problems in developing countries. Dr. Leonard is author of several recent books, including *Pollution and the Struggle for the World Product, Natural Resources and Economic Development in Central America,* and a Conservation Foundation book, *Are Environmental Regulations Driving U.S. Industries Overseas?* He is also editor of *Divesting Nature's Capital: The Political Economy of Environmental Abuse in the Third World,* and *Business and Environment: Toward a Common Ground.* He is a member of the Council on Foreign Relations, the Society for International Development, and the World Affairs Council.

Valeriana Kallab is Vice President and Director of Publications of the Overseas Development Council and co-editor of the ODC's U.S.-Third World Policy Perspective series. She has been responsible for ODC's published output since 1972. Before joining ODC, she was a research editor and writer on international economic issues at the Carnegie Endowment for International Peace in New York. She was co-editor (with John P. Lewis) of *Development Strategies Reconsidered* and *U.S. Foreign Policy and the Third World: Agenda 1983;* and (with Guy F. Erb) of *Beyond Dependency: The Third World Speaks Out.*

Richard E. Feinberg is Executive Vice President and Director of Studies at the Overseas Development Council. Before joining ODC in 1981, he served as the Latin American specialist on the Policy Planning Staff of the U.S. Department of State, and as an international economist in the Treasury Department and with the House Banking Committee; he is also co-editor of the Policy Perspectives series. He is an adjunct professor of international finance at the Georgetown University School of Foreign Service. He has written numerous articles and books on U.S. foreign policy, Latin American politics, and international economics, including *The Intemperate Zone: The Third World Challenge to U.S. Foreign Policy* (W. W. Norton); (as editor) *Central America: International Dimensions of the Crisis;* and *Subsidizing Success: The Export-Import Bank in the U.S. Economy.*

Contributing Authors

Montague Yudelman is an agricultural economist who has been involved in research, teaching, and advising and directing efforts in agricultural development and related fields. He has been a technical officer at FAO, Assistant Director for Social Sciences at The Rockefeller Foundation, Vice President of the OECD Development Center in Paris, and Director of Agriculture and Rural Development at the World Bank from 1972 to 1984. Dr. Yudelman retired from the World Bank in September 1984. From 1984 to 1987, he was a Distinguished Fellow at the World Resources Institute. Since 1987 he has been a Fellow at the World Wildlife Fund/The Conservation Foundation. Dr. Yudelman has been a Professor of Economic Development at the University of Michigan/Ann Arbor, a visiting lecturer and Fellow at the Center for International Affairs at Harvard, and he is currently a Woodrow Wilson Visiting Fellow. Dr. Yudelman's publications include: *Africans on the Land* (1965), *Agricultural Development and Economic Integration in Latin America* (1970), and *Employment and Technological Change in Developing Countries* (OECD, Paris, 1972). Since retirement he has published *The World Bank and Agricultural Development—an Insider's View* (World Resources Institute, 1986), *Forty Years of Agricultural Development* (ICIPE Science Press, Nairobi, Kenya, 1986), and *Prospects for Agricultural Development in Sub-Saharan Africa* (Winrock International, 1988). He is currently working on a book on the economics of low-cost soil conservation.

John O. Browder is Assistant Professor of International Development in the Urban Affairs and Planning Program at Virginia Polytechnic Institute and State University, where he has been teaching since 1988. Previously he has conducted various consulting assignments for the World Bank, the World Resources Institute, and the Brazilian government and undertaken contracted research under the sponsorship of the National Science Foundation and the Organization of American States. His research has focused on the social and economic aspects of tropical deforestation, smallholder agriculture, and livestock production in the Brazilian Amazon. He is the author of numerous articles and editor of *Fragile Lands of Latin America: Strategies for Sustainable Development* (1989).

A. John De Boer is Chief of Party for the Winrock International Institute for Agricultural Development team supporting the Agricultural Research and Production Project in Nepal. From 1978 through 1986, he worked at Winrock International headquarters as a Program Officer, Director for Asian Programs, and Deputy Director for Technical Cooperation Programs. Prior to that, he was Lecturer in Agricultural Economics at Queensland University, Brisbane, Australia. He has published widely on animal production economics in developing counties, crop-livestock systems, and household economics, and has served as a consultant to the Food and Agriculture Organization (FAO), the World Bank, Asian Productivity Organization, Asian Development Bank, and USAID in Asia, Africa, Latin America, and the Caribbean.

J. Dirck Stryker is President of Associates for International Resources and Development and Associate Professor of International Economic Relations at the Fletcher School of Law and Diplomacy, Tufts University. He is currently completing a research project, Linkages Between Policy Reform and Natural Resource Management in Sub-Saharan Africa, for USAID. From 1983 to 1988, he directed a Tufts University team providing technical assistance to the Integrated Livestock Project in Niger. He has conducted major studies of agricultural price policy and marketing in Ghana, Guinea, Madagascar, Mali, Morocco, and Nigeria. Over the past twenty years, he has been a frequent consultant to African governments, USAID, and the World Bank. He is co-author of *Rice in West Africa: Policy and Economics* and has written numerous journal articles, papers, and reports dealing with agricultural development.

Tim Campbell is a Senior Urban Planner at the World Bank, where he has worked since 1988 on urban policy, decentralization and water supply for Latin America and Guatemala. Before joining the World Bank, he worked for twelve years as a private consultant to the World Bank, the Inter-American Development Bank, the United Nations, the World Health Organization, governments, and engineering companies. His fields of expertise include urban planning and growth strategies, compulsory relocation around hydropower dams, and the impact of low-cost technologies for water supply, waste disposal, and renewable energy on the urban and rural poor. Mr. Campbell has served on a variety of expert groups and assignments concerning development issues in Third World cities, including earthquake reconstruction and decentralization in Mexico City for the Government of Mexico; analysis of environmental impacts in the Valley of Mexico for the United Nations; and renewable energy fuels in Pakistan for the United Nations. He has also served as a Research Associate at the University of California at Berkeley and as a Consulting Assistant Professor in the Department of Civil Engineering at Stanford University. He is the author of numerous articles and technical reports in his field.

Alison Jolly has been Visiting Lecturer at Princeton University's Department of Biology since 1987. From 1982 to 1987, she was Guest Investigator at The Rockefeller University. In the 1960s and 1970s, she held academic and research appointments at the University of Sussex, Cambridge University, and the University of Zambia. From 1962 to 1964, she was also Research Associate at the New York Zoology Society. Dr. Jolly's recent books include *A World Like Our Own: Man and Nature in Madagascar* (1980) and *Madagascar* (1984).

PULLING TOGETHER: THE INTERNATIONAL MONETARY FUND IN A MULTIPOLAR WORLD

Catherine Gwin, Richard E. Feinberg, and contributors

The global economic environment in which we now live is radically different from the one foreseen when the International Monetary Fund was created in the wake of World War II. The important changes have to do not only with the end of U.S. economic hegemony and the demise of the fixed exchange rate system, but also with the internationalization of financial markets, shifting patterns of global production and trade, and a prolonged slowdown in global economic growth.

The Fund has not kept pace with the changes and has not been fulfilling its needed role. This volume poses the fundamental questions regarding the responsiveness of Fund policies and practices to change, and the member countries' willingness to let the Fund play a more constructive role in coping with the new realities of international monetary and financial matters. It also addresses the overarching question of the Fund's dual role—its systemic role and its role as a financial institution for countries that do not have market access, or whose access is temporarily interrupted. The study sets out a plan for revisions that must be made in light of the major changes in the global economy.

Contents:

Catherine Gwin and Richard E. Feinberg—Overview: Reforming the Fund

Jacques J. Polak—Strengthening the Role of the IMF in the International Monetary System

Peter B. Kenen—Providing Access to IMF Credit

C. David Finch—Comment: Conditional Finance for Industrial Countries

Jeffrey D. Sachs—Strengthening IMF Programs in Highly Indebted Countries

Guillermo Ortiz—The IMF and the Debt Strategy

Louis Goreux—The Fund and the Low-Income Countries

Joan M. Nelson—Comment: The IMF and the Impact of Adjustment on the Poor

Catherine Gwin has been a consultant to The Ford Foundation, Rockefeller Foundation, and Asia Society. She also served as a consultant for the Group of Twenty-Four's 1987 report on the future of the International Monetary Fund. From 1981-83, she was a Senior Associate at the Carnegie Endowment for International Peace, where she directed a Study Group on international financial cooperation and the management of developing-country debt. From 1980-81, she was North-South issues coordinator at the U.S. International Development Cooperation Agency. From 1976 to 1978, she was on the staff of the 1980s Project of the Council on Foreign Relations; in 1978-79, she was Staff Director of the project. Dr. Gwin has taught at the School of International Affairs of Columbia University and she has published widely in the field of development economics.

Richard E. Feinberg is vice president of the Overseas Development Council. He served as the Latin American specialist on the Policy Planning Staff of the Department of State from 1977 to 1979. He has worked as an international economist in the Treasury Department and with the House Banking Committee, and has been an adjunct professor of international finance at the Georgetown University School of Foreign Service. Dr. Feinberg has written numerous articles and books on U.S. foreign policy, Latin American politics, and international economics, including *The Intemperate Zone: The Third World Challenge to U.S. Foreign Policy* (W. W. Norton); (as editor) *Central America: International Dimensions of the Crisis* (Holmes and Meier); and *Subsidizing Success: The Export-Import Bank in the U.S. Economy* (Cambridge University Press).

U.S.-Third World Policy Perspectives, No. 13
Summer 1989, 256 pp.

$24.95 (cloth)
$15.95 (paper)

FRAGILE COALITIONS:
THE POLITICS OF ECONOMIC ADJUSTMENT

Joan M. Nelson and contributors

The global economic crisis of the 1980s forced most developing nations into a simultaneous quest for short-run economic stabilization and longer-run structural reforms. Effective adjustment is at least as much a political as an economic challenge. But political dimensions of adjustment have been much less carefully analyzed than have the economic issues.

Governments in developing countries must balance pressures from external agencies seeking more rapid adjustment in return for financial support, and the demands of domestic political groups often opposing such reforms. How do internal pressures shape external bargaining? and conversely, how does external influence shape domestic political maneuvering? Growing emphasis on "adjustment with a human face" poses additional questions: Do increased equity and political acceptability go hand in hand? or do more pro-poor measures add to the political difficulties of adjustment? The capacity of the state itself to implement adjustment measures varies widely among nations. How can external agencies take such differences more fully into account? The hopeful trend toward democratic openings in many countries raises further, crucial issues: What special political risks and opportunities confront governments struggling simultaneously with adjustment and democratization?

The contributors to this volume explore these issues and their policy implications for the United States and for the international organizations that seek to promote adjustment efforts.

Contents:

Joan M. Nelson—The Politics of Long-Haul Economic Adjustment
John Waterbury—The Political Management of Economic Adjustment and Reform
Stephan Haggard and Robert R. Kaufman—Economic Adjustment in New
    Democracies
Laurence Whitehead—Democratization and Disinflation: A Comparative Approach
Joan M. Nelson—The Politics of Pro-Poor Adjustment
Thomas M. Callaghy—Toward State Capability and Embedded Liberalism in the Third
    World: Lessons for Adjustment
Miles Kahler—International Financial Institutions and the Politics of Adjustment

Joan M. Nelson has been a visiting fellow at the Overseas Development Council since 1982; since mid-1986, she has directed a collegial research program on the politics of economic adjustment. She has been a consultant for the World Bank, the Agency for International Development, and for the International Monetary Fund, as well as a staff member of USAID. In the 1970s and early 1980s, she taught at the Massachusetts Institute of Technology, the Johns Hopkins University School of Advanced International Studies, and Princeton University's Woodrow Wilson School. She has published books and articles on development assistance and policy dialogue, political participation, migration and urban politics in developing nations, and the politics of economic stabilization and reform.

U.S.-Third World Policy Perspectives, No. 12 $24.95 (cloth)
Summer 1989, 192 pp. $15.95 (paper)

U.S. FOREIGN POLICY AND ECONOMIC REFORM IN THREE GIANTS: THE USSR, CHINA, AND INDIA

Richard E. Feinberg, John Echeverri-Gent, Friedemann Müller, and contributors

Three of the largest and strategically most important nations in the world—the Soviet Union, China, and India—are currently in the throes of historic change. The reforms in the giants are transforming global economic and geopolitical relations. The United States must reexamine central tenets of its foreign policy if it is to seize the opportunities presented by these changes.

This pathbreaking study analyzes economic reform in the giants and its implications for U.S. foreign policy. It assesses the impact of the reforms on the livelihood of the nearly half the world's population living in their societies. Each of the giants is opening up its economy to foreign trade and investment. What consequences will this new outward orientation have for international trade, and how should U.S. policy respond to these developments? Each giant is attempting to catch up to global technological frontiers by absorbing foreign technologies; in what areas might cooperation enhance American interests, and in what areas must the U.S. protect its competitive and strategic assets? What role can key international economic institutions like the GATT, the IMF, and the World Bank play to help integrate the giants into the international economy?

Economic reform in the giants has important consequences for their political systems. What measures can and should the United States take to encourage political liberalization? How will the reforms affect the foreign policies of the giants, and what impact will this have on U.S. geopolitical interests?

The contributors suggest how U.S. foreign policy should anticipate these new circumstances in ways that enhance international cooperation and security.

Richard E. Feinberg, John Echeverri-Gent, and Friedemann Müller—
Overview: Economic Reform in the Giants and U.S. Policy
Friedemann Müller—Economic Reform in the USSR
Rensselaer W. Lee III—Economic Reform in China
John Echeverri-Gent—Economic Reform in India
John Echeverri-Gent, Friedemann Müller, and Rensselaer W. Lee III—
The Politics of Economic Reform in the Giants
Thomas Naylor—Economic Reforms and International Trade
Richard P. Suttmeier—Technology Transfer to the Giants: Opportunities
and Challenges
Elena Borisovna Arefieva—The Geopolitical Consequences of Reform in the Giants

---

Richard E. Feinberg is vice president of the Overseas Development Council and co-editor of the U.S.-Third World Policy Perspectives series. From 1977 to 1979, Feinberg was Latin American specialist on the policy planning staff of the U.S. Department of State.

John Echeverri-Gent is a visiting fellow at the Overseas Development Council and an assistant professor at the University of Virginia. His publications are in the fields of comparative public policy and the political economy of development in India.

Friedemann Müller is a visiting fellow at the Overseas Development Council and a senior research associate at Stiftung Wissenschaft und Politik, Ebenhausen, West Germany. His publications on the Soviet and Eastern European economies have focused on economic reform, energy policy, and East-West trade.

U.S.-Third World Policy Perspectives, No. 14
Winter 1989, 256 pp.

$24.95 (cloth)
$15.95 (paper)

STRENGTHENING THE POOR: WHAT HAVE WE LEARNED?

John P. Lewis and contributors

"bound to influence policymakers and make a major contribution to renewed efforts to reduce poverty"
—B. T. G. Chidzero, Minister of Finance,
Economic Planning, and Development,
Government of Zimbabwe

"deserves wide readership within the broader development community"
—Barber B. Conable, President,
The World Bank

The issue of poverty alleviation—of strengthening the poor—is now being brought back toward the top of the development policy agenda.

The current refocusing on poverty is not just a matter of turning back the clock. Anti-poverty initiatives for the 1990s must respond to a developing world and a policy environment that in many ways differs dramatically from that of the 1970s and even the 1980s. Much has been accomplished during and since the last thrust of anti-poverty policy. The poor themselves have in some cases become more vocal, organized, and effective in pressing their own priorities. A great deal of policy experience has accrued. And national governments, donor agencies, and non-governmental organizations now employ a much wider range of tools for poverty alleviation.

Strengthening the Poor provides a timely assessment of these changes and experience. In an overview essay, John Lewis draws important policy lessons both from poverty alleviation's period of high salience in the 1970s and from its time of lowered attention in the adjustment-accentuating 1980s. An impressive cluster of U.S. and developing-country authors react to these propositions from diverse points of view.

Contents:

John P. Lewis—Overview—Strengthening the Poor: Some Lessons for the International Community
Norman Uphoff—Assisted Self-Reliance: Working With, Rather than For, the Poor
Samuel Paul—Governments and Grassroots Organizations: From Co-Existence to Collaboration
Uma Lele—Empowering Africa's Rural Poor: Problems and Prospects in Agricultural Development
Mohiuddin Alamgir—Some Lessons from the IFAD Approach to Rural Poverty Alleviation
Sartaj Aziz—A Turning Point in Pakistan's Rural Development Strategy
Nurul Islam—Agricultural Growth, Technological Progress, and Rural Poverty
Sheldon Annis—What Is Not the Same About the Urban Poor: The Case of Mexico City
Mayra Buvinić and Margaret A. Lycette—Women, Poverty, and Development
Richard Jolly—Poverty and Adjustment in the 1990s
Thomas W. Dichter—The Changing Role of Northern NGOs
S. Guhan—Aid for the Poor: Performance and Possibilities in India
Joseph C. Wheeler—Sub-Sector Planning and Poverty Reduction: A Donor View

---

U.S.-Third World Policy Perspectives, No. 10
1988, 256 pp.

ISBN: 0-88738-267-3 (cloth) $19.95
ISBN: 0-88738-768-3 (paper) $12.95

DEVELOPMENT STRATEGIES RECONSIDERED

John P. Lewis and Valeriana Kallab, editors

"First-rate, comprehensive analysis—presented
in a manner that makes it extremely valuable
to policy makers."
—Robert R. Nathan
Robert Nathan Associates

Important differences of opinion are emerging about the national strategies
best suited for advancing economic growth and equity in the difficult global
adjustment climate of the late 1980s.

Proponents of the "new orthodoxy"—the perspective headquartered at the
World Bank and favored by the Reagan administration as well as by a number
of other bilateral donor governments—are "carrying forward with redoubled
vigor the liberalizing, pro-market strains of the thinking of the 1960s and
1970s. They are very mindful of the limits of government." And they are "em-
phatic in advocating export-oriented growth to virtually all comers."

Other prominent experts question whether a standardized prescription of
export-led growth can meet the needs of big low-income countries in the latter
1980s as well as it did those of small and medium-size middle-income countries in the 1960s and 1970s. They are concerned about the special needs of
low-income Africa. And they see a great deal of unfinished business under the
heading of poverty and equity.

In this volume, policy syntheses are proposed to reconcile the goals of
growth, equity, and adjustment; to strike fresh balances between agricultural
and industrial promotion and between capital and other inputs; and to reflect
the interplay of democracy and development.

Contents:

John P. Lewis—Overview —Development Promotion: A Time for Regrouping
Irma Adelman—A Poverty-Focused Approach to Development Policy
John W. Mellor—Agriculture on the Road to Industrialization
Jagdish N. Bhagwati—Rethinking Trade Strategy
Leopoldo Solis and Aurelio Montemayor—A Mexican View of the Choice Between
  Inward and Outward Orientation
Colin I. Bradford, Jr.—East Asian "Models": Myths and Lessons
Alex Duncan—Aid Effectiveness in Raising Adaptive Capacity in the Low-Income
  Countries
Atul Kohli—Democracy and Development

John P. Lewis is Professor of Economics and International Affairs at Princeton Uni
versity's Woodrow Wilson School of Public and International Affairs. He is simultaneously senior advisor to the Overseas Development Council and chairman of its Program Advisory Committee. From 1979 to 1981, Dr. Lewis was chairman of the OECD's
Development Assistance Committee (DAC). From 1982 to 1985, he was chairman of the
three-year World Bank/IMF Task Force on Concessional Flows. He has served as a
member of the U.N. Committee for Development Planning. For many years, he has alternated between academia and government posts (as Member of the Council of Economic Advisors, 1963-64, and Director of the USAID Mission to India, 1964-69), with
collateral periods of association with The Brookings Institution, The Ford Foundation,
and the World Bank.

Valeriana Kallab is vice president and director of publications of the Overseas
Development Council and series co-editor of the ODC's U.S.-Third World Policy Perspectives series. She has been responsible for ODC's published output since 1972. Before
joining ODC, she was a research editor and writer on international economic issues at
the Carnegie Endowment for International Peace in New York.

U.S.-Third World Policy Perspectives, No. 5   ISBN: 0-88738-044-1 (cloth) $19.95
1986, 208 pp.   ISBN: 0-87855-991-4 (paper) $12.95

BETWEEN TWO WORLDS:
THE WORLD BANK'S NEXT DECADE
Richard E. Feinberg and contributors

"essential reading for anybody interested in the Bank"
—The Economist

"well-researched analysis of some of the problems confronting the World Bank in the 1980s"
—The Journal of Development Studies

In the midst of the global debt and adjustment crises, the World Bank has been challenged to become the leading agency in North-South fiwhich must be comprehensively addressed by the Bank's new presinance and development. The many dimensions of this challenge are the subject of this important volume.

As mediator between international capital markets and developing countries, the World Bank will be searching for ways to renew the flow of private credit and investment to Latin America and Africa. And as the world's premier development agency, the Bank can help formulate growth strategies appropriate to the 1990s.

The Bank's ability to design and implement a comprehensive response to these global needs is threatened by competing objectives and uncertain priorities. Can the Bank design programs attractive to private investors that also serve the very poor? Can it emphasize efficiency while transferring technologies that maximize labor absorption? Can it more aggressively condition loans on policy reforms without attracting the criticism that has accompanied IMF programs?

The contributors to this volume assess the role that the World Bank can play in the period ahead. They argue for new financial and policy initiatives and for new conceptual approaches to development, as well as for a restructuring of the Bank, as it takes on new, systemic responsibilities in the next decade.

Contents:
Richard E. Feinberg—Overview: An Open Letter to the World Bank's Next President
Gerald K. Helleiner—Policy-Based Program Leading: A Look at the Bank's New Role
Joan M. Nelson—The Diplomacy of Policy-Based Lending
Sheldon Annis—The Shifting Grounds of Poverty Lending at The World Bank
Howard Pack—The Technological Impact of World Bank Operations
John F. H. Purcell and Michelle B. Miller—The World Bank and Private Capital
Charles R. Blitzer—Financing the World Bank

Richard E. Feinberg is vice president of the Overseas Development Council and co-editor of the U.S.-Third World Policy Perspectives series. From 1977 to 1979, Feinberg was Latin American specialist on the policy planning staff of the U.S. Department of State. He has also served as an international economist in the U.S. Treasury Department and with the House Banking Committee. He is currently also adjunct professor of international finance at the Georgetown University School of Foreign Service. Feinberg is the author of numerous books as well as journal and newspaper articles on U.S. foreign policy, Latin American politics, and international economics.

U.S.-Third World Policy Perspectives, No. 7   ISBN: 0-88738-123-5 (cloth) $19.95
June 1986, 208 pp.   ISBN: 0-88738-665-2 (paper) $12.95